Policing Passengers

Justice, Power, and Politics

Heather Ann Thompson and Rhonda Y. Williams, *editors*

The Justice, Power, and Politics series publishes new works in history that explore the myriad struggles for justice, battles for power, and shifts in politics that have shaped the United States over time. Through the lenses of justice, power, and politics, the series seeks to broaden scholarly debates about America's past as well as to inform public discussions about its future.

A complete list of books published in Justice, Power, and Politics is available at https://uncpress.org/series/justice-power-politics.

Policing Passengers

Black Women and the Fight Against Bus Violence

MARY-ELIZABETH B. MURPHY

The University of North Carolina Press Chapel Hill

This book was published with the assistance of the Thornton H. Brooks Fund of the University of North Carolina Press.

Set in Charis by Westchester Publishing Services

Library of Congress Cataloging-in-Publication Data
Names: Murphy, Mary-Elizabeth B. author
Title: Policing passengers : Black women and the fight against bus violence / Mary-Elizabeth B. Murphy.
Other titles: Justice, power, and politics
Description: Chapel Hill : The University of North Carolina Press, [2026] | Series: Justice, power, and politics | Includes bibliographical references and index.
Identifiers: LCCN 2026043608 | ISBN 9781469698304 cloth | ISBN 9781469698311 paperback | ISBN 9781469696515 epub | ISBN 9781469698328 pdf
Subjects: LCSH: Segregation in transportation—United States—History—20th century | Civil rights movements—United States—History—20th century | African American women civil rights workers—History—20th century | Bus occupants—United States—History—20th century
Classification: LCC E185.61 .M978 2026 | DDC 323.1196/073—dc23/eng/20260921
LC record available at https://lccn.loc.gov/2026043608

Cover art: *Washington, D.C. Greyhound bus terminal on the day before Christmas. Waiting to board the bus to Richmond*, 1941, by John Vachon. Library of Congress, Prints & Photographs Division, Farm Security Administration/Office of War Information Black-and-White Negatives. https://lccn.loc.gov/2017813725.

For product safety concerns under the European Union's General Product Safety Regulation (EU GPSR), please contact gpsr@mare-nostrum.co.uk or write to the University of North Carolina Press and Mare Nostrum Group B.V., Doelen 72, 4831 GR Breda, The Netherlands.

This book is dedicated to my sister, Maggie Murphy. She started, and finished, law school while I researched this book and fights for justice, always.

By 1940 the Commonwealth of Virginia had become sophisticated in handling racial incidents on interstate buses. While it would tolerate no breach in its wall of segregation, it would also make sure that there was no basis for a charge of police brutality.

—Pauli Murray, *Song in a Weary Throat: An American Pilgrimage*

Addressing the historical injustices of the twentieth century is the project of the twenty-first century.

—Margaret A. Burnham, *By Hands Now Known: Jim Crow's Legal Executioners*

Contents

Illustrations

Figures

Tables

Policing Passengers

Introduction

Before Rosa, a Rosie

In July 1944, as World War II raged across Europe and Asia, Black women waged their own battles with white bus drivers. These violent struggles stretched across the country, from city buses in Birmingham, Alabama, to interstate carriers in Missouri and Virginia. One of those fighters was Irene Morgan. During World War II, she secured the most coveted position for Black women: she became a "Rosie"—an industrial worker. On a summer day, Irene Morgan boarded a Greyhound bus in Gloucester County, Virginia, bound for her home in Baltimore. In accordance with the Virginia segregation statute, she selected a seat in the middle. But a few miles into the trip, the driver requested that Morgan move to accommodate a white couple. She refused. The bus driver snapped that racial segregation was the law in Virginia. After Morgan rejected this order a second time, the driver tapped his well-worn police powers and called the sheriff. When the sheriff arrived, he read Morgan a warrant, but she grabbed it out of his hand and hurled it behind the seat. She kicked the sheriff, stating that she would "neither change her seat nor get off the bus." Officers arrested Morgan, placed her in jail, and fined her $10 for violating Virginia's segregation laws. A few days later, she entered the offices of a Black attorney to challenge her arrest.[1] After a long and protracted legal battle, Irene Morgan's case traveled to the Supreme Court of Virginia and eventually the United States Supreme Court, which ruled in 1946 that segregation on interstate buses posed an undue burden on interstate commerce.[2]

Irene Morgan is not as iconic as Rosa Parks. The *Morgan* decision was decided on narrow grounds and rarely enforced. In 1955—eleven years after Morgan's bus experience—Rosa Parks had a similar exchange with a bus driver in Montgomery, Alabama, but her arrest precipitated the Montgomery Bus Boycott and the court case *Browder v. Gayle*, which ended segregation on city buses. Since that era, Parks has symbolized bus segregation. An elementary school myth depicts a timid and tired Rosa Parks, whose spontaneous refusal to move sparked the Black freedom struggle. A nuanced narrative reveals that Parks was not the first Black woman to resist segregation, activists had been threatening a boycott, and the bus driver was violent.[3] But starting the story in the middle erases the beginning.[4] Rosa Parks was part of the second generation of passengers. By 1955, when Parks defied segregation, the violent bus industry was in its fourth decade, hundreds of Black women had already been arrested, and drivers had amassed significant policing power.

Policing Passengers presses back to the beginning, revealing that Black women riders dominated bus travel and bus protest from the outset. Scholars have recognized that Black women constituted a significant cohort of passengers in the early days of the bus industry.[5] But this history has complex layers. The threat, and hypervisibility, of Black women riders prompted white bus executives to recruit drivers from law enforcement, training them to administer white supremacy by elevating white women passengers and policing Black women passengers. When this first generation of Black women passengers boarded buses, they resisted this violent policing and fought tirelessly for their right to be treated as *women*. Black women passengers filed at least forty-three lawsuits against the bus industry in the 1920s, 1930s, and 1940s, which revolutionized the early campaign for Black equality in the United States. Black women passengers' foundational, if forgotten, activism transformed the bus industry and the law while drafting blueprints for the postwar Black freedom struggle. This history began right after World War I, when buses began to wheel on American roads and Black women traveled across these same routes.

The First Generation of Passengers

The bus industry and the Great Migration came of age together. And they shaped each other. In the 1910s, as white businessmen in the United States traced the first bus routes, thousands of African Americans left the South in the Great Migration. Between 1910 and 1950, over three million Black Southerners streamed into Northern cities.[6] The Great Migration put Black women on the road, while the Great Depression made inexpensive travel a necessity, resulting in thousands of Black women passengers in the earliest days of buses. Interstate buses were transformative for African American women in this era, unlocking a world of travel that had once been elusive.[7] Some Black women rode buses in their journeys northward, but many seized on the convenience and affordability of buses to return home.[8] In Southern Black communities, women served as the cultural workers in their extended families. It was expected that Black women would travel home for summer visits, holidays, illnesses, and funerals. Excited by the possibilities of affordable travel, Black women purchased bus tickets to attend conferences and conventions, tour the United States for vacations, and advance their education.[9] By 1935, more Americans were riding buses than trains. And one year later, Victor H. Green began to publish *The Negro Motorist Green Book*, which informed Black travelers about the restaurants, hotels, beauty parlors, and tailors they could patronize.[10] Even though this guide was primarily aimed at Black drivers, the recommendations were relevant for bus passengers as well, reflecting the broader trend of Black mobility in this era of migration.

While interstate lines connected Black women across great distances, municipal buses facilitated local transportation. As many cities switched from streetcars to buses in the 1930s and 1940s, thousands of Black women rode city buses in their daily work commutes. During World War II, ridership on all bus lines surged as Black women visited military bases and labored in factories, government offices, and hospitals. As soon as they purchased bus tickets on interstate or municipal lines, Black women encountered a rigid color line, whether it was segregation, exclusion, or even violence. And they did not accept this treatment as a fact of life.

Long before thousands of Black women marched against bus segregation in the 1950s or sat in the white section to enforce the *Morgan* decision in the 1960s, at least forty-three filed lawsuits against bus companies.[11] This first generation of lawsuits began with Laura Fischer in Indiana in 1927, and ended with Irene Morgan in Virginia in 1944. Some passengers contacted the National Association for the Advancement of Colored People (NAACP) to inquire about legal recourse, but many initiated lawsuits on their own, educating NAACP lawyers about strategy. Black women litigants received surprising legal victories and defeats in both regions of the country, winning approximately one-half of their cases and receiving thousands of dollars in damages. These cases illuminate the complexity of the law, underscore the richness of early struggles against racial discrimination, and demonstrate how segregation was practiced and enforced in both the Jim Crow North and the Jim Crow South.[12] But not all Black women had the time or resources to file lawsuits. Aggrieved passengers also narrated their experiences to the Black press, wrote blistering letters to bus companies, notarized affidavits, pressed the government to investigate incidents, and called for boycotts. In this first generation of bus riding, it was not unusual for a Black woman to board the bus as a passenger and then exit as a criminal.

In this era, Black women bus passengers had the least amount of money or power of any group of riders, including white men, white women, and

Black men. Most Black women riders labored in low-wage service jobs as cooks, domestics, and laundresses. At times, they boarded buses because they were fleeing violent situations. But buses were not safe spaces for Black women riders. With a few exceptions during World War II, white men drove the buses and enforced racialized and gendered codes with violence. In no other site of consumption—whether department stores, hotels, theaters, or restaurants—did Black women experience such a stark sexual and racialized dynamic. Businesses also practiced a color line, but the larger space, coupled with a hierarchy of operations, often defused conflict.[13] If a Black woman customer contested her treatment at a department store, she first interacted with a saleswoman and then was directed to a store manager. Violence was a last resort. But on a cramped bus, the white male driver was often the only employee. The bus industry outfitted him with a police-inspired uniform and accessories that could be weaponized. Violence was always on the table.

White male bus drivers subjected Black women riders to a range of abuses. Drivers knowingly misplaced luggage, exposed passengers to dangerous fumes, or denied them entry onto the bus altogether. For these Black women passengers, losing their luggage, paying a doctor's bill, or arranging alternative transportation had devastating financial consequences. Bus drivers and white passengers also violated Black women's bodies. Wielding billy clubs, pipes, ticket punchers, guns, and their own fists, white drivers violently assaulted Black women passengers.[14] As bus trips pressed into the evening and the moon eclipsed the sun, these rides became more dangerous. Buses were dimly lit, and it was not uncommon for white passengers to board buses intoxicated. In dark rows, white men thrust themselves on Black women's bodies. And when buses emptied of most passengers, white male drivers raped Black women, sometimes in broad daylight. There is no question that Black women represented the most poorly treated passengers at the outset of the bus industry. Bus lines also followed a strict hierarchy across race and gender, hiring Black women only for the most servile positions to ensure that they would never interact with white passengers, while eagerly recruiting white men and women—and even some Black men—to be conspicuous on buses.[15] These labor practices were not a mere afterthought; they were part of a deliberate strategy to make Black women invisible in the bus industry.

While this first generation of Black women bus passengers and workers has been forgotten, the history of their resistance is not surprising. Black women had a robust presence in the early civil rights movement.[16]

But if Black women's resistance to white supremacy was persistent, did their bus protests differ significantly from other forms of political activism in the interwar era? *Policing Passengers* demonstrates that Black women's experiences as bus passengers was explicitly gendered. Beginning in the late 1920s, Black women became a striking presence in this brand-new industry, constituting a disproportionate number of passengers on the bus and litigants in the courtroom. It was Black women riders who led the African American community in these transformative campaigns against bus segregation. Black women forcefully protested their treatment on buses because they demanded the right to be treated as women. This was not new. Whether as bus passengers, train riders, or streetcar travelers in previous generations, Black women had *always* been on the front lines against segregated transportation and racial violence.[17] But it was their fight on buses that forged the precise links between early struggles for civil rights and the postwar Black freedom movement. Black women were so vocal about their violent mistreatment on buses precisely because they understood on a visceral level that they were never the desired passenger in the first place.

Policing Passengers

When white men formed the first commercial bus lines in the United States, they worked to exclude Black women riders at every turn.[18] Many bus founders and executives were connected to the railroad industry, well versed in the dynamics of mass transportation, and seasoned in its racial configurations.[19] By the 1840s, railroads had transformed American life at the height of antebellum slavery.[20] As the historian Miriam Thaggert argues, trains were the first "mass form of technology actively policed in an effort to assert and maintain white political, social, and economic dominance."[21] Even though the United States' racial order underwent massive transformations from slavery to Reconstruction to Jim Crow, the railroad industry was nimble, creating different spatial configurations to accommodate the changing contexts of racialized and gendered hierarchies. From the beginning, passenger trains were capacious, featuring regular cars, a first-class car, a Ladies car, and a short car, also known as the "Negro car," the luggage car, or the smoking car.[22] The ladies' car was designed for white women, featuring padded seats and restrooms.[23] When slavery was a legal institution, free African Americans mostly rode in the luggage car but occasionally slipped into the regular passenger car or even the first-class car.[24]

But these iron railroad cars bent under the weight of racial ambiguity. Light-skinned African Americans—free and enslaved—avoided the luggage car through racial passing, even using those cars as their portal to freedom. And when Black servants accompanied white families, many argued that their labor required them to be present in the passenger and first-class cars. Most train segregation laws mandated that at least one or two passenger cars be designated for Black train riders.[25] As railroad passengers, Black women sued for the right to ride in the ladies' car, forcing white judges to contemplate the enforcement of racial segregation, and ultimately succeeded in securing significant damages from the railroads.[26]

By the 1910s and 1920s, when white men founded the bus lines in the United States at the height of Jim Crow, that racial system informed every consideration in the new industry. Designing a Jim Crow bus was significantly more difficult than a Jim Crow train because it was one large vehicle. There was no ladies' car and no luggage car. In subtle and overt ways, industry executives used the bus experience to construct white women as the desired passenger and Black women as the deviant one. These decisions stretched from the content of their printed and promotional materials to their hiring practices to the spatial configurations of rest stops. The bus industry hired Black women to perform the most menial of service labor, relegated them to the back of the bus, and often banned them from lavatories, restrooms, and restaurants. Industry executives designed the bus experience to reflect African Americans' second-class citizenship rights in the United States. While evidence indicates that Indigenous people and Mexican migrants also experienced a color line, white executives positioned anti-Blackness in both the Jim Crow South and the Jim Crow North as the overarching racial classifications in the bus industry.[27]

Long before Black women riders ever boarded the first bus, white industry executives felt so threatened by the prospect of their presence and their visibility on buses that they created a new category of worker to enforce and subsequently police the racialized and gendered color line with brute force: the bus driver. This new worker had very different responsibilities from a train conductor.[28] Bus drivers had to steer the bus, manage passengers, oversee luggage, check tickets, and enforce Jim Crow in a very tight space. These expanded duties, compounded by the high stakes of the job, prompted bus executives to recruit white drivers and safety managers from law enforcement industries, especially the military and the police. The bus industry trained its drivers to uphold racialized and gendered codes with brute force. When Black women riders protested this rough treatment, white bus drivers escalated their intensity. It was not a coincidence that by the late 1930s, many bus drivers carried guns, were deputized to conduct citizen arrests, and frequently steered buses toward police stations at the slightest moment of conflict. Activist Pauli Murray stated that by 1940, Virginia buses had become "sophisticated" in handling incidents. Bus drivers and police officers mistreated and abused Black women passengers, but the system had been devised so that these riders could not contest the brutality they experienced. What Murray did not say was that Black women riders—both the threat of their presence and their visibility on buses—prompted bus companies to develop these powerful systems of passenger policing.[29]

In 1929, Greyhound, the largest and most powerful bus company in the United States, tapped Marcus Dow from the New York Metropolitan Police Department to become its director of safety, a role that entailed supervising all bus drivers. Dow had spent three years in the Bureau of Public Safety in the New York City Police Department, which explains how Greyhound, the largest and most iconic bus company in the nation, modeled its bus drivers on the police.[30]

One illustration that graced the cover of Greyhound's in-bus magazine, the *Highway Traveler*, from 1936 was meant to be gentle and charming, demonstrating how a white bus driver with a gun in his holster interacted with two white boys on a sandy beach in Florida. But a political cartoon from the *Baltimore Afro-American* in 1944 painted a different picture—that of World War II bus drivers as violent figures who routinely sparred with, and occasionally killed, Black soldiers.[31] Importantly, this cartoon showed a frightened Black woman, shielding her baby from the wrath and force of the bus driver, who has just shot a man.

Law enforcement institutions inspired the look and mannerisms of all bus drivers in the United States. Drivers wore uniforms modeled on those of police officers and soldiers, sometimes carried guns, and wielded authority that resembled that of law enforcement. Like police officers, bus drivers were considered pleasant and nonthreatening figures in white America. But in African American communities, white police officers routinely assaulted and policed—and overpoliced—Black women and girls.[32] Buses represented another important site of violence. While drivers were the most iconic employees, the industry also trained ticket agents and other company workers to enforce a color line and traumatize thousands of Black women passengers. Buses were unique workspaces because of the racialized and gendered patterns of labor. *Policing Passengers* critically interrogates the dynamic

These images demonstrate two different depictions of a white bus driver. In the *Highway Traveler* (*above*), the bus driver is kind and gentle, even though he looks like a police officer and is armed with a gun, which was legal in Florida. In the image from the *Baltimore Afro-American* (*opposite*), he is wielding power over Black passengers and is aiming his gun at the body of a Black soldier during World War II. *Sources: Highway Traveler* Collection, Western Reserve Historical Society, Cleveland, Ohio; *Baltimore Afro-American*, July 22, 1944. Courtesy of the AFRO American Newspapers Archives/Afro Charities.

between white bus drivers laboring in this violent industry and the Black women who boarded these buses. Black women's unrelenting opposition to their treatment transformed the early bus industry, prompting executives to expand their violent policing tactics.

While Black women passengers provoked this heightened culture of violence in the bus industry, they simultaneously challenged it by filing at least forty-three lawsuits, which forced bus companies and the government to grapple with passenger experiences and the legal complexities of racial segregation. This dynamic process between the bus industry's violent practices of domination and Black women's unrelenting patterns of resistance escalated steadily every year and can be mapped across three decades and hundreds of passenger stories, stretching from the start of the industry in the 1920s to the height of bus power by World War II.

The law was both clear and ambiguous about the color line on buses. Between 1928 and 1943, most Southern states had added statutes to their state constitutions, stating that racial segregation on trains, trolleys, and streetcars now applied to buses.[33] Maryland, Tennessee, and Kentucky never passed these statutes even though segregation was practiced in those states. In several cases, Black women won their lawsuits because they experienced racial segregation when state statutes did not include the word "bus." Even though these types of lawsuits cracked open a window, state legislatures soon slammed the door shut by amending their constitutions to make bus segregation legal. But even if bus segregation was the law, its enforcement was unclear. Mississippi was the only state that required buses to install partitions composed of "metal, wood, or cloth" to separate Black and white passengers.[34] In other Southern states, buses merely put white passengers in the front and Black passengers in the back, sometimes adjusting the ratios in accordance with the bus population. Conversely, fifteen Northern states and the District of Columbia had civil rights statutes, which banned segregation in public accommodation. In theory, buses traveling within these states could not segregate passengers, but in practice, enforcement was limited.[35] And on interstate buses that traveled across state lines, these vehicles were technically under the jurisdiction of interstate commerce, not state laws mandating segregation or civil rights. But most interstate carriers, especially buses that wheeled into Southern states, enforced racial segregation.[36]

Aware of the legal ambiguity of segregation on buses and the legal category of tort, or personal injury, Black women litigants plunged ahead with vigor. Middle- and working-class Black women used the law as an instrument to counter the power of the bus industry, forcing bus lines to compensate them for poor passenger experiences. Throughout the Jim Crow South and the Jim Crow North, Black women filed forty-three lawsuits for segregation and bodily harm. In cases that traveled to state supreme courts, white judges issued verdicts that shaped legal precedent on these matters. In the 1930s, judges issued appellate decisions ruling that all-white buses were illegal, that drivers had to enforce racial segregation fairly between Black and white passengers, that the bus industry was required to transport passengers to their final destination, even if they were impoverished, and that bus carriers were liable for lost luggage.[37] Additionally, in local courts in the Jim Crow North, Black women successfully used their state's civil rights statutes to sue against bus segregation. All of these lawsuits put the industry in a defensive position.

When the United States entered World War II, the federal government created the Office of Defense Transportation and partnered with the bus industry, marking a critical shift from commercial-based violence to state-based violence. Bus drivers seized on the violent policing tactics they had perfected on Black women passengers and applied them to Black male soldiers and Black women war workers, nurses, civil servants, and soldiers' wives, sometimes to deadly ends. By World War II, the United States was fully complicit in these bus abuses but would neither acknowledge this reality nor hold the bus industry accountable. During World War II, Black women war workers and soldiers' wives—not the soldiers themselves—made the right to ride the right of American democracy. Drawing on lessons they had learned in the 1930s, Black women filed five lawsuits that reached the Supreme Court of Virginia and ultimately the US Supreme Court in the landmark ruling *Morgan v. Virginia* in 1946. Uncovering the racist and violent origins of the bus industry in the United States fastens the crucial link between the birth of buses after World War I and the explosion of Black protest against segregated transportation in the postwar era. This first generation of Black women passengers used bus travel to press for citizenship rights in the United States.[38]

But in this first generation, Black women's protest against racial discrimination on buses and claims to citizenship rights was not a nationally coordinated movement. In cities and especially in migrant neighborhoods, women traded stories about bus discrimination and created legal networks. And on buses themselves, women passengers forged close bonds. Cooks, maids, and teachers rode buses every day, and this experience knit them together. But in other instances, Black women passengers who had never even met became allies and, in a few instances, co-litigants or cellmates, bonded by their shared experiences of violence. In this era, there were only two resources with a national reach that addressed bus segregation: the Black press and the NAACP. By the 1930s, at least twenty Black newspapers and periodicals covered discrimination on buses. As Black women told reporters about the violence of the bus industry, their stories linked passengers in activist reading cultures across the country. Reading a newspaper article about an episode of discrimination or a successful lawsuit inspired other Black women to speak out or contemplate a lawsuit. Black women also alerted the NAACP about their passenger experiences. The NAACP's officers, some of whom were lawyers, advised Black women on the next legal steps to take and sometimes contacted bus companies. Even though these Black women were battling bus segregation at the same time, most were not aware that the struggle was collective. It is only in dusty archival documents, trial transcripts, and newspaper exposés where patterns began to appear.

Silence, Violence, and Testimony in the Archive

Like any historical project, the research in this book was not linear. I began with a simple question: What were African American women's experiences on buses in the early days of the industry? After spending three years immersed in newspapers and the NAACP's vast archive, I had gathered many sources about Black women's experiences on buses, including letters, articles, and even legal affidavits. These documents were rich, furnishing insights into Black women's interiority as bus passengers. I then visited the Chicago History Museum to investigate Greyhound Corporation records. When I pulled company histories, financial documents, and speeches out of the boxes, I realized that this collection had been swept clean. Greyhound executives had carefully curated this archive, presenting a capitalist narrative of economic growth devoid of racial conflict. The power was present, and the silence was telling.[39]

But box 3 contained two periodicals: a passenger magazine, *Greyhound Traveler*, and an employee newsletter, the *Highway Log*. When I cracked open the pages, the perspective shifted from silence to violence. In the text and images of these periodicals, I found racist caricatures and offensive travel articles about Black Southerners, Indigenous Americans, Latinx people, and residents of Africa and Asia. Not only was I surprised that Greyhound had circulated these racist periodicals among its passengers and employees, but I began to understand these texts and images as an epistemic form of violence. By dehumanizing people of color in their publications, Greyhound and other bus lines made it clear that they had already determined who people of color were, how they behaved, and, implicitly, how acts of brutal racist violence could be justified.[40] Visiting this archive inspired me to add a new layer to the book and position the bus industry as a historical actor. It was impossible to investigate Black women's experiences on buses without first understanding the white men who founded these early bus companies and illuminating the powerful business culture they created.

I then located other bus industry periodicals: *Transit Journal* and *Bus Transportation*. All businessmen in the industry read these trade journals, which chronicled topics ranging from automotive technology and bus routes to passenger recruitment and driver uniforms. These periodicals covered *all* buses, including massive interstate corporations like Greyhound, regional companies, and municipal lines. None of the bus periodicals I examined ran a single article explicitly focused on Black women passengers, but the specter of their presence appeared in fleeting references and disturbing fragments. These industry periodicals echoed a similarly violent narrative about Black women passengers, demonstrating that the color line was just as insidious on local buses and regional lines as it was on interstate carriers. Inspired by the methodological insights from Black feminist history, I determined that these sources formed a core part of the research.[41] There is a reason why historians have distinguished between interstate and municipal bus companies, but reading these industry publications convinced me to write about first-generation Black women passengers on all bus lines.[42]

I then gained access to a legal database and began searching for lawsuits. Newspapers and letters were littered with references to court cases, but I was uncertain whether I could actually locate them. To my utter surprise, I uncovered a treasure trove of Black women's lawsuits against bus lines that traveled to Southern appellate courts in the 1930s and 1940s. I then discovered that many state supreme court archives and libraries had even preserved the briefs and trial transcripts for many of these lawsuits. These trial transcripts roared with Black women's animated testimony and vivid descriptions as bus passengers in the Jim Crow South.[43] It was in these legal archives where Black women narrated their experiences with bus violence, including sexual assault and rape, which never appeared in the published opinions. The silence and fragments in the bus industry sources contrasted sharply with the noise and breadth of this legal evidence.

These searches furnished me with a range of materials, including organizational records, personal papers, Black and white newspaper articles, bus industry periodicals, court cases, and census records. And yet as in any historical project, there is still an unevenness. Most of the Black women in this book were working-class residents of either the Jim Crow South or the Jim Crow North, who lived on the economic margins and rode buses as part of their daily survival. The lives of some of them can be illuminated through archival, census, or legal records, while the lives of others appear only as fragments—a faint signature in a tattered letter or a single frustrating sentence in a newspaper article. There are no perfect sources, and silences can be as telling as testimony.

Policing Passengers is a work of historical restorative justice. "Addressing the historical injustices of the twentieth century," writes the legal scholar Margaret Burnham, "is the work of the twenty-first century." It is "still within the United States' power to provide reparation for the violence that made Jim Crow possible."[44] *Policing Passengers* reckons with the violence that Black women experienced at the hands of the bus industry. I have chosen to keep every woman's name in the book because all somehow spoke truth to power. I am eternally grateful that at least forty-three women navigated a white legal system to tell their story and seek justice from the bus industry so that we can hear from this first generation of passengers.

Chapter Outlines

Policing Passengers is divided into three parts, each one illuminating a different dimension of Black women's interactions with the bus industry. Part 1 analyzes Black women's experiences with the bus lines. Chapter 1 peels back the curtain to expose the racialized and gendered imaginaries of bus companies, analyzing the periodicals they disseminated, the labor practices they followed, the advertisements they circulated, and the rest stops they designed. Chapter 2 turns to Black women passengers' resistance. Black women bus riders articulated claims to consumer citizenship as they worked with the early civil rights community to protest their unequal treatment. Black male leaders celebrated Black women's defiance and simultaneously downplayed the brutal violence that these passengers experienced.

Part 2 examines Black women's lawsuits against the bus companies. Chapter 3 chronicles lawsuits in the Jim Crow North. Southern migrant women hired Black attorneys to take Northern bus lines to court and test the boundaries of citizenship rights in their new states of residency. Pointing to their state's civil rights statutes, Black women received surprising legal victories in the late 1920s and early 1930s. But as bus travel gained popularity and violence became more normalized, Black women began to lose their lawsuits. Chapter 4 investigates the tort lawsuits that Black women filed in the Jim Crow South. This chapter documents the delicate dance Black women had to perform in Southern courts: suing for bodily injury on buses without ever discussing race relations or the humiliation of segregation.

Part 3 chronicles Black women's bus rides during World War II, as the stakes on buses escalated when the federal government began partnering with the bus industry. Chapter 5 examines the thousands of Black women who rode buses in the Deep South during World War II, including war workers, nurses, soldiers' wives, members of the military, and ordinary citizens. This chapter analyzes Black women's exclusion from most wartime opportunities, demonstrating how they channeled that frustration into pointed resistance on city buses: cursing at drivers and passengers, fighting back against violence, and politicizing the wartime climate on the bus. Bus drivers drew on the policing tactics they had perfected when dealing with Black women passengers and applied them to Black male soldiers, sometimes to deadly ends. Chapter 6 demonstrates the profound difference that region made in the war, revealing how Black women in the North, the Midwest, and the Washington, DC, metropolitan region engaged in similar types of resistance but successfully linked their wartime labor with the right to ride in dignity, making claims to war citizenship. By the middle of the war in 1943, rows of city buses sat idle in parking lots because there were no white Americans to drive them. In Cleveland, Detroit, and New York City, this crisis of transportation reached such a breaking point that it forced municipal bus companies to do the unthinkable and hire Black women as bus drivers. Around this same time, five Black women brought cases of bus segregation to the Supreme Court of Virginia and worked to make the right to ride the right of American democracy, paving the way for the landmark ruling *Morgan v. Virginia*.

Researching and writing civil rights history of the long twentieth century presents many challenges. It is nearly impossible to select a point of origin that establishes a definitive beginning. It is equally difficult to assess the significance of the early and passionate struggles for Black freedom before the passage of national legislation in the 1950s and 1960s.[45] *Policing Passengers* presses back to the first generation of riders, peering into the lives of women who first heard the word "bus" and imagined it as the means to sustain their familial networks in the era of migration, travel to and from work, and tour the United States for pleasure. This new form of technology would have a fraught history around race and sex and would ultimately become a crucial part of the postwar Black freedom struggle, when the second generation of riders boarded buses. And yet the struggles and triumphs of the first generation made the second generation possible. Black women's early bus rides made bus seats a powerful symbol of American democracy, which persists to this day. Instead of beginning with Rosa Parks, let us start with a passenger named Violet Mohand, whose violent encounter on a bus in Clarksdale, Mississippi, has until now been lost.

Part I Bus Companies and Their Customers

We recognize women as our natural customers.

—Frank J. Noll, President, Sommerset Bus Company, 1932

It is most deplorable when decent self-respecting, law-abiding colored people receive such services from bus companies. I hope something can be done in a general way to alleviate such treatments which are most humiliating to women.

—Leila Payne, New York City, 1941

1 Selling Sarah and Violating Violet

Racialized Constructions of Womanhood in the Bus Industry

In 1932, an article in *Bus Transportation* proclaimed, "Sell Sarah," telling industry leaders that profits would surge if they catered to women riders. Women, the article noted, "are just as important to transportation as they are to department stores." With the recent economic depression, automobile sales had declined, prompting bus industry leaders to court women riders.[1] The article profiled Frank J. Noll, a white veteran of World War I, who had founded the New Jersey–based Somerset Bus Company in 1925.[2] Noll tailored Somerset to satisfy women passengers. "We recognize women as our natural customers," Noll stated, noting that women constituted the "backbone" of his bus business. Women were more discerning than men and often demanded "better service." Somerset made bus timetables clear enough that women passengers could understand them, trained drivers to treat women with courtesy, assured women about the reliability of bus transportation, and kept their buses clean. It was women customers who controlled the "purse strings" and were the "world's back-seat drivers," paying just as much attention to driving on buses as they did in cars. If companies like Somerset satisfied women customers, this business strategy would also attract men. "There's not a better bet today," the article concluded, "than to sell Sarah."[3]

"Sarah" did not exist. She was a figment in the imagination of the bus industry, created at this historically specific moment when transportation in the United States was changing at a rapid pace and bus lines raced to convince Americans to start riding these modern vehicles. By enshrining a definition of Sarah through words and images, the bus industry both explicitly crafted the normative bus passenger as a white woman and implicitly determined the deviant bus passenger as the antithesis of Sarah. Her name was Violet. And she was not imagined.

In June 1935, Violet Mohand journeyed over nine hundred miles from her home in Chicago to visit family in New Orleans. Mohand was one of thousands of Black women who traveled to sustain familial connections in the Great Migration. Following her summer stay, she purchased a

Greyhound bus ticket back home. It was not surprising that Mohand had opted for Greyhound. Over the past seven years, Greyhound had tripled in size and published glossy advertisements, promising women passengers a seamless, comfortable ride on modern buses.[4] At the height of the Great Depression, as Americans were crushed by unemployment and lower wages, a bus was more affordable than a train. Over three hundred miles into Mohand's trip, in Clarksdale, Mississippi, the bus filled with passengers. Mohand remained in her assigned seat near the front of the bus. When the white driver ordered her to vacate her seat so a white woman could sit down, she refused. Mohand's actions enraged the driver, prompting him to curl his fingers into a tight fist and punch her in the face. He then called the police, who arrived and swiftly arrested Violet Mohand, charging her with disorderly conduct. A judge sentenced her to either $125 in fines or thirty days on a chain gang, a form of imprisonment almost always reserved for Black women. Ironically, or not, her work on the chain gang would pave the very roads that this bus had traveled, underscoring how the bus industry intersected with the carceral state for Black woman passengers.[5]

It is unclear which punishment Mohand selected, but when she returned to her hometown, she immediately contacted the city's Black-owned *Chicago Defender*, which ran an exposé of her story.[6] Not only did this article describe Mohand's ordeal, but it also featured her photograph. When the broad swath of *Defender* readers living across the country scanned the latest issue, they were greeted with the startling headline "Visits 'Hell.'"[7] Readers stared at Violet Mohand's arresting portrait. Dressed in a stylish hat, Mohand gazed seriously and sorrowfully into the camera.

Pressing back to the formation of the first bus lines in the United States, white industry executives sold to Sarah and violated Violet: They used the category of womanhood to create racial divisions in their company culture as a business strategy to increase profits and uphold white supremacy. Black women *haunted* the bus industry. As capitalists, bus executives knew that the presence of Black women bus passengers might deter the patronage of white passengers, so they took deliberate steps to ensure that Black women's bodies would not be welcome on this new form of transportation except as servants. In their printed materials—including bus magazines, company newsletters, and industry periodicals—writers and illustrators denigrated Black women and waxed poetic about white women. Executives only hired Black women in a servile capacity, while

The *Chicago Defender* was a vital source for reporting incidents of bus segregation and violence in the first generation. By taking the care to include a photograph, readers across the country could gaze into Violet Mohand's eyes and envision her traumatic experience on a bus. *Source*: "Visits 'Hell,'" *Chicago Defender*, July 20, 1935, 3.

they elevated white women to a range of paid positions. They designed different experiences for women passengers across racial lines, stretching from their treatment at the hands of ticket agents and bus drivers to the design of rest steps.

Just as buses needed constant maintenance to ensure a smooth ride, so did the systems of white supremacy and racialized constructions of womanhood that undergirded the industry. Divisions between Black and white women passengers were not necessarily natural; the bus industry had to create, maintain, and reinforce these differences. More than any other figure, the white bus driver maintained these categories. He revered white women passengers while he wielded instruments of terror on Black women passengers.[8] If a white bus driver brandished a weapon on a white woman passenger, the system of "Selling Sarah" would be crushed. By vesting a bus driver with absolute authority, the bus industry granted him the power to fictionalize Black women's behavior and conveniently justify his brutality toward a Black woman passenger by claiming that she was disorderly, violent, or unreasonable, reinforcing the mythology that Black women passengers were inherently deviant. Black women tried to evade these oppressive systems at every turn by asserting claims to womanhood, and at every turn, they were rejected.[9]

This chapter chronicles the formation of the early bus industry in the United States, underscoring how executives wove their anxieties around Black women riders and workers into their industry practices. Illuminating this racialized and gendered culture is essential for understanding why thousands of Black women, such as Violet Mohand, experienced such a traumatic bus experience. The bus industry, like any new economic enterprise, did not appear overnight and grew in fits and starts. It involved reams of paper, thousands of vehicles, glossy advertisements, the construction of rest stops, and hiring blitzes. The threat of Black women riders and workers lurked at every corner. I begin with text and images, critically investigating the racialized and gendered imaginaries of bus industry executives who evoked Black women in their everyday discourses. These materials shed light on the origins of the bus industry. I then turn to work, analyzing the hiring practices of the bus industry and the racialized and gendered implications of this labor. Shifting to advertisements, I analyze how the bus industry recruited white women riders. Much to their horror, however, the bus industry's shiny ad campaigns also reached cohorts of Black women, who eagerly climbed aboard these new buses and soon discovered that they were not the bus industry's desired passenger. I conclude with a discussion of the spatial configurations of rest stops and waiting rooms, casting them as architectural sites to reinforce Black women's exclusion from the bus industry and white women's inclusion in it. Let us begin with an ordinary article about the bus industry. Why did an advertising executive in New York City begin his article about corporate growth in the bus industry with Topsy, a fictional enslaved girl?

Selling Sarah: Racialized and Gendered Cultures in the Bus Industry

In July 1932, Ralph K. Wadsworth, a New York City advertising professional, wrote a feature in *Bus Transportation* titled "Who Rides Buses Most, Men or Women?"[10] Here, Wadsworth traced women's growing visibility in the bus industry. "Like Topsy," Wadsworth wrote, "the bus business just 'growed up.'" Topsy referred to an enslaved Black girl in *Uncle Tom's Cabin*, an abolitionist book that contained many racist caricatures. In the novel, Topsy frequently misbehaved and required frequent beatings. Her counterpoint was an angelic white girl named Eva, who helped to save her. Wadsworth then described the increasing numbers of women bus riders and the ways that the industry might cater to women, whether it was adding touches of luxury to waiting rooms or advertising bus lines on the Women's page of the newspaper rather than the Sports page.[11] There was no space for subtlety in this piece. By beginning an article about the expansion of bus companies with a derogatory reference to an African American girl who needed to be tamed and policed—and implicitly a white girl who helped to save her—this piece revealed that the denigration of Black women was situated at the heart of the bus industry in the United States.

The bus industry began in the 1910s at the height of Jim Crow. The first buses were jitneys, small vehicles that could transport people across short distances. In 1913, Swedish immigrant Carl "Eric" Wickman moved to the town of Hibbing, Minnesota, where he opened the Mesaba Transportation Company (later rebranded as Greyhound), which ran a taxi that traveled four miles to the nearby town of Alice. After the success of this venture, Wickman broadened his ambitions and began to schedule bus routes from Hibbing to other destinations. The rides were so inexpensive that dozens of men and women eagerly clamored to travel in these vehicles, demonstrating the real consumer demand for mass transportation.[12] Wickman originally envisioned the Mesaba Transportation Company to merely improve the lives of white workers, but gradually the company expanded its customer base to serve white businessmen, housewives, and families. While Carl Wickman was experimenting with bus rides in Minnesota, business leaders in California were also testing out customer routes. In 1912, Charles Wren, a native of Missouri, incorporated the Pickwick Bus Line in Southern California. Pickwick ferried passengers from the Pickwick Theatre to different destinations in San Diego, California, but soon expanded throughout the region, running lines that dipped into Texas.[13] And in San Francisco, businessmen in the

American Motor Transport Corporation began running the Yelloway Bus Line, named for its distinctive yellow color.[14] Mesaba, Pickwick, and Yelloway became the largest interstate bus companies in the 1910s.[15]

In the 1920s, the business climate, government investment in transportation, and a handful of Supreme Court rulings nurtured the growth of bus companies throughout the United States. The federal government did not exercise much regulation over business in this decade, which led to tremendous economic expansion for both the automobile and the bus industries. The government also poured money into infrastructure. In 1921, Congress passed the Highway Act, which allocated $75 million for the construction of highways and channeled this money through state governments to match these funds.[16] Not only did the government fund highways, but the Supreme Court also issued a set of rulings that bolstered the economic climate for commercial buses, ruling that "states could not prevent the use of motor buses in interstate commerce."[17] Individual states recognized buses as common carriers and imposed their own regulations.[18]

The 1920s ushered in an era of prosperity and expansion for bus lines in the United States. The front page of the *New York Times* proclaimed, "Motor Bus Expansion Big Feature of Year," highlighting the endless possibilities of this new bus transportation.[19] At that time, 6,500 bus lines traveled across 7,800 routes throughout the nation, stretching from large interstate companies to local and regional lines.[20] Universities even began to offer classes for enterprising men to learn about the bus industry.[21] The United States manufactured 63 percent of all buses in the world. American workers built the bus chassis, or structural framework, and shipped them abroad, where the rest of the bus was assembled.[22] As bus lines flourished in the United States, mostly white businessmen formed networks and published periodicals to adopt standardized practices for the industry. In 1926, white businessmen affiliated with the American Automobile Association founded an auxiliary organization, the Motor Bus Division, which became the National Association of Motor Bus Operators (NAMBO) in 1930. Every year, industry leaders gathered at NAMBO meetings, where they viewed vehicle exhibitions, fingered upholstery swatches, discussed traffic patterns, and learned about the latest laws and regulations in the bus industry.[23] Bus executives shared industry information through publications. McGraw-Hill published two periodicals for the bus industry: *Transit Journal* and *Bus Transportation*. *Transit Journal* was initially focused on streetcars and subways but gradually shifted to buses. *Bus Transportation*, founded in 1922, centered on the growing bus industry, profiling different bus lines across the country and offering information about legislation and best company practices.[24]

Articles in *Bus Transportation* celebrated the growth of the bus industry in this decade, documenting the expansion of interstate and municipal lines. The bus industry reached such a pinnacle that some interstate companies designed their buses to be luxurious and even glamorous, rivaling the amenities of fancy trains. These buses were outfitted with reclining chairs, plush pillows, towels, dining service with fine china, and waiters to care for passengers.[25] Just as elegant department stores and train stations offered their customers many opulent touches, including beauty parlors, high-end retail, and restaurants, some of the most enterprising bus lines aspired to this level of service. In 1929, the Pickwick Corporation introduced the Nite Coach—a double-decker bus modeled on sleeper trains, especially luxury Pullman cars. Bus passengers boarded the bus in the afternoon or evening, climbed into a sleeping compartment, enjoyed turn-down service by a Black porter, and were able to sleep for most of the bus ride. The Nite Coaches became the "Pullmans Plus," offering passengers a sixty-eight-hour bus trip from Los Angeles to Chicago.[26] Interstate bus lines such as Pickwick and Greyhound typified the nation's capitalist abundance in the 1920s.

Not only did interstate bus companies grow at a rapid pace, but many American cities began to replace streetcar lines with buses. Urban leaders recognized the mass appeal of buses over streetcars because of their faster speeds, ability to travel across roads, and quieter rides.[27] Large cities, such as New York, Boston, Chicago, and Philadelphia, as well as smaller cities, such as Atlanta, Birmingham, Baton Rouge, Cincinnati, Cleveland, Kansas City, and Pittsburgh, all introduced buses for urban residents, or ran a mixture of streetcars and buses.[28] By 1932, there were 14,333 buses running in cities with a population of fifty thousand or more.[29] Municipal bus companies were commuter lines, ferrying passengers to and from work, school, and shopping. Even though municipal lines modeled their operations on interstate buses by adopting the same bus driver uniforms and systems of stops and transfers, amenities were spartan, featuring durable seats and modest waiting rooms.

Local lines expanded so rapidly in the 1920s that white women and African American men even established their own bus lines. In the Midwest, Helen M. Schultz, Iowa's "Bus Queen," operated the Red Ball Transportation Company, which ran routes across Northern Iowa, until she sold the business in 1930.[30] Black businessmen also incorporated their own bus companies to serve an exclusively Black clientele. In 1921, Black men in Virginia invested $10,000 to launch the Brooks Bus Company to avoid segregation on white lines. Just two months after the company's founding, the Brooks Jitney bus was ferrying Black passengers on twenty trips a day between Washington, DC, and Alexandria, Virginia.[31] This worked in the short term, but sustaining a bus company required capital that most Black businessmen simply did not have, and the Brooks Bus Company dissolved. Ten years later, in 1931, the Rialto Bus Company opened its doors in New York City's Harlem with the explicit purpose of transporting Black passengers, and especially chartering buses to other cities, but it also folded after only a few years.[32]

The only Black bus line that survived longer than a decade was the Safe Bus Company in Winston-Salem, North Carolina. Safe emerged out of longstanding patterns of racial disparities in transportation. In the 1910s, North Carolina's Duke Power Company had introduced a streetcar in Winston-Salem but refused to extend routes into Black neighborhoods.[33] To transport Black workers to the Camel Cigarette Factory, taxi driver E. L. Richardson purchased a truck, installed seats in the vehicle, and created a jitney for Black riders. Demand was high, and hundreds of workers clamored for rides each day, causing conflict and skirmishes. To solve this transportation problem, a group of Black businessmen incorporated the Safe Bus Company in 1926, making this line synonymous with security and protection. It is possible that Safe might have been subtly coded to indicate that passengers would not experience violence or assault at the hands of its bus drivers.[34] Remarkably, the Safe Bus Company defied the odds and ran until the early 1970s, when the city of Winston-Salem purchased it.[35] These Black bus companies shared several characteristics. They all crafted their identity around the service of an exclusively Black clientele, generating goodwill by offering African American passengers a bus ride free from the humiliation of segregation. And because they were based in New York, Virginia, North Carolina, they had a natural base of Black passengers. Being able to ride a Black-owned bus afforded African Americans a ride in dignity with attentive customer service. Boarding these buses—and shopping at Black-owned department stores—marked a transformative experience for Black consumers.[36] But Safe was the only Black-owned bus company to last longer than five years, which demonstrates not only the fluid nature of the industry but also the structural disadvantages of Black lines against the enormous capital of white lines.

In 1930, the United States slipped into the Great Depression, ridership fell by 10 percent in the United States and Canada, and many of these local bus lines collapsed.[37] Seizing on this historic opportunity, Greyhound purchased

TABLE 1.1 Greyhound-affiliated lines in North America, 1936

Name	*City*	*State*
Greyhound Management Company	Cleveland	Ohio
Pacific Greyhound Lines, Inc.	San Francisco	California
Canadian Greyhound Lines, Inc.	Windsor	Canada
Central Greyhound Lines, Inc.	New York City	New York
Atlantic Greyhound Lines, Inc.	Charleston	West Virginia
Capitol Greyhound Lines, Inc.	Cincinnati	Ohio
Pennsylvania Greyhound Lines, Inc.	Philadelphia	Pennsylvania
Dixie Greyhound Lines, Inc.	Memphis	Tennessee
Northland Greyhound Lines, Inc.	Minneapolis	Minnesota
Southwestern Greyhound Lines, Inc.	Fort Worth	Texas
Southeastern Greyhound Lines, Inc.	Lexington	Kentucky
Richmond Greyhound Lines, Inc.	Richmond	Virginia

Source: *Highway Traveler*, February–March 1936, Western Reserve Historical Society, Cleveland, Ohio.

California Transit, Southern Pacific Motor Transport, and, most importantly, Pickwick Stages. By purchasing Pickwick, Greyhound absorbed the largest bus company in the United States. With these acquisitions, Greyhound buses wheeled across forty states as well as Canada and Mexico, transported 1.8 million people per year, and served forty-five thousand towns across the country. Not only did Greyhound expand its business empire, but it also purchased minority interests in other bus companies and joined the New York Stock Exchange.[38] In 1931, the newly formed Greyhound Management Company moved from Chicago, Illinois, to Cleveland, Ohio, and opened a sprawling new headquarters on Superior Avenue. The Greyhound Management Company oversaw Greyhound's twelve affiliated lines, and the company's board of directors appointed a seasoned team of white executives to lead it. By the early 1930s, it was clear that Greyhound commanded enormous power and influence in the bus industry.

Since it was mostly white men who formed bus lines in the 1920s and 1930s, evidence indicates that all executives—whether they worked at Greyhound or a local municipal line—worked to sell Sarah and market an inexpensive product for discerning white women consumers. Many legal, economic, and racial considerations influenced this bus industry culture. Jim Crow laws governed the South but shaped the nation. Southern bus companies were legally obligated to enforce racial segregation on their buses and could be fined if they resisted. But even for bus lines outside the South, it was logical to follow their own system of racial exclusion, even though the Jim Crow North had civil rights statutes. These legal considerations intersected with economic and racial anxieties. White bus executives feared that the presence of Black passengers on a bus—whether in front seats or far in the back—would deter white women from boarding. And they worried that their bus lines would start to lose profits if they gained the reputation of transporting large numbers of Black passengers or if white riders complained about Black riders. And these were only the economic and legal concerns. Most business executives were white men who had been born in the United States, steeped in the nation's racial attitudes and prejudices. Segregation and anti-Black exclusion were reflexive positions that they incorporated into their bus lines. Whether they were adhering to the law, applying a business principle, or following their own racial instincts, white executives in the bus industry elevated white women passengers and degraded Black women passengers. In creating this gendered and racialized bus industry culture, white bus executives stamped Jim Crow practices onto a brand-new form of transportation in the United States. Executives did not know the future in the 1920s and 1930s, but their deliberate decisions about the bus industry ultimately shaped the course of American travel and became the lightning rod in the Black freedom struggle. Even as the ink dried on these bus industry publications, it was clear that white executives were laser focused on selling Sarah.

In 1932, *Bus Transportation* published a revealing article titled "She Wanted Repairs, Not Damages," describing the importance of vehicle maintenance. Strangely, or perhaps not, this article offered a fictional vignette about a Southern Black woman who had just been hit by a car. A friend asked her if she was going to sue for damages, and she replied, "I've got plenty of damages already, what I wants is repairs." The article then went on to offer bus companies strategies to prevent these types of accidents through bus maintenance and upkeep. But the subtext was that this elderly Black woman was not savvy enough to file a lawsuit, even though by 1932, more than ten Black women had already sued bus companies throughout the country. Her poor grammar and her malapropism—confusing damages and repairs—was racially coded, evoking Black characters on a minstrel stage.[39] This placement of a Black woman depicted in racist caricature served as a humorous yet quotidian reminder for bus companies to conduct regular bus maintenance. But on a more substantive level, this racist vignette typified how the bus industry viewed Black women: as poor, unsophisticated, and dim people. By denigrating Black women in a thoroughly ordinary article about bus maintenance, the bus industry granted all bus companies implicit permission to treat Black women with humor and derision. Just as another article about industry growth had referenced Topsy, both pieces in *Bus Transportation* demonstrated that Black women loomed large in the cultural imagination of the white bus industry.

Executives in the bus industry printed magazines for passengers and company employees to read, and many brimmed with racialized and gendered overtones. The Greyhound Management Company published the *Highway Traveler* in the 1920s, 1930s, and 1940s, and whenever a customer purchased a Greyhound bus ticket, an agent would hand them a copy of the magazine. Since Greyhound had its corporate headquarters in Chicago and Cleveland, it used the pages of the *Highway Traveler* to encourage Midwestern white women to imagine vacations to warmer climates, whether in the US South, Mexico, Cuba, or the Southwest. Covers of the *Highway Traveler* always featured white women enjoying these tourist adventures.[40] Not only did Greyhound circulate this magazine to its bus passengers, but it also sold it to 750,000 subscribers across the country for $1 and mailed it to chambers of commerce, travel agencies, libraries, medical waiting rooms, steamship companies, schools, and US consuls.[41] Greyhound cast a wide net, making sure that its periodical reached a broad audience of readers throughout the United States.

Articles in the *Highway Traveler* centered whiteness as they racially othered Black Southerners, Indigenous people, Mexican Americans, and Bahamian immigrants.[42] Through this culture of reading, bus industry executives used the pages of the *Highway Traveler* to take white women passengers on racial tours through exotic parts of the United States.[43] In its inaugural issue, Greyhound's magazine profiled Jackson, Mississippi, detailing the city's "picturesquely colorful negro life," remarking on the "dusky and primitive faces" of the Black residents who performed songs in the streets. While the citizens of Jackson "appreciated" the "charm of their colored folks," this article observed that their "laws limit[ed] the negro's privileges."[44] This seemingly generic travel article was bursting with racialized and gendered assumptions. It presumed that all African Americans lived in the Deep South, ignoring the thousands of Black Americans who had recently migrated to Chicago. This article also depicted African Americans in a language of cruel racial stereotypes, whether it was physical features or musical talents. But most importantly, this article cast Jim Crow laws as gentle, conflating rights with "privileges." By publishing such a blatant piece, Greyhound not only gave white women passengers explicit permission to denigrate African Americans but also articulated its company identity.

In addition to customer magazines, bus companies published employee periodicals, which openly denigrated Black women in vicious caricature. One of the worst offenders was Pickwick's *Highway Log*. In October 1930, this magazine featured a cartoon with the intriguing headline "NiteCoaching Through Swaziland." As the accompanying article explained, businessmen from Swaziland (near South Africa), China, and Japan had all contacted Pickwick about their iconic Nite Coach buses and wanted to purchase this vehicle for their countries. Donald Shongwe, the private secretary to King Sobhuza II of Swaziland, wrote to Pickwick President Charles Wren about the possibility of purchasing Nite Coaches.[45] King Sobhuza was the ruler of Swaziland in the British Empire's High Commission territories, and he practiced polygamy to integrate different clans into the nation.[46] The *Highway Log*'s cartoon imagined the sheer lunacy of a Black man in Southern Africa bringing bus travel into his home nation. "We judge from this information," the cartoon stated, "that the chief of Swaziland must plan to take his harem on his trips through the country." Not understanding Southern African culture, this cartoon assumed that the chief was Muslim and had "harems" he would need to transport by bus.

Pickwick used this cartoon to dehumanize Black women and Southern African culture in cruel and derogatory stereotypes. By focusing so much on Black women's loose sexuality, the artist gave readers permission to gaze at their bodies.[47] Every Black woman in this cartoon is scantily clad in grass skirts and garments that barely cover their breasts, and their lips and hair are exaggerated. This cartoon confuses Southern African and Hawaiian cultures by dressing the figures in grass skirts and listing the bus's destination as "Hula Hula." The cartoon evokes Hawaii because it was a popular tourist destination in the late 1920s and early 1930s.[48] Pickwick's casual racism in this cartoon epitomized the company's racist politics. By depicting Black women as ugly, primitive, and ignorant, the Pickwick Corporation granted its employees explicit permission to assault and abuse Black women passengers.[49]

A sampling of these periodicals reveal that bus industry executives crafted racist mythologies about Black women and stamped them onto their publications. These denigrating depictions of Black women—Topsy, a dim car accident victim, stereotyped residents of Mississippi, and scantily-clad South African wives—told white bus employees and white women passengers that the bus industry reviled Black women. According to these periodicals, Black women were not intelligent, could communicate only in broken English, and were sexually licentious (and therefore not worthy of protection). These visual and textual representations cannot simply be

NiteCoaching Through Swaziland

Mr. Charles F. Wren, President of the Pickwick Corporation, recently received a letter from Donald Shongwe, private secretary to the chief of the Swazi nation in South Africa. The letter bears the postmark of Mbabane, capital of Swaziland, and asks for full particulars and prices on the Pickwick NiteCoach.

We judge from this information that the chief of Swaziland must plan to take his harem along on his trips through the country.

Also, a high governmental official of one of China's most populous provinces, now in this country on a business mission, plans to visit Los Angeles this month for the primary purpose of inspecting the Pickwick motor coach works at El Segundo.

Japan likewise is showing a lively interest in Pickwick built motor coaches, as the company's plant was recently inspected by a delegation of Japanese engineers and transportation experts.

Pickwick's *Highway Log* was a publication for company employees. By openly writing and illustrating such racist depictions, Pickwick created a bus company culture that permitted its white employees to treat Black passengers with violence and derision. *Source*: *Highway Log*, Greyhound Collection; image courtesy of the Chicago History Museum, Chicago, Illinois.

attributed to the cultural attitudes of white Americans in this era. They illuminate a deliberate strategy on the part of the bus industry to emphasize that Black women and men did not have the respectability, acumen, or even language skills to be dignified bus passengers. These discursive representations are not merely fragments or aberrations but also constitute a critical part of the cultural and intellectual history of the bus industry, illuminating the thoughts and practices of industry executives.[50] These materials created a body of knowledge that dictated the position of Black women and men in the bus industry: The only way that they could be affiliated with the industry was in service positions.

Serving Sarah: Race and Gender in the Bus Industry's Labor Practices

Despite the variety of bus lines formed during the interwar era, the white industry limited Black women's employment to bus cleaners, maids in

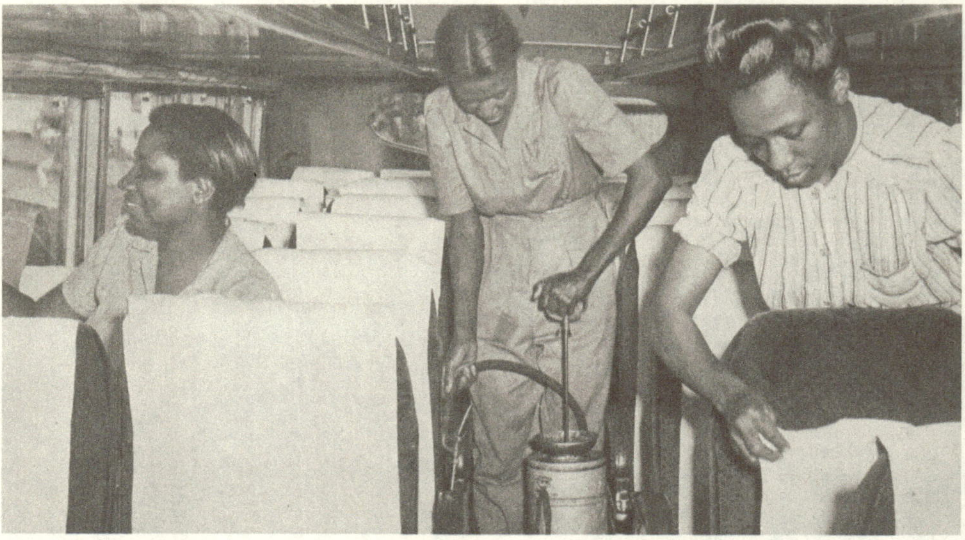

From the very beginning, Greyhound maintained a racialized and gendered hierarchy in employment, only permitting Black women to labor as cleaners, cooks, and maids in the bus industry and never interact with white passengers. In this image from World War II, Black women clean and sanitize a bus in Florida after bus passengers have departed. *Source*: *Highway Traveler* Collection, Western Reserve Historical Society, Cleveland, Ohio.

waiting rooms, or cooks in warehouse cafeterias.[51] Hiring Black women in these roles ensured that they would rarely interact with white bus passengers and remain hidden as workers in the industry, a deliberate strategy to serve Sarah. An image in Greyhound's *Highway Traveler* depicted Black women bus cleaners in Florida. Even though this photograph demonstrated Black women's physical labor of cleaning and sanitizing by showing them on the bus, it was obvious that this activity occurred after passengers had departed. Greyhound, and most bus lines, created a labor schedule to ensure that Black women employees would never interact with white passengers.

For Black women workers, there were some benefits to working as maids, cooks, and cleaners in the bus industry. These jobs provided Black women with a steady paycheck and allowed them to avoid white people's houses, and might have offered some discounts on bus tickets or the opportunity to travel. But the industry's rigid culture of white supremacy thwarted opportunities for advancement. It was only at Black-owned bus companies where Black women were employed in positions beyond service labor. By the 1930s, the Safe Bus Company was transporting sixteen thousand passengers daily and had hired Black women to work as cashiers, clericals, and stenographers.[52] In fact, over the company's five-decade history, two Black women served as president of the company, a rarity for any woman in the 1950s.[53] These opportunities at Safe—in customer service, clerical, and administrative positions—contrasted sharply with the narrow employment prospects in the white bus industry, which confined Black women workers to service positions.

Black women's limited opportunities in the bus industry also differed from the more diverse jobs they performed in the railroad industry: as food vendors, maids, nannies, and beauty culturists. When trains first debuted, most did not have dining cars. At station stops, many passengers would exit trains for food. In Mississippi and Virginia, Black women entrepreneurs gathered outside train stations as vendors or "waiter carriers," selling fried chicken, biscuits, hard-boiled eggs, cakes, pies, and coffee. Working as peddlers at train stations allowed Black women to have a modicum of control over their labor and showcase their talents for cooking. Purchasing food from a waiter carrier was a crucial part of the tourist experience in these states, and there is no evidence that the train industry discouraged these entrepreneurial activities.[54] In addition to peddling food for passengers, Black women also worked on trains, especially Pullman cars. In 1867, train magnate George Pullman had introduced his luxurious sleeping cars and recruited formerly enslaved Black men to work as porters, rationalizing that they were familiar with good service. Pullman porters were desirable positions, offering Black men comparatively higher wages and the opportunity to travel across the country.[55] In 1901, the Pullman Company expanded its services and hired Black women to labor as train maids. Black women cleaned train cars, but they also interacted directly with passengers by styling hair, administering manicures, and caring for children. As Pullman maids, Black women connected with white passengers and received tips for their services. In the interwar era, Black Pullman workers unionized as the Brotherhood of Sleeping Car Porters and Maids and subsequently gained more economic and political power.[56] Not only did Black women enjoy a range of labor opportunities in the white train industry, but they were valued for their talents in food service and beauty culture.

Bus lines hired Black men and gave them more opportunities to interact directly with bus passengers. Black male workers cleaned warehouses, shined the shoes of white bus drivers, or worked as porters and redcaps to assist passengers with their luggage. Whether located in the North or the South, many white lines used the Black male porter to convey Southern hospitality. In a telling article titled "Said a Southern Operator to a Northern

Operator," the manager of Dixie Coaches Inc. in Alabama told a Northern manager that courtesy was the key to good business. He recommended that this Northern manager hire "baggage porters who are real southern negroes . . . the kind of negroes who grin and say yassum. You'll see business pick up."[57] This anecdote demonstrates not only that the bus industry valued the culture of the Jim Crow South but also that Black workers might have followed a precise script to fit in this racial context.[58] During the Great Depression, train stations and bus depots stopped paying redcaps a salary, forcing them to rely solely on tips. But in 1938, the redcaps affiliated with the Congress of Industrial Organizations to form the International Brotherhood of Red Caps, which was interracial. Even though it was a major victory that redcaps were able to unionize, they continued to be some of the lowest paid workers in the transportation industry, always fighting for salaries.[59]

Interstate buses hired Black men to serve white passengers on special lines. In the late 1920s and early 1930s, Pickwick and the Great Eastern Stages experimented with night trips, tapping African American men to perform the same work as a Pullman porter, but this practice was short-lived. Pickwick even called their buses "Pullman Plus," to emphasize that passengers could enjoy the comforts of a Pullman car on an interstate bus.[60]

In 1931, *Bus Transportation* profiled a bus line in Portland, Oregon, featuring photographs of the company workers, demonstrating that Black workers labored as servants for the white employees. One staged image, "Keeping the Bus Driver on His Toes," depicted a smiling Black man as he polished the boots of a white bus driver, who was dressed in a uniform that resembled that of a law enforcement officer.

Another photograph featured a warehouse kitchen where a white woman waitress was situated in the foreground while a Black woman cook was in the background. The handkerchief on the cook's head evoked the figure of "mammy"—a stereotype of enslaved Black women. In both these photographs, the racialized and gendered hierarchies were palpable: Black women and men were the servants for the white bus industry, workers who would never interact with white passengers. By framing these workers in a language of stereotypes, these images dehumanized Black workers while also giving white workers permission to treat them with hostility and disdain.[61] Bus lines reinforced these racialized labor hierarchies in their socialization practices. The Virginia Transit Company, a municipal bus line, held separate picnics for its Black and white employees, demonstrating that these workers were not located on the same footing.[62]

Racialized and gendered hierarchies were palpable throughout the bus industry, even on this bus line in Portland, Oregon. Here a Black man shines the shoes of a white driver while a Black woman cook is depicted with a kerchief in the kitchen. Images of both Black women and men working in the industry at the time evoked racial stereotypes. *Source*: "Keeping the Driver on His Toes," *Bus Transportation*, November 1931, 581.

But if bus lines had a narrow imagination about the labor that Black women and men could perform, they had expansive and creative visions about white women's employment. In the 1920s and 1930s, the bus industry hired white women to work as ticket agents, clericals who tabulated drivers' reports, ticket printers, bus attendants, and tour guides.[63] Some companies even elevated white women to leadership positions.[64] The Washington Motor Coach Company, a bus line in Spokane, Washington, tapped white women to perform the new role of "conductorettes" to sell tickets and assist women customers, the first time that any bus line had hired women in such a capacity. Operating on the assumption that buses were perceived to be masculine modes of transportation, the Washington Motor Coach Company framed conductorettes as a business strategy to attract more women bus passengers, reasoning that white women would be more comfortable receiving bus services if they were attended to by a conductorette.[65] The Santa Fe Transportation Company in New Mexico hired white women to work as couriers, taking bus passengers on three-day trips through the dwellings of Indigenous Pueblo people and the neighborhoods of Mexican Americans. Speaking both English and Spanish, these white women served as the "diplomat between traveler and native." An article praised these white women for their sensitivity, which allowed them to perform the role of cultural translator in the "exotic" parts of Florida and New Mexico and warn passengers not to "displease the natives."[66] In the 1920s and 1930s, white women held a surprisingly diverse set of roles in the bus industry.

But the bus industry envisioned the most expansive employment opportunities for white male employees, who were tasked with enforcing the color line. Bus lines hired white men to serve in executive and managerial positions, drive the bus, sell tickets, and make automotive repairs. Buses provided a brand-new form of transportation in the American economy, and companies tried to staff these positions with workers who had experiences in similar types of industries. The ticket agent was the customer's first interaction with the bus line. The bus industry trained ticket agents to determine if a passenger was racially eligible for travel, if they would have a seat near the back, and whether their luggage would be safely transported to their final destination.[67] In hiring bus agents, companies favored workers who had experience selling train, steamboat, and even theater tickets.[68] But other lines were not as large and merely added ticket sales onto the already hefty responsibilities of the driver.[69]

The bus driver position was a demanding one. These men administered the color line, drove the bus, collected tickets, distributed change and transfers, and managed passengers. Buses were small, cramped spaces, requiring drivers to be fit, nimble, and efficient in corralling passengers. Since this was a new labor position, the bus industry devoted significant resources to training drivers. Prospective drivers had to complete a mixture of written coursework and on-the-bus education and were evaluated for courtesy, safety, and cleanliness.[70] Most bus companies maintained large mechanical warehouses where drivers deposited their buses after every trip, vehicles were repaired and serviced, and drivers and executives shared company information. These serious responsibilities, compounded by the high stakes of the job, prompted industry executives to recruit drivers and safety managers from the military and the police.

One of the largest bus companies to follow this path was Greyhound, who tapped Marcus Dow from the New York City Police Department (NYPD) to become its director of safety, a role that supervised all bus drivers. Born in Michigan in 1878, Dow had moved to New York City in the 1910s, where he became a safety expert for the New York Central Railroad. In 1922, Police Commissioner Richard Enright recruited Dow to join the NYPD's newly formed Bureau of Public Safety to reduce street accidents.[71] By the time Dow joined the department, this institution was a thoroughly modern and professional enterprise. The department vigorously trained its police officers, emphasizing nutrition, fitness, hygiene, and the use of brute force, especially on nonwhite residents of the city. The historian Matthew Guariglia traces the growing militarization of police officers in New York City, noting that the department drew inspiration from imperial campaigns in the Philippines. By introducing militarized khaki unforms, officers in the Metropolitan Police Department mirrored the culture of law enforcement and US imperialism.[72]

There were several practices within the NYPD that Marcus Dow took with him to his new role at Greyhound. First, Commissioner Enright had followed a strict racial hierarchy in the department, publicly stating that policing was a "white man's job." Under Commissioner Enright's tenure, the department hired Southern and Eastern European immigrants as police officers but never African Americans.[73] Dow followed this practice, making bus driving at Greyhound a white man's job.[74] He had also learned about the latest trends in policing, especially physical combat training for officers. In 1923, New York City hosted the third-annual International Police Conference, at which Marcus Dow spoke. Police chiefs from around the world discussed the latest methods of policing. In New York City, officers were all trained in "jujitsu, wrestling, boxing, gymnastics, and guns."[75] The department also developed a reputation for overpolicing Black residents of the city.[76] Even though Dow spent only a few years in the NYPD, this experience shaped him deeply in that he incorporated many of these police techniques into his new position at Greyhound.

In addition to modeling bus drivers on law enforcement, Dow specified the precise requirements for Greyhound bus drivers: they had to be between twenty-five and thirty-five years of age and citizens of the United States. This citizenship requirement for drivers likely reflected hostility toward new immigrants from Southern and Eastern Europe and migrant workers from Mexico. Additionally, Greyhound drivers had to pass a written test, practice excellent penmanship, undergo a mental exam, list neighbors and former teachers as references, and participate in a thirty-day training program, in which they learned about buses and the rigors of the road.[77] Greyhound also required each driver to carry a set of tools and perform basic bus repairs, including tire changes, when needed.[78] It is difficult to overstate the significance of Marcus Dow's influence on Greyhound and, in turn, the culture of the bus industry. To honor his legacy, Greyhound began to bestow Marcus Dow Safety Awards to bus drivers with the fewest accidents per mile, and it continued to grant these awards into the 1950s.[79] By memorializing Dow through a safety award, Greyhound honored his outsized legacy at the company.

Other bus lines followed Greyhound by establishing employment standards for bus drivers and aligning their companies with law enforcement, the military, and the newly formed United States Border Patrol.[80] For example, John A. Ritchie, the president of the Chicago Motor Coach Company, outlined a set of criteria to hire bus drivers. In addition to selecting drivers who were over the age of twenty-five and in good physical shape, with strong mental fitness, he preferred men who were married or had served in the military. Military veterans made good bus drivers because they had a "familiarity with discipline." Ritchie worked to build community among drivers by organizing fishing expeditions and boxing matches, noting that these events enabled drivers to "demonstrate their ability in the 'manly' art." To retain these employees, the bus line also sponsored a fraternal order, which allowed workers to pay into medical care and life insurance benefits, which allowed them to be breadwinners for their family.[81] Bus driving at the Chicago Motor Coach Company was men's work. Similarly, J. A. Phelan, the president of Colonial Coach Lines in Watertown, New York, remarked that his lines liked to hire "former state troopers and county officers," noting that these men were "substantial citizens of the communities where they lived."[82] This evidence demonstrates that at least three bus lines—Greyhound, with a national reach, and Chicago and Colonial, with more local routes—looked to the military and the police to recruit a set of white male bus drivers.

Even if the bus industry could not recruit every driver from law enforcement, they all outfitted them in police-inspired uniforms. In 1925, an article in *Bus Transportation* polled 150 of these companies, reporting that most bus driver unforms consisted of the following items: leg breeches, coats, caps, puttees, and Sam Browne belts. Most were khaki or olive brown.[83] These sharp uniforms helped brand bus drivers, giving them an air of professionalism and denoting their company's "responsibility, prosperity, and progressiveness."[84] In this era, most middle-class white women viewed police officers as a source of protection. But for Black women, white police officers surveilled, patrolled, and overpoliced Blackness, and Prohibition and the Great Depression only exacerbated the white policing of Black women's bodies.[85] By teaching white drivers to look and behave like police officers, the bus industry created a culture of policing for Black women passengers and a culture of safety for white women passengers.

The bus industry trained its drivers to police the color line across the nation. Bus companies appropriated the racialized practices and accoutrements of police officers—including their uniforms, their quick enforcement of "order," and sometimes even their blackjacks and pistols—and outfitted

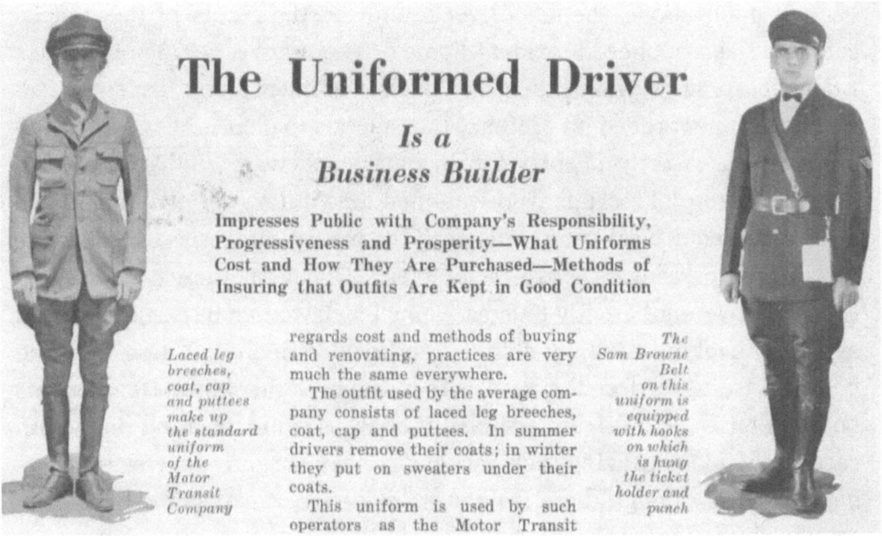

The Uniformed Driver

Is a

Business Builder

Impresses Public with Company's Responsibility, Progressiveness and Prosperity—What Uniforms Cost and How They Are Purchased—Methods of Insuring that Outfits Are Kept in Good Condition

Laced leg breeches, coat, cap and puttees make up the standard uniform of the Motor Transit Company

regards cost and methods of buying and renovating, practices are very much the same everywhere.

The outfit used by the average company consists of laced leg breeches, coat, cap and puttees. In summer drivers remove their coats; in winter they put on sweaters under their coats.

This uniform is used by such operators as the Motor Transit

The Sam Browne Belt on this uniform is equipped with hooks on which is hung the ticket holder and punch

The bus industry throughout the United States drew inspiration from the military and the police in outfitting bus drivers. In the 1920s, 1930s, and 1940s, these uniforms were styled on law enforcement. *Source*: "The Uniformed Driver Is a Business Builder," *Bus Transportation*, November 1925, 538.

their new bus drivers in these militarized uniforms. These accessories and training ensured that drivers could handle unruly riders, isolate criminals, and, most importantly, enforce the color line with brute force, which racially policed Black bus passengers. In the early 1930s, Durham, North Carolina, switched from streetcars to buses. Fares increased by two cents, and passengers boarded one large bus instead of individual streetcars. African Americans composed 35 percent of the city's population and an even greater proportion of the bus riders, since many relied on public transportation to labor in tobacco factories and white people's houses. In a profile of Durham's new bus line, *Bus Transportation* praised the city's "tactful drivers," who had been "properly trained" to solve the "problem."[86] Although this article opted for subtext, the message was clear: The bus industry trained its drivers in racial policing, which implicitly elevated white women passengers and degraded Black women passengers.

By simply using these technologies of racial policing on Black women passengers and rarely, if ever, on white women passengers, the bus industry crafted the mythology that Sarah was a passenger entitled to courteous and gentle service, while Black women riders, such as Violet, were dangerous and required violence. While the bus industry constructed this narrative in their publications, the bus driver reinforced the reality of these racial categories as he policed his riders. Some drivers were eager to police Black women passengers, while others did not exert as much force. Just as the federal government relied on ordinary bureaucrats to determine whether immigrants were worthy of entry, low-income people were eligible for welfare relief, or potential recruits were qualified for military service, the bus industry trained drivers to administer to the binary categories of normative and deviant passengers across racial lines.[87] Of course, these racialized dichotomies were inherently blurred. Some Black women passengers passed as white, evoking the light-skinned enslaved women and men who had boarded trains to freedom.[88] At other times, light-skinned passengers boarded buses, and drivers assumed they were white, treating them with care. Only upon realizing their race did drivers abruptly reverse their behavior.[89] Even though there is no overt evidence, it is possible that Black women riders passed as men.[90]

The labor practices of the bus industry offer a revealing window into the values of these companies. Bus lines granted white men absolute authority to drive the buses, sell the tickets, check the luggage, and oversee the routes, while they enlisted white women for a range of positions, stretching from conductorettes to tour guides. The bus industry hired African Americans as servants and hid Black women workers from white passengers. Before Black women ever boarded the first bus, the industry had already crafted a culture of white supremacy in its printed materials and labor practices. These racialized and gendered worldviews of the bus industry ensured that Black women riders and workers would never be treated with respect on these vehicles or even permitted to board them in the first place. Greyhound and other bus lines spent thousands of advertising dollars publicizing the comfort and convenience of their modern vehicles, all geared to white women. Irene Davis saw one of these ads and purchased a ticket, but she was precisely a rider that Greyhound did not want: a Black woman.

Policing Irene: Serving White Women and Rejecting Black Women

In December 1931, Irene F. Davis, a resident of Philadelphia, purchased a Greyhound bus ticket to travel to Norfolk, Virginia, for a Christmas visit with her extended family. As a woman and an aspiring bus passenger, Irene Davis had been led to believe that this trip would be relaxing and that she would enjoy comfortable accommodations and be treated as a respected customer. But once she boarded the Greyhound bus, her expectations were dashed. "I had previously associated the word 'Greyhound' with comfort and ease in travel," Davis wrote to the company, "but I am about to change my opinion." The ride from Philadelphia to Virginia was uneventful. She praised the bus driver for his "courteous" treatment of all passengers and his "careful" driving. But the return trip to Philadelphia was not as pleasant. The bus driver policed her as a deviant passenger. He forced five Black passengers to sit on a small seat in the back of the bus, making her long trip deeply uncomfortable. The driver was also "reckless," and Irene Davis spent the trip "frightened" for her life. Not only was the bus ride terrifying, but it was nine hours long with two scheduled stops.

At the rest stop in Salisbury, Maryland, Greyhound reinforced Irene Davis's exclusion from the category of womanhood and solidified her subject position as a deviant bus passenger.[91] Black passengers were denied service at the restaurant and banned from the lavatory facilities. White managers directed them to an area behind a building where there was only a "dirty toilet" for both Black women and men to use. By providing modern and separate accommodations for white customers according to sex but only a crude shared toilet for Black passengers, Greyhound demonstrated that only white women passengers were worthy of such accommodations. Irene Davis concluded her customer service letter by threatening that if she was ever to ride Greyhound again, she hoped that the company would provide better conditions for its Black passengers. Here, Irene Davis articulated a discourse of consumer citizenship, contending that her hard-earned money entitled her to a safe and dignified bus ride.[92]

Greyhound did not ignore Irene. J. Cumming, Pennsylvania Greyhound's regional manager, responded to Davis's letter, thanking her for drawing his attention to the lack of modern restrooms and promising that "steps are being taken to remedy the various conditions outlined in your complaint.[93] But Irene Davis was unaware that Greyhound and other bus companies were invested in "Selling to Sarah" and far less interested in dealing with these types of customer complaints from Black women. The early bus industry in the United States was actively working to attract aspiring white women passengers and exclude Black women, but Irene Davis's letter revealed a core flaw in their plan. By engaging in advertising blitzes aimed at generic "women" passengers, Greyhound inadvertently attracted the dollars and patronage of Black women. And Irene Davis was not the only one.

Beginning in the late 1920s, African American women began to spend their hard-earned money on bus tickets. Through bold advertisements in magazines and newspapers, the bus industry promised to make the prospect of interstate and city travel more of a reality for working-class and middle-class Americans, and they especially courted women passengers. Even though these companies did not actively solicit Black riders in their advertising campaigns, African Americans nonetheless felt excited about the accessibility, affordability, and modernity of commercial buses. For Black women, especially Southern migrants, these vehicles could facilitate family visits, promote long-distance education, streamline travel to organizational and religious conferences, and transport riders on vacations. But as passengers like Irene Davis discovered, the bus industry used the category of womanhood to create racial divisions in their treatment of customers, whether it was organizing the racialized space of the bus, policing and assaulting Black women passengers, or putting white supremacy at the center of their practices.

As bus lines began to advertise in newspapers and magazines across the country, they joined a longer tradition of branding products for white women consumers, even cars. In the 1920s, manufacturers mass-produced automobiles to appeal to women. The big three—Chrysler, Ford, and General Motors—all competed for women's patronage by designing their cars in a variety of colors and upholstery fabrics. As women exercised more preference about their consumption habits, manufacturers worked to attract women customers by inviting them to declare a fondness for a particular color or style.[94] Automobile advertisers stressed the reliability of the vehicles and emphasized how easy it was to both drive and park their cars.[95] The growing popularity and affordability of auto travel in the 1920s coincided with the era of the New Woman.[96] The New Woman was a product of the decade, personified by white women's growing independence. The New Woman had bobbed hair, wore short skirts, exercised the new right of suffrage, earned an independent income, and enjoyed more sexual freedom.[97] Driving—and by extension, owning a car—fit into this new discourse of independence and empowered white womanhood. But by 1930, only 21 percent of the licensed drivers in the United States were women. Because there were fewer women drivers, it was logical that interstate and municipal bus lines would recruit women passengers.[98]

In the late 1920s, bus companies unveiled advertising campaigns aimed at women. In 1929, Greyhound spent $100,000 on full-page advertisements in national publications, such as the *Saturday Evening Post*, *Liberty*, and *American Magazine*. The *Saturday Evening Post* was the crown jewel for showcasing products and the most circulated weekly in the country.[99]

Greyhound tried to persuade travelers to reject automobiles, noting that buses enabled passengers to enjoy a pleasant trip, with no concerns over parking or driving, for one-third of the cost of car ownership. Buses charged the lowest fares of any form of public transportation.[100] When the United States slipped into the Great Depression in the early 1930s, the number of Americans who purchased automobiles dropped precipitously. This economic climate prompted bus companies to recruit consumers who might have purchased automobiles but were now only able to afford bus tickets. This campaign was known as "convert private car users." In a fitting nod to the economic crisis, these advertisements touted buses' affordable fares. This branding strategy fit within broader advertising campaigns during the Depression, when supermarkets and bargain stores emphasized the values of thriftiness and economizing.[101] As opposed to the luxury of department stores, hotels, and even automobiles, the bus industry promised consumers an exciting yet affordable experience. Most bus lines assumed that men wanted to ride buses to "save time and money," whereas women were more interested in travel and enjoyment.[102] Bus lines also worked to recruit different cohorts of women riders, including teachers and housewives.[103]

Even though these advertisements centered on the most ordinary of bus features—seat size, compartments, fabric textures, and levels of cleanliness—these discussions, in fact, revealed core assumptions about how the bus industry viewed the bodies of white women. Advertisements waxed poetic about their prospective white women passengers, highlighting their physical delicacy, their attention to cleanliness, their expectations for safety, and their sensitivity.[104] One Greyhound advertisement featured a glamorous and attractive white woman, who stated, "From the feminine point of view, the new Greyhounds are marvelous."[105] Catering to these delicate and discerning white women passengers, bus advertisements depicted bus travel as luxurious and glamorous, featuring reclining chairs, plush pillows, towel service, and stewardesses and waiters to care for passengers.[106] A revealing article in *Bus Transportation*, titled "These Women and Their Damn White Gloves," described the importance of keeping buses pristine for women customers. Reminding readers that women made up half of the bus customers, the article concluded that "it is wise to keep buses clean and inviting."[107]

At the same time, the bus industry constructed Black women passengers as the antithesis of white women. Bus lines imagined Black women as physically imposing, and this discourse stretched from a discussion of

Black women's "rough" bodies to their violent tempers. If white women were clean and demanded immaculate riding accommodations, Black women were inherently dirty and needed to be separated from white women passengers. If white bus drivers were expected to treat white women customers with courtesy and respect, the presumption was that they were to police and assault the bodies of Black women passengers who refused to comply with the racial orderings of the bus. These imagined qualities translated to concrete realities for Black women who engaged with the bus industry. As Black women purchased tickets and boarded buses, they reported passenger experiences that mirrored these cruel stereotypes.

The bus industry instructed ticket agents to enforce Jim Crow, first with a light touch. In the 1930s, 90 percent of Greyhound ticket agencies were located inside hotels, restaurants, drugstores, and confectionaries. Large interstate companies constructed terminals in urban hubs, including Cleveland, New York City, and Washington, DC. All of these bigger terminals had a newsstand and a lunch counter, as well as a counter where white agents sold tickets and checked luggage.

Since these agents determined bus seating arrangements, they printed tickets that separated Black and white passengers, refused to allow Black riders to board certain buses, and resorted to violence when necessary.[108] Bus terminals were public places, so ticket agents tried to keep violence to a minimum. But because the bus industry prioritized the enforcement of a color line at all costs, violence was inescapable. In the early 1940s, Lottie Johnson—a twenty-nine-year-old divorced cook living in Columbus, Ohio—purchased a Greyhound ticket to visit relatives in Kentucky. When she arrived in Kentucky, she exited the bus and walked to the terminal to retrieve her luggage. She presented her stub to the white ticket agent and waited for her bags. After many minutes, she reminded the agent that she had given him her stub and was still awaiting her luggage. Even though this was an ordinary customer follow-up, the ticket agent escalated the situation. He reached for his club and threatened to "crack her skull" if she did not leave. This encounter left Johnson terrified. As a cook, a lodger, and a divorced woman, she lived on the edges of poverty and it would be costly to replace her checked bags.[109] When she returned to her home in Columbus, she contacted a lawyer and recounted her experience to a reporter at the *Cleveland Call and Post*. Although rare, this episode illustrates that Greyhound even armed its *ticket agents* with weapons to

Greyhound ticket counters were the first opportunity for the company to police the color line. Ticket agents frequently sold Black women and men seats in the back of the bus. *Source*: "Selling the Bus Passenger," Greyhound Collection, Western Reserve Historical Society, Cleveland, Ohio.

wield on Black women passengers, and they only sold tickets and handled luggage.

In 1928, William and Elizabeth Mimms, a Black couple from Kansas, boarded a Pickwick-Greyhound bus in Topeka bound for Lawrence. The Mimms knew a thing or two about good service, because William Mimms worked as a Pullman porter. The bus driver forced William and Elizabeth Mimms to sit in the back of the bus, even though Kansas did not have a segregation law. When they protested this seating arrangement, the driver flicked on the ventilator, announcing that he would "freeze them out." The bus traveled the twenty-eight miles from Topeka to Lawrence with the couple shivering in the back. This callous and cruel behavior demonstrated that Pickwick trained its drivers to assault and abuse Black passengers. Within two years, Pickwick would publish the dehumanizing image of the Swaziland chief and his "wives" as a visual way to reinforce and justify its treatment of Black passengers. When the couple finally returned home, Elizabeth Mimms was so ill that she was in bed for two weeks.[110] As bus passengers, Black women quickly learned that bus drivers could deploy the technology of the bus to be violent and sadistic toward passengers of color. These experiences contrasted sharply with the promises of the bus industry.

While the early bus industry claimed to desire the patronage of women, that passenger was racially coded as a white woman. Unaware of this industry culture, Black women seized on this new automotive technology to book bus travel across the country. Once on the bus, they discovered that bus drivers policed them, viciously pressed a ventilator to "freeze them out," and uplifted white women passengers as they degraded Black ones. Not only did the bus industry design the bus experience around the sensitive minds and bodies of white women riders, but it also constructed rest stops as architectural sites to reinforce racialized categories of womanhood. Gertrude Pryor learned this firsthand.

Most Humiliating to Women: Excluding Black Women Passengers Outside the Bus

In July 1932, Gertrude Pryor booked a bus trip from her home in Leavenworth, Kansas, to Washington, DC. Her travel experiences revealed a core truth: Greyhound did not desire Black women's patronage and refused to spend money accommodating Black riders. At a rest stop in St. Louis, Missouri, she was denied service at the restaurant and did not eat for the duration of the trip. At the rest stop, two white soldiers remarked, "I don't see why the Greyhound management sells tickets to N******, they know there is no provision made for them along the route." Detailing this experience in a letter to the NAACP, she concluded that Greyhound was an "evil" bus company.[111]

As Gertrude Pryor explained, the bus industry used rest stops and restaurants to encode and reinforce racial divisions among their women passengers. Previously, the railroad industry had introduced a first-class ladies' car as a place from which to bar Black women.[112] But modern buses had no such compartments. Most buses were small and had only one large car. Since buses lacked the amenities of trains—including restrooms, dining cars, and parlors—bus lines employed rest stops to give passengers an opportunity to use the lavatories, eat a meal, stretch their legs, and inhale fresh air. Some rest stops had food services, ranging from basic provisions to full-scale restaurants. Greyhound mandated that every trip have a rest stop after 150 minutes on the road. At Greyhound-managed rest stops, customers could eat a meal; use the restroom; and purchase candy, gum, tobacco products, food, soft drinks, and beer.[113] If bus lines did not operate their own rest stops, they partnered with local hotels, restaurants, and gas stations to fill in the service gaps in the early days of the industry. Of course, by outsourcing their rest stops to third-party vendors, Greyhound and other bus lines could always evade claims of racial discrimination, merely pointing to the established practices of these businesses.

All rest stops were equipped with lavatory facilities, and many banned Black women from the ladies' room. If bus lines did provide a bathroom for Black passengers, it was almost always a single shared toilet, intended for both women and men. Black women's exclusion from the ladies' room was a form of violence. It refused to acknowledge that Black women were women. This barring of Black women's bodies from the restroom resembled other oppressive systems in the Jim Crow South. In the convict lease system in Georgia, authorities forced Black women to wear men's clothing.[114] Not only was it traumatic to deny Black women the privilege of womanhood, but requiring these passengers to share a restroom with men made them deeply vulnerable to sexual violence.

Black women rode buses in the era of migrations. These were journeys of hope, but they were always tinged with sadness, uncertainty, and trauma. Some passengers had boarded buses to escape not only the interracial violence of the Jim Crow South but also intraracial sexual violence in their own families and communities.[115] Denying Black women the privilege of a women's restroom put Black women at risk of assault and potentially retraumatized them if they were fleeing violent situations. At every rest stop, the bus industry was determined to deny Black women passengers the privilege of womanhood.

Even though the bus industry furnished white women with their own lavatories, many passengers were dissatisfied. White women complained to bus companies that the ladies' room did not have mirrors to apply their makeup, hooks to hang their purses, or towels to dry their hands.[116] In March 1936, an article in *Bus Transportation*—titled "Still No Towels (and No Soap Either)"—discussed these conditions. The article depicted a glamorous white woman, stylishly dressed, who was displeased with the spartan accommodations of these rest stops. She struggled to apply lipstick and had no hook to hang her fur coat.

This article was written by a "feminine patron who occasionally rides Intercity buses." In a playful tone, the writer called the bus company "Mr. Bus Operator," noting that his profits would increase if he paid more attention to women customers. The article observed, "The 'Ladies Room' in many bus terminals, even in the larger cities, is certainly no place fit for a lady." In a cheeky conclusion, she ended, "It's a Hell of a Way to Treat a Lady."[117] By publishing this criticism, the bus industry committed to making improvements, which would allow white women to clean up, apply their makeup, and perform their femininity. Of course, this article did not acknowledge that most Black women were excluded from the facilities at most bus rest stops.

In August 1935, Ada Montgomery, a twenty-one-year-old maid in Pittsburgh, purchased a Greyhound bus ticket to visit her family in Wytheville, Virginia.[118] At a rest stop, she noticed that Black women were not able to use the restrooms. When she inquired why there were no lavatories for Black passengers, Greyhound officials informed her that "the colored and white had been fighting and it could not be avoided." By adopting this stance, Greyhound opted for exclusion rather than a racial solution. When Montgomery returned to her home in Pittsburgh, she was ill for five days and had to be medically treated.[119] In September 1941, New York City resident Leila Payne boarded a Greyhound bus to travel to the South. At a rest stop, she walked into the lunchroom and sat at the counter. She observed that waitresses were serving customers quickly. But "after waiting for about ten minutes, noting that persons on either side of me were being served, I finally was told that colored people were not served inside." African American customers could eat at a separate restaurant, but it was not open yet. At the rest stop in Philadelphia, she was able to order a meal, but the service was hostile. Payne reflected on her experiences, opining that "it is most deplorable when decent self-respecting, law-abiding colored people" had to contend with such services from bus companies. She concluded that she "hope[d] something can be done in a general way to alleviate such treatment which are [*sic*] most humiliating to women."[120] Here, Leila Payne called out Greyhound, remarking that a company that ostensibly catered to (white) women had created intolerable circumstances for her as a Black woman customer. Leila Payne worked hard to secure the privileges of womanhood, but Greyhound, and the bus industry as a whole, refused to acknowledge that identity.

The bus industry used rest stops to reinforce divisions between women passengers. White women registered dissatisfaction that they did not have shiny mirrors in which to apply their lipstick or hooks on which to hang their purses, while Black women reported that they were not allowed into this restroom at all. This exclusion forced Black women to share a toilet with Black men (if they were lucky) and made them vulnerable to violence and assault. White women may have been upset that the food did not meet their culinary standards, while Black women reported that cooks handed them food from a crack in the door of a restaurant. Black women, including

Gertrude Pryor, Ada Montgomery, and Leila Payne, all wrote blistering letters protesting these conditions. When Leila Payne told the NAACP that these exclusions were "most humiliating to women," she asserted claims to womanhood as a strategy to shame the bus industry into treating her as a woman. What she did not know was that her Blackness would never give her the privilege of womanhood in the eyes of the bus industry. As far as it was concerned, she would always be a deviant passenger.

All of these women evinced a heightened political consciousness, making claims that their respectability, their American citizenship, and especially their dollars and cents entitled them to decent and dignified service. Now that we have peeled back the layers of the bus industry—in printed words and images, labor practices, advertising campaigns, and facilities—we can now reconstruct Violet Mohand's visit to Hell with more precision and clarity.

Visited Hell: How the Bus Industry Violated Violet

In June 1935, Violet Mohand, like many Black women, was navigating two worlds. Her roots stretched between her past in New Orleans and her present in Chicago. As a woman in her family, it was her responsibility to tend these ancestral branches. After a rich and restorative stay with her family in New Orleans, she decided to return to Chicago by bus. When she entered the Greyhound terminal in New Orleans to purchase her ticket, she might have observed that it was all white male agents who took her money, handed her a copy of *Highway Traveler*, and checked her bag. Violet Mohand was able to select a seat near the front and settled in for the nearly nine-hundred-mile trip back to her new home of Chicago. If Mohand chose to read the *Highway Traveler*, she would have noticed articles that racialized the cultures of nonwhite people, including African Americans, Indigenous people, and Bahamian and Mexican migrants. Every ninety miles, the bus pulled into a rest stop. By 1935, these rest stops likely included well-appointed restrooms for white women passengers. But Mohand had to share facilities with Black male passengers, and if she wanted food, she had to eat outside. It is unclear what types of interactions Mohand had with the bus driver, but she might have observed that his actions and mannerisms resembled the police officers who surveilled her, both in her former home of New Orleans and in her new city of Chicago.

Over three hundred miles into the trip, the bus pulled into the city of Clarksdale, Mississippi, and that is when the trouble erupted. When a white woman passenger boarded the bus, the driver turned to Violet Mohand and demanded that she vacate her seat. She refused. It is impossible to know why Mohand resisted, but a few theories can be surmised. Since she had been able to sit near the front for the first leg of the trip, she might have assumed that she would be able to keep her seat. This was an interstate bus, and Mohand might have argued that segregation was not legal. Finally, as a new resident of Illinois, Mohand might have pointed to her state's civil rights statute. Nevertheless, her interiority will always be unknown.

Violet Mohand's refusal to move enraged the driver, prompting him to draw on his police-based training to curl his fingers into a tight fist and punch her in the face. In assaulting her, the driver crafted the subject positions of white women as the normative bus passenger and Black women as the deviant passenger. The driver quickly called the police and Mohand was arrested, charged with disorderly conduct and assault, and sentenced to either $125 in fines or thirty days on a chain gang.[121]

But the bus industry violated Mohand long before she entered the Greyhound terminal in New Orleans and boarded the bus. When white businessmen formed the bus industry in the United States, executives made deliberate decisions to sell to Sarah and violate Violet. Every inch of their industry—stretching from employment practices to bus driver etiquette to advertisements to the bus experience itself—put white women at the center. The bus industry assumed, often rightly so, that white women wanted a bus experience predicated on racial purity and segregation.[122] The bus industry hired Black women to perform menial tasks, while it celebrated the intelligence and career aspirations of white women. The bus industry evoked the figure of a generic Black woman through humor and derision, whether it was writing vignettes of Black women speaking in broken English or drawing racist cartoons satirizing Black women's bodies. By crafting these derogatory stereotypes, the bus industry articulated to both its workers and its customers where it stood on the matter of race. By modeling its bus drivers on law enforcement officials, the industry created a figure who would honor white women and assault Black women. And by denying Black women access to single-sex restrooms and the comforts of a restaurant, the bus industry used rest stops to crystallize Black women's exclusion from womanhood. This chapter has chronicled the ways that the bus industry sought to dominate Black women—in its periodicals, through its labor practices, and as deviant passengers. Chapter 2 investigates the archive of Black women's unrelenting resistance to the bus industry.

2 They Sure Treat Us Shameful

The Archive of Black Women's Everyday Resistance in the Interstate Bus Industry

Pearl Johnson Hooper did not stay in one place. A native of Opelousas, Louisiana, she married her husband in the 1920s and the couple moved throughout the South. They first settled in Beaumont, Texas, and then New Orleans, where she gave birth to their only child. By the 1930s, the daily indignities of life in the Jim Crow South prompted Hooper and her family to imagine a brighter future in Chicago.[1] But as a daughter, she always knew she would return. In 1939, Pearl Hooper traveled back to Louisiana to bury her mother and grieve with her family. After a few weeks had passed, it was time to go home. Her husband mailed her a ticket on the Teche Greyhound Lines. When she entered the bus, she discovered that she had been assigned the worst seat: the very back over the wheel. One hundred miles into the trip, the bus reached Hammond, Louisiana, and the driver ordered Hooper to vacate her seat for a white man. She refused.[2] At the next stop, the driver shoved Hooper out of her seat and kicked her off the bus into a rainstorm, throwing her luggage at her. Her watch and ring, valued at one hundred dollars, were missing. In this era of migration, family heirlooms were precious jewels.

When she finally arrived home, she alerted the *Chicago Defender* and contacted the local branch of the National Association for the Advancement of Colored People (NAACP) to consider a lawsuit against Teche Greyhound. Pearl Hooper told a reporter this bus ride marked "her last trip in Mississippi."[3]

Migrant women like Pearl Hooper kept their Southern family close. In Black communities, women served as cultural workers to sustain their ancestral connections.[4] The Great Migration pushed Black women far away from their Southern homeland, but they always felt a familial pull. In December and the summer months, crowds of Black women stationed themselves in long lines to board interstate buses in order to visit with their extended family. A sudden illness or funeral also prompted Black women to purchase bus tickets and return home to care for their loved one or to grieve. Visiting was Black women's work, marking an important, if unexplored, dimension of the gendered history of the Great Migration.[5]

Even though Black women entered stations as paying customers, riding a segregated bus was more labor than leisure. It was exhausting to shuffle seats, deal with stern drivers, inhale fumes, and wait in the very back of the line to retrieve luggage. Bus technology was modern, but interstate bus trips were long and arduous. Violence could erupt at any moment, creating a tense atmosphere for every Black rider. Most Black women riders simply wanted to disappear and travel from one destination to the next in dignity. Instead, interracial bus conflicts created emotional and psychic encounters that could linger for life. The insults and dangers of segregated bus travel sapped Black women's energy and eroded their patience.

This chapter investigates the archive of Black women bus riders and their everyday resistance to these passenger experiences. By writing letters, talking to reporters, and filing affidavits, Black women passengers spoke back to the powerful and unrelenting domination of the bus industry. They articulated several different discourses of citizenship rights. Many expressed the identity of a consumer citizen, contending that their dollars and cents entitled them to ride in safety and dignity.[6] Others broadened this language, connecting their experiences on buses with aspirations for Black equality in the United States. I term these statements "textual acts of citizenship." In vivid letters and crisp affidavits, Black women detailed their harrowing bus rides and then appropriated strident language from the abolition movement, vowing to destroy systems of segregation and discrimination. Even though Black women described some truly horrific experiences, many remained optimistic that the bus industry—and, by extension, the nation—could overcome its racist practices. This rich archive of affidavits, letters, and newspaper exposés illuminates Black women's everyday experiences on buses but also reveals their complex theoretical assessments about race relations, capitalism, equality, and political strategies in the early civil rights movement. Their clear-headed calls for justice in the bus industry were never published anywhere else, and the Black women who crafted these textual acts of citizenship have long been forgotten. But as the historian Crystal Moten argues, everyday documents, such as these letters and affidavits, brim with Black women's rich intellectual thought, which demands rigorous engagement.[7]

When Black women expressed their resistance against the bus industry, they often turned to the early civil rights community for support, defined here as reporters and editors in the Black press and officers in the NAACP's national office.[8] This community was largely male and middle class. These men were sympathetic to the plight of Black women passengers but often failed to understand how gendered violence, the threat of sexual assault, and even an everyday bus conflict could affect a Black woman for life.[9] Most Black women who rode interstate buses were Southern migrants like Pearl Hooper, who already lived on the economic margins and were vulnerable to physical violence and sexual assault. By encouraging Black women to persist in their resistance to the point of arrest, the civil rights community taunted the bus industry, tempting them to double down on their domination of Black passengers, which necessarily meant Black women passengers.

By the late 1930s and 1940s, the number of Black women who were arrested on buses began to surge. As more and more cases were reported, the NAACP and Black press slowly realized what Black women passengers knew the second they entered the station: The bus industry built its business strategy around the recruitment and comfort of white women customers and the simultaneous degradation of Black women passengers.

Black Women and Consumption in the Great Migration

As Black women like Pearl Hooper wrestled with the difficult decision to migrate out of the South, they had to strategize about how they would return, weighing affordability and convenience alongside safety considerations. Visiting the South was an expensive prospect, one that required months, or even years, of savings. It was almost always Black women who performed this labor, and yet as service workers in the Jim Crow North, they were the ones with the least amount of money. By the 1920s, transportation options had broadened to include private automobiles, trains, and interstate buses, which were still in the infancy stage. Since most women visited the South alone or accompanied by young children, it was dangerous to drive a car and secure roadside accommodations.[10] In the Jim Crow South, the Highway Patrol could surveil and harass Black drivers across the region's newly built roads.[11] Most Black women purchased train tickets for their Southern visits. On trains, especially Pullman cars, the presence of Black workers meant that African Americans might receive better service and be protected from violence, even if accommodations were segregated.[12] But by the late 1920s and early 1930s, the interstate bus industry had expanded, promising accessible routes and affordable fares. These shiny advertising campaigns, coupled with the Great Depression, convinced more

The holidays were a busy time for bus travel. Here a Black woman traveler in Washington, DC—carrying presents and dressed in a fancy dress, hat, and a striking fur coat—waits to board a bus bound for Richmond, Virginia. Black women bus passengers always bore a burden to embody respectability in their clothing and overall decorum. *Source*: John Vachon, *Washington, D.C. Greyhound Bus Terminal on the Day Before Christmas. Waiting to Board the Bus to Richmond*, December 24, 1941, Farm Security Administration Photographs, Prints and Photographs, Library of Congress, Washington, D.C., LC-USF34- 064205-D [P&P].

and more Black migrant women to opt for bus travel. For shorter trips, there was little financial difference between a train and a bus. It cost $1.50 to travel between New York City and Philadelphia on a bus, and $1.80 on a train. But for longer trips, it was more economical to ride a bus. A bus trip between New York and Chicago cost $12.95, but on a train, it was $18.20.[13] That $5.25 was a significant amount of money for migrant travelers, resulting in thousands of Black women who began to purchase their first bus tickets.[14]

When Black women walked into the bus station, they tapped their identities as modern consumers in a capitalist world. By the 1910s and 1920s, modern mass culture had proliferated in cities across the United States, enabling women to shop for consumer goods for themselves and often their families. Department stores and catalogs featured a world of goods, stretching from clothing, radios, and furniture to linens and cleaning supplies. Newly built chain grocery stores began to appear in urban neighborhoods, stocked with a variety of foodstuffs.[15] As Black women migrated to Northern cities, they encountered a more extensive landscape of consumer and leisure culture. Although most women labored in low-paying jobs as domestic servants, waitresses, laundresses, and cooks, they had more free time and disposable earnings.[16] These circumstances enabled Black women to spend money on movie tickets, a new article of clothing, or a trip to the beauty parlor. Not only did migration give Black women more opportunities for consumption, but it enabled them to exercise choice, electing to buy certain brands over others and map their individual preferences onto their purchases.[17]

As much as Black women might have wanted to patronize Black-owned bus companies, whether it was Brooks, Rialto, or Safe, most of these bus lines were short-lived and could not accommodate their travel needs during the Great Migration. Even though most Black women had poor customer experiences with Greyhound, it was the largest interstate bus line in that era, with regular routes and ride schedules, meaning it could facilitate Black women's travel in the era of migration. Or so it seemed.

"Show Some Manhood and Womanhood": Gendered Resistance in the Early Bus Industry

In the early days of interstate bus travel, Black women passengers began to report four principal dissatisfactions: racial segregation, illness, desertions in unfamiliar locations, and a lack of accommodation at rest stops. Most of these experiences can be traced to a color line in the bus industry, but others were related to the uneven early days, when bus service was still scattered and companies were refining their operations.[18] Many Black women purchased bus tickets in Northern states with civil rights laws. But when they boarded the bus, they were stunned to find that drivers forced them to sit in the very back, threatening violence if they did not comply. Early buses were flimsy vehicles. In seats toward the back, it was more difficult to control temperature, and many riders were exposed to the elements, including rain, wind, and snow. Black women frequently reported illness after sitting in these back seats and subsequent doctor's bills. But illnesses were not always temporary and inconvenient. In the late 1920s, four African Americans boarded a Gregory bus, transporting them from rural Mississippi to St. Louis, Missouri. Sixteen white passengers sat up front, and four Black ones in the back. When the bus wheeled into St. Louis the next morning, the driver discovered that a pipe had been leaking carbon monoxide. One Black passenger died, and three others were hospitalized.[19] In this era, bus companies like Gregory were brand new, and drivers were still learning the technology. But the fact that Black passengers were the ones who died or became ill demonstrated the deadly consequences of racial segregation on bus lines. The Gregory Bus Lines went into bankruptcy later that year, and Pickwick purchased the company. Greyhound bought Pickwick one year later.[20]

As these disturbing stories about passenger experiences spread, the Black press began to investigate the bus industry. Journalists and editors sensed that bus travel would figure prominently in the lives of African Americans in this era, and they devoted significant resources toward investigating claims of discrimination. No newspaper was more vigilant than the *Chicago Defender.* By 1930, Chicago had over two hundred thousand African American residents, including many Southern migrants. Not only did many of Chicago's Black residents ride interstate lines, but many buses established their corporate headquarters in the city.

In 1927, the *Chicago Defender* hired the white journalist Albert A. Libby to pose as a white Southerner and ask different bus lines in the city about their racial practices.[21] In his undercover reporting, Libby found that the Inter-State Motor Stages "stick the n****** in the back," that the Ni-Sun and Shore lines excluded Black passengers altogether, that the Yelloway Lines preferred to sell to passengers of lighter complexions, and that the Purple Swan–Greyhound–Oriole limited the number of Black riders on each bus to four. Importantly, Libby also conversed with a white woman who worked as an agent for Shore Line, who told him that the company banned Black passengers from the waiting room and restrooms. "They get offended," she reported, "but then go away." Libby concluded that Shore Line was "doing its best to get rid of colored."[22] This investigation revealed that most Chicago-based bus lines enforced the color line during this period.[23]

Following the publication of this exposé, Black women wrote to the *Chicago Defender,* recounting their own experiences. Victoria Watson, a Black woman in Ypsilanti, Michigan, told the *Defender* that her mother purchased an Oriole bus ticket to travel from Chicago to Detroit. When the bus pulled up, the driver refused to allow her to board, telling her another bus would be along shortly. That was a lie. Her mother had to wait for eight hours, and when she finally boarded the bus, she was forced to ride in the back, and the windows were open for the entire ride. When her mother reached her destination, she was ill.[24]

The civil rights community learned about these incidents but was not always attuned to the complex gendered dynamics between white male drivers and Black women passengers. Male civil rights leaders and newspaper editors and reporters celebrated Black women's defiance against bus segregation but at times marginalized the dangers that they encountered. In an editorial published in the *Chicago Defender* about bus travel in Illinois, the editor remarked, "Women traveling alone have found themselves the butt of all sorts of vicious and smutty remarks from bus conductors and drivers." While Black men had also been forced to occupy seats in the rear, the editor argued that it was women riders who "had shown the most daring in attempting to assert their rights to any seat available in these coaches." Indeed, as the editorial correctly stated, Black women were on the front lines against segregation in the early days of bus travel. The editorial called on Black women and men to persist in their protest, noting, "It is time that we were beginning to show some manhood and womanhood about the things for which we have suffered in this country." Articulating a discourse of consumer citizenship, the editorial implored citizens to recognize that Black residents were tax-paying citizens who deserved "fair treatment" on all forms of transportation in the state.[25] Pieces such as this one not only reported gendered patterns of opposition to bus discrimination but also educated new migrants to the city about civil rights that they, as residents of Illinois, were entitled to receive. And yet this editor did not necessarily understand that for women passengers, there were hidden dangers to standing up to the bus industry.

By the late 1920s and early 1930s, two things about Black women and the bus industry had become clear: Even though services were uneven, Black women passengers needed this affordable option for travel in order to sustain their familial connections in this era of financial precarity. At the same time, discrimination against Black women passengers was unrelenting. In this context, Black women and leaders at the NAACP searched for a solution to address these mounting patterns of injustice.

"Stamp Out This Insult to Our People": The NAACP Intervenes Against Greyhound

Leaders at the NAACP recognized that they needed to put an end to the mistreatment of Black women passengers on buses. Reeling from the Great

Depression, membership in the organization hovered at only twenty thousand, and the NAACP was dangerously close to bankruptcy.[26] But the mounting injustices on buses were not going to disappear. African Americans reported discrimination on nearly every bus line, but it was clear that Greyhound not only dominated the interstate market but zealously enforced the color line with brute force. In 1931, the NAACP announced that it was partnering with the American Civil Liberties Union and the Garland Fund to file lawsuits testing segregation on interstate transportation, including buses and trains.[27] Black women from across the country immediately wrote to the NAACP, detailing discrimination on buses. The organization received so many letters about Greyhound that legal assistant William Andrews wrote an internal memo, asking that the office "make a separate file of cases dealing with discriminations on bus lines."[28] After some reflection, NAACP leaders realized that they needed to focus their campaign on one of Greyhound's eleven lines. Executive Secretary Roy Wilkins picked Pennsylvania Greyhound, a shrewd choice. Pennsylvania had a civil rights law, and Philadelphia and Pittsburgh were cities with growing populations of Black Southern migrants. In a call announcing this campaign, the NAACP asked Black passengers to send in accounts of their experiences on Greyhound buses, particularly affidavits. The NAACP printed this call in at least three Black newspapers, including the *Philadelphia Tribune*, the *Kansas City Call*, and the *Pittsburgh Courier*.[29]

Over thirty Black women from across the country heeded this call. Writing on religious stationery, organizational letterhead, translucent looseleaf, greeting cards, and thick, cream-colored paper, Black women filled every inch of their letters with vivid detail. Narrating their experiences on Greyhound buses, Black women highlighted the financial, physical, and emotional tolls of these trips. Many ended their descriptions with a hope that discrimination might end in the United States. Sealing their accounts in envelopes, women mailed their testimony to the NAACP's office in New York City. Their letters filled canvas mail bags, furnishing unequivocal evidence about Greyhound's widespread patterns of discrimination against passengers. Even though every account was different, each woman took the time to write a letter so that her experience could be part of the NAACP's organizational fight against Greyhound.

Black women articulated claims to consumer citizenship, contending that as paying customers and dignified, well-dressed bus passengers, they were entitled to decent service on Greyhound buses. For instance, Mrs. Woodson, a resident of Philadelphia, traveled on a Greyhound bus bound for New

York City, where the driver forced her to take a seat "over the wheel," which was in the back and very uncomfortable. When the bus rolled into New York City, Woodson was ill from inhaling the bus fumes. On the return trip home, she refused to sit over the wheel and was given a seat on the back bench, which did not recline, for the two-and-a-half-hour trip. These seats contrasted with the luxurious benches Greyhound promised its women passengers. "I hope you all will try to make all the colored race to stop riding the Greyhound Bus line," she told the NAACP, "as they surely treat us shameful." Woodson charged that Greyhound treated all Black passengers in this manner, "no matter about how nice you are dressed." As a passenger, Woodson understood that the bus industry sold to Sarah, asserting that Greyhound "don't think you're good enough in having a decent seat or being comfortable in it."[30] As a consumer citizen, she had expected that her dollars, her nice clothing, and her respectability would allow her to ride the bus in dignity. But her Blackness meant that she would never be afforded the privilege of womanhood.

Others echoed these sentiments, detailing the very particular ways that the bus industry violated them as working-class Black women. In the 1930s, Augusta Saunders, a native of Alabama, took a Greyhound bus from New York City to Los Angeles, California, where she worked as a maid. This was a very long trip, lasting nearly a week. As the lone Black rider, she reported that a driver was "very ugly" in his interactions with her. Not only was Saunders disappointed that she had to sit in the back the entire time, but she was shocked that the American West and Southwest also enforced racial segregation against African Americans. "In New Mexico and Arizona, to my surprise," she told the NAACP, "I was segregated, even in Southern California." She also recounted how, at a rest stop, a Black girl was banned from the women's restroom and had to use the men's restroom.[31] Augusta Saunders's letter was laden with references to violence, whether it was the rough behavior of bus drivers or the prospect of men assaulting a young girl in the restroom.

Other letters revealed how bus trips could result in devastating financial impacts for migrant women. For example, Detroit resident Nerline Brown and her twin sister had traveled to visit family in Missouri. Both sisters worked as maids and shared a room in a boardinghouse. During the trip, the Greyhound driver had threatened to seat them in the back, and when they changed buses in Chicago, Brown realized that her handbag was missing. After a week, she recovered the bag, but not the forty dollars inside it. Brown contacted the bus station and was told to "drop it" and warned not to "start any trouble." The Greyhound Management Company in Cleveland never responded to her inquiries. Nerline Brown told the NAACP that she hoped her story "will help some" in their case against Greyhound.[32] Ida B. Richardson recounted a similar experience. A migrant from South Carolina, she was in her late twenties, worked as a bar maid in a hotel, and lodged in Harlem. On a bus trip to visit her family in the South, the driver forced her to take a seat in the rear, she was not permitted to use the restroom or restaurant at the rest stop, and her suitcase was lost. When she arrived at her destination, she had to purchase new clothes.[33] Not only did Nerline Brown and Ida Richardson experience hostile service on Greyhound, but these bus trips resulted in a financial loss. Forty dollars and the cost of new clothes were devastating amounts of money for migrant women.

In addition to the financial toll of bus trips, Black women told NAACP officers how encounters over the most mundane matters put them face-to-face with hostile bus drivers. This racialized sexual dynamic enabled bus drivers to police them as passengers, whether it was issuing sharp verbal threats, using brute force to move them to other parts of the vehicle, or creating an overall culture of fear. White drivers ejected them from the bus with their small children in tow, refused to retrieve their bags, and threatened them with arrest when they declined to move assigned seats.[34] White male passengers, often drunk, also abused and taunted Black women.[35]

Some women even completed the extra step by filing affidavits, which required them to notarize their testimony with a clerk or attorney. In their affidavits, Black women identified their legal name, residence, and all persons involved. Paragraph by paragraph, they listed the facts of the event. They then appeared before a notary public, who administered an oath, stamped their testimony, and asked them to sign the affidavit, making it a legal document.[36] While not part of a court case, these affidavits can be read as small textual claims to citizenship, in which Black women not only recounted their experiences with the bus industry but also articulated their visions for equality and justice in the United States. By notarizing their testimony through affidavits, Black women eagerly inserted their narratives into the NAACP's campaign against Pennsylvania Greyhound, expressing optimism that their experiences might offer compelling evidence.

As Black women described their individual cases, they pinned their stories of bus discrimination onto the larger canvas of civil rights. In her affidavit, E. Pauline Myers detailed a bus trip from Washington, DC, to Virginia, where she was forced to endure segregation in the back even though there were numerous empty seats toward the front. "I trust that this experience of mine along with any other similar experiences of other Negroes," Myers wrote, "may serve as an instrument in the associational fight against the degradation of segregation."[37] Here, Myers outlined a vision for the future of the United States as a nation where the system of segregation might be abolished. Similarly, Baltimore resident Ethel Brooks argued, "The embarrassment that I and others experienced was terrible and I can never forget. I wish you victory in your endeavor. We can only crush such circumstances by sticking together and defending our rights regardless."[38] Brooks bolstered her letter with references to the nineteenth-century movements to abolish slavery and enact Black equality through Reconstruction. Adele Grymes of Bridgeton, New Jersey, hoped that her testimony would "help stamp out this insult to our people."[39] Los Angeles resident Augusta Saunders evoked religion, predicting "there will come the day and very soon when God will enable the Black man to rise up against these ignorant whites of America."[40] And in her letter, West Virginia resident Mattie Bradshaw described a missionary trip, where the bus driver forced her and her friend to sit in the very back of the bus on top of the luggage for the duration of the ride. Signing her letter on religious stationery, Bradshaw concluded that she was a "real fighter against all evil" and begged the NAACP to "stop the madness."[41] By selecting verbs like "crush," "stamp out," "rise up," and "stop," Black women articulated the abolitionist contours of their fight for citizenship rights, noting that these patterns of discrimination must be banished in the bus industry.

Analyzing these letters and affidavits demonstrates what the historian Julie Greene calls a "tactile experience."[42] These letters are historical sources, but the substance cannot be separated from the subjective presence of these Black women, pulsing in every document—for example, Pauline Myers's clipped, precise handwriting. Her letters were so neat that she must have earned the highest marks in penmanship as a young girl. When she was practicing her *Q*'s and *R*'s, did she ever imagine she would summon her handwriting talents to write a letter about discrimination on a bus—a vehicle that had not yet been invented? Or the exaggerated loops and flourishes in Ethel Brooks's dramatic handwriting. The vivid ink in Ida Richardson's letter suggests that she wrote with a fountain pen, giving it a touch of luxury. As a bar maid in a hotel, she might have borrowed this writing instrument or purchased one for herself. In the creases of the paper, the bold ink of their words, and the flourishes of their signatures, Black women layered these letters with sorrow and anger at the discrimination they had experienced as bus passengers. But they always ended with a dose of optimism, hoping that racism in the United States would recede. It was likely a cathartic act for migrant women to write such letters, knowing that their accounts might have been surveilled and silenced in the Jim Crow South.

Black women believed that discrimination on Greyhound buses represented an injustice that could be reversed. Since buses were a brand-new invention, it was easier to envision abolishing segregation on a bus than integrating an elementary school or dismantling the rigid structure of economic inequality. Black women were paying customers, and they were eager and impatient for the NAACP to take up the case. As Goldie Washington of Kansas City told the NAACP, "I am certainly glad to know that someone has taken the case of Greyhound Bus Lines."[43] Ending discrimination on Greyhound made logical sense for these aggrieved passengers.

In the spring of 1932, Roy Wilkins testified before the Pennsylvania Public Service Commission. Carrying these letters and affidavits laden with Black women's textual claims of citizenship, Wilkins described how Greyhound's blatant policies of racial discrimination violated Pennsylvania's civil rights law. Despite this mountain of evidence documenting widespread patterns of racial discrimination, the Pennsylvania commission granted Greyhound its certificate of service.[44] The NAACP had lost this battle.

In the aftermath of this defeat, Roy Wilkins exchanged several letters with John B. Walker, the vice president of the Greyhound Management Company in Cleveland. In them, Wilkins had a frank conversation about the bus line's racist practices. After Wilkins reached out about an individual case of bus passenger discrimination, Walker assured him that the incident could be traced to the actions of a single bus driver, whose behavior was not part of any broader company policy or culture. Walker told Wilkins that he welcomed any feedback about his company and that Greyhound desired the patronage of Black customers and had, in fact, hired several African Americans to work as passenger agents.[45] This was blatantly false. There is no evidence that Greyhound ever recruited Black passengers or hired Black ticket agents. In fact, Greyhound only employed African Americans to labor as porters and cleaners.[46] At this precise moment, while John B. Walker was assuring Wilkins that Greyhound desired Black passengers, local officials from the Central Greyhound Lines Inc. approached the NAACP for a bus contract for the national conference. The NAACP publicly rebuffed the offer.[47]

In another letter, Wilkins told Walker that bus drivers policed Black passengers because Greyhound sanctioned this culture of discrimination—an understanding Wilkins had come to after reading the outpouring of testimony from Black women.[48] Greyhound did not take this accusation lightly. In a follow-up letter, Walker denied this claim but noted that it would be nearly impossible to "stamp out" the discriminatory attitudes of some Greyhound employees, ironically echoing the precise language of Adele Grymes in her textual act of citizenship. Walker assured Wilkins that while the NAACP would likely keep hearing reports of discrimination, he predicted that "they will become more and more infrequent."[49]

Leaders at the NAACP were unsure of the next steps to take. The Pennsylvania Public Service Commission did not acknowledge the blatant patterns of intolerance, while Greyhound assured the NAACP that it did not practice discrimination. The NAACP had worked within established, respectable channels, and the strategy had failed. The only solution to address this intractable problem would be individual lawsuits and direct action resistance. By 1932, at least six Black women had filed lawsuits against bus companies in the North and Midwest. Some ended in defeats, but several won their cases. The NAACP's national office supported these lawsuits from afar and began to recognize that individual judges, especially in the North, were willing to rule against bus companies in moments of blatant discrimination.

In July 1932, the NAACP issued a wide-ranging press release that instructed Black riders to take direct action measures against racial discrimination. The NAACP advised Black passengers that they should "insist on their rights and refuse to allow bus drivers" to order them to move to rear seats. The NAACP instructed African Americans to "sit tight," daring bus drivers to either eject them from the bus or call the police. When bus employees or police officers tried to abuse Black passengers, they could file lawsuits against bus lines and sue for damages, reminding riders to save their ticket stubs. While companies might "try to talk rough and scare Negroes into surrendering their rights," the NAACP predicted that few bus drivers would go "so far as use violence."[50]

The NAACP's press release brimmed with naivete about both the violence of the bus industry and Black women's vulnerability as passengers. At this moment, most male leaders in the NAACP had not even boarded a bus. They were unaware that the bus industry modeled its bus drivers on the police, and they were oblivious to the racial violence at the heart of bus companies. By training their drivers to act like police officers, instructing them to use force, and discursively othering African Americans, Greyhound and other companies did not hesitate to enforce the color line with violence, especially toward Black women. Black women passengers were well-versed in this reality. They had experienced this violence firsthand, and for some, it continued to linger. NAACP leaders were more naive. This 1932 memo represents where the gendered blind spots of the early civil rights community were most visible.

While this memo offered a clarion call for passengers' unrelenting opposition to the domination of the bus industry, it highlighted how male civil rights leaders placed their implicit trust in both police officers and the courts. Inviting Black passengers, especially women, to be arrested created dangerous scenarios for racial and sexual violence. At this point, the NAACP had reason to believe that Black women could continue to receive victories in their favor in US courts, based on a string of recent cases. Plus, the NAACP still maintained a moderately cordial relationship with the bus industry and seemed to express faith in John B. Walker's prediction that episodes of racial discrimination would become more "infrequent." But by the late 1930s and early 1940s, this optimism would dissipate as Black women passengers continued to bear the brunt of the violence. In one devastating letter after another, Black women riders informed the NAACP about the true intentions of the bus industry.

Arresting Passengers: Violence Escalates, 1935–1941

Not only did Black women return to the South to nurture their family connections, but they also had to participate in proceedings about property and other legal matters. In 1938, Rebecca Ferguson, a domestic worker in Brooklyn, had to return to Sumter, South Carolina, to testify in a civil case about land. She was ordered to appear alongside fellow migrant Jacqueline White.[51] The two women boarded a bus in New York City and sat near the front. Jacqueline White had recently been hospitalized and was in a frail state. When their bus wheeled into Richmond, Virginia, the driver explained that racial segregation was the law and ordered the two women to move to the back. White and Ferguson heeded the NAACP's instructions and refused to move. The driver returned with police officers, who arrested them. The police officers were rough in their demeanor. Ferguson wrote that the officers "pulled and pushed us and snatched us around as if we were cattle" and then deposited the two women in jail. In police court, the two women were fined and charged with disorderly conduct. Because of their arrest and jail time, the two women were unable to reach their final destination and appear in court. When they returned to New York, Rebecca Ferguson contacted the NAACP and explained the circumstances, but there was little that the organization could do.[52]

By the mid-1930s, Black women passengers reported more cases of discrimination, violent assault, and arrest. Several factors contributed to this uptick in cases. In 1935, bus travel became more popular than train travel, which meant that an increased number of Black women boarded these vehicles. Since bus companies deliberately catered to white women, the increased presence of Black women—especially passengers who expressed resistance and frustration—empowered drivers, ticket agents, and company officials to impose the color line with greater force. As bus travel surged in popularity in the United States, it became an indelible part of the American economic and cultural landscape. The Pennsylvania Public Service Commission had rejected the NAACP's claim that Pennsylvania Greyhound had exercised discrimination in 1932. That victory emboldened Greyhound, granting the company explicit permission not only to persist in business as usual but, in fact, to accelerate their racist policing of Black women passengers. As more Black women filed lawsuits against Greyhound and other bus lines, these companies became savvier at evading them. The bus industry began to blatantly contradict Black women's narratives of discrimination and violence. Rather than acknowledging episodes of racial discrimination or moments of a bus driver's intolerance, executives at bus lines now crafted false accounts that Black women passengers were abusive and disorderly. Sometimes they even encouraged bus drivers to threaten Black women and intimidate them against taking legal action.

The citizenship status of African Americans was also shifting. By the mid-1930s, African Americans had begun to receive some benefits from New Deal programs, whether it was a federal arts project, public housing, the Civilian Conservation Corps, or even the Social Security Act. With the Wagner Act, some Black workers organized into powerful labor unions and began to receive higher wages. In Northern cities, activists staged "Don't Buy Where You Can't Work" campaigns, withholding patronage at stores and restaurants that did not hire Black workers. And cities like Chicago, New York, and Detroit were starting to develop large Black electorates who could send representatives to Congress. This changing context of Black citizenship rights likely created feelings of animosity and hostility in the bus industry, especially among white bus drivers.[53] On individual buses, drivers routinely assaulted Black women passengers with greater force, issued threats, and brought in law enforcement. This policing behavior became normalized in bus driver etiquette. Cumulatively, by the mid-1930s, these shifting circumstances contributed to a more violent dialectic between Black women's resistance and bus companies' and bus drivers' aggression.

As they boarded buses, Black women noticed that the most ordinary ride had become fraught and dangerous. In August 1938, Lucille Lewis booked a Greyhound trip from New York City to Washington, DC, where she sat in the back next to a fellow Black passenger. A group of eight white men boarded the bus. They were all drinking whiskey and began to heckle Lewis. When they put their luggage in the overhead compartment, they crushed her hat. She asked a fellow Black passenger to notify the bus driver, but he stated that he didn't want any "disturbances." The white passengers then began to attack the Black male passenger. The driver suddenly appeared in the back of the bus, jumped across Lewis's lap, and pinned down the Black male passenger while the white men attacked him. After the white men assaulted the Black passenger, they began vomiting in the aisles. They continued to taunt Lewis and the Black man for the rest of the bus trip. When they reached New York, the driver had the white men sign "papers."[54] Lucille Lewis's letter reached the NAACP, which called it "one of the most vicious cases we have had in our office in quite some time."[55] Lewis's letter illuminates the degree to which white passengers abused Black riders and the complicity of white bus drivers to permit this behavior to occur. The fact that the driver asked these white passengers to sign papers indicates that he intended to keep this incident a secret. This behavior reflected a shift on the part of bus drivers, who were determined to evade any responsibility for incidents on board.

In 1941, Viola Barren, a housemaid in Chicago, wrote a letter to the *Chicago Defender* describing a violent bus experience. A migrant from South Carolina, she and her husband were raising her niece. When she learned that her brother in Memphis, Tennessee, was ill, she and her niece traveled down South to care for him and later bury him. She booked a Dixie Greyhound bus to return home, and every employee at Dixie Greyhound treated her with disrespect, prompting her to remark, "Conditions are not changing very fast for the good of the Negro people." Barren noted that both the reservations agent and the driver "pushed and abused her." The bus had many empty seats near the front, but the driver insisted that she sit in the back over the wheel, where water poured into the bus. On three occasions, she told the driver that she was getting wet, and he became more abusive to her each time. When she and her niece arrived in Chicago, they were both ill.[56] Viola Barren was not the only Black woman to be dismissed by a bus driver.

Another bus driver ejected Alice Byrd and Francina Coleman and their young children into an ice storm. Migrants from rural Virginia, these women had settled in Queens.[57] Alice Byrd's life had recently fallen apart when her husband had abandoned the family, a common occurrence in the era of migration.[58] Coleman and Byrd planned a trip to visit relatives in Lancaster, Virginia, with two children in tow. Any trip down to the South was dangerous, so it is possible that they traveled together for safety. The bus ride from New York to Baltimore was uneventful, but when they had to transfer in Baltimore, they were forced to move to the segregated section, and they refused. When the bus stopped at Colonial Beach, Virginia, the driver ejected them into an ice storm, forcing the four evicted passengers to take two expensive taxi rides to reach Lancaster. In her letter to the NAACP, Byrd noted the irony that while they were paying for this extra transportation, they still had their round-trip bus tickets.[59]

When the women returned to New York, they reached out to the NAACP. Their letter reached the desk of the NAACP's Legal Defense Fund, and Milton Konvitz—a Jewish lawyer in the office—seized on the case.[60] Konvitz contacted the Pennsylvania Greyhound Lines as well as the general manager of the Greyhound Management Company. Greyhound gaslit Alice Byrd and Francina Coleman, stating that they were "abusive and disorderly" and insisting that Greyhound was "in no way liable for [the] incident alleged."[61] This episode was telling. Previously, Greyhound often sided with the customer. Now, as bus travel grew in popularity, racial discrimination had become more routine, and the bus industry became more powerful, the company institutionalized a racist corporate approach. Since Greyhound had endowed white bus drivers with absolute authority, these men had the privilege to craft false narratives about Black women passengers' behavior on the bus.

Conditions became so dire that Bradford Gibson, a traveling salesman, wrote a letter to the *Chicago Defender* in which he proposed that African Americans across the country boycott Greyhound. "Race people," Bradford pleaded, "show your race pride by traveling on buses that are courteous to you."[62] For Black women living across the country, a boycott was unsustainable. No Black bus company was able to survive for very long except for the Safe Bus Company in Winston-Salem, North Carolina, and there were no interstate Black lines in the industry. As reports from Black women continued to pour into NAACP offices, leaders recognized that violence on buses was metastasizing, and there was no clear answer. In the 1930s, NAACP attorney Charles Hamilton Houston's desk brimmed with reports from Black women detailing discriminatory passenger experiences. In a revealing letter, Houston acknowledged that he was "very anxious" to find a solution to the problem of discrimination. In the Great Depression and the Great Migration, buses were "becoming more and more important to the masses of our people."[63]

Beginning in the mid-1930s, the arrest of Black women bus passengers began to surge. Bringing in law enforcement allowed the bus industry to triangulate these conflicts and shift the blame for violence from the bus driver to the police officer. It also enabled the bus industry to reinforce its narrative that Black women were disorderly passengers. For Black women passengers, the stakes escalated. The presence of law enforcement officers created more opportunities for physical and sexual assault. Police officers arrested at least seventeen Black women in the period before World War II. Most of these women were Southern migrants who had to navigate a fraught landscape, performing respectability while facing economic marginalization, danger, and assault at every turn. For these women, jail time, criminal records, and the psychological trauma of arrest only made bus travel more precarious.

In 1938, Edna Reed, a single migrant from South Carolina in her fifties, purchased a ticket on the Great Eastern Bus Line to travel from New York City to Greensboro, North Carolina.[64] When the bus wheeled into Washington, a white man, his wife, and their child boarded the bus, and the driver brusquely ordered Edna Reed to relinquish her seat, which she did. But when the bus arrived at Alexandria, four state troopers boarded and escorted Edna Reed off, leaving her stranded.[65] She was forced to take another bus back to Washington, DC, where she booked a train to Greensboro. As a domestic servant, purchasing this train ticket strained Reed's budget, and experiencing harassment at the hands of both the bus driver and the state troopers frayed her nerves.[66]

One year later, another pair of women ran into legal trouble. In August 1939, two migrant women in Pittsburgh planned a visit to the Deep South. Odell Moore was twenty-seven and Mahalia Webster was thirty-nine, and both labored as domestic servants for white families. Moore had planned to visit family in Alabama, while Webster was traveling farther down South to Jacksonville, Florida. In Birmingham, Alabama, the two women boarded another bus bound for the city of Dothan. The driver ordered both women to take seats in the back, and they refused. The driver called the police, who arrested Moore and Webster with force, depositing them in the city jail. At the sentencing the next morning, Judge Henry D. Martin accused the women of defying segregation to sue the bus company or initiate a test case.[67] This allegation demonstrated that white judges were increasingly aware of the NAACP's advice that Black passengers should resist. At the time of their arraignment, the judge gave them each fifty-dollar fines and thirty days in jail. Local leaders in the city tried to get them parole. Both Webster and Moore admitted to their misunderstandings about the etiquette of racial segregation in Alabama.[68]

Cumulatively, the cases of Edna Reed, Mahalia Webster, and Odell Moore demonstrate how bus drivers had begun to escalate their tactics of racial violence against Black women and reinforce their power with police officers. All three of these women were Southern migrants. All three bore the scars of white supremacy and had purchased bus tickets to travel back to the South. But instead of a comfortable bus ride, they encountered hostile bus drivers, police officers, and, in some cases, jail cells. And it would only get worse.

In 1940, police officers arrested at least five Black women on buses traveling in the South. As the United States inched closer to war, bus travel surged in popularity, more Americans were on the road, and bus drivers and police officers targeted Black women for arrest. Virginia even adjusted its segregation statute to deputize bus drivers as officers of the peace, permitting them to carry guns and conduct citizen's arrests. In March, two young African American women, Pauli Murray—the future civil rights activist—and her friend, Adelene McBean, were traveling between New York City and Durham, North Carolina, to spend a holiday with relatives. In Hopewell, Virginia, a bus driver ordered the two women to move to the back of the bus. They refused. The white driver pushed Murray to the ground and arrested both women. Murray was taken to the jail in Petersburg, Virginia, and McBean, who was ill, was taken to the hospital. Upon her release, she joined Murray. Both women would later complain of "vulgar and abusive treatment" from the corrections officers.[69] For Pauli Murray, this bus arrest would be a galvanizing moment in her political consciousness, inspiring her to wage a campaign in the struggles for women and Black freedom until the 1970s.

In 1940, Brooklyn resident Sara Wilson purchased a Greyhound ticket to visit South Carolina. At a stop in Goldsboro, North Carolina, a new bus driver started a shift and demanded that Wilson move to the back, and she refused. The driver swiftly called the police, who arrested her. The next morning in police court, she was convicted of violating the state's segregation statute and given the options of paying a fine or serving thirty days in jail. When Wilson returned to New York City, she contacted the NAACP. Staff lawyer and future Supreme Court justice Thurgood Marshall agreed that the case represented a devastating situation but glumly noted that it was "another instance of injustice which is difficult for us to meet."[70] This attitude reflected a sea change. In 1932, the NAACP had urged Black women passengers to resist racial segregation and be arrested, if necessary. But now, eight years later, the NAACP finally understood the unrelenting power and violence of the bus industry in the United States.

By 1940, on the eve of World War II, the bus industry was a violent well-oiled machine. The NAACP had encouraged Black women passengers to practice direct action resistance by remaining in their seats, demanding their rights, and getting arrested, if necessary. Black women passengers had complied with this strategy, but it had not produced the desired results. Bus drivers and police officers continued to assault Black women. After these episodes, migrant passengers not only had scars; they also had criminal records. Individual Black women bore the brunt of this violence. The arrest and prosecution of so many Black migrant women reinforced the narrative in the eyes of both the bus industry and law enforcement that African American women were deviant passengers.

The Price of Resistance

Beginning in the late 1920s, thousands of Black women in the United States viewed bus travel as their affordable transportation solution in the era of mass migration. Lured by appealing advertisements promising comfort and safety, Black women instead discovered that bus drivers forced them to sit in the most uncomfortable seats. They also discovered that buses were not safe for Black women. Not only did Black women endure violence at the hands of bus drivers and fellow white passengers, but many experienced illness, whether it was from the exhaust fumes, the lack of restrooms, intense heat and cold, or exposure to the elements—especially when they were kicked off the bus.

Black women passengers did not treat bus abuse as another frustrating contradiction of the Black experience in the United States. These working-class migrants, with little money or formal education, alerted the NAACP, the Black press, and bus companies. They tried to work with the NAACP to bring a case against Greyhound. Through their letters and testimony, they pressed for claims to consumer citizenship, stating that their hard-earned dollars entitled them to ride in dignity. These Black women riders occupied a fragile place in the American economy. They were the lowest paid workers in the United States, and they saved and saved to purchase bus tickets to visit family, attend conventions, travel the country as tourists, and nurture their communities. A mishap on a bus was not merely an inconvenience; it cost Black women thousands of dollars to replace lost luggage, purchase train tickets, reserve taxis, or pay medical bills. Black women also completed textual acts of citizenship, connecting their experiences on buses with clarion calls to abolish racial discrimination in the United States. The Black women discussed in this chapter were the ones who had the time and resources to voice these customer experiences. Thousands of other Black women likely experienced these same scenarios, but their stories have not reached the archive.

Protest had a price. Black women's massive resistance prompted the bus industry to reinforce its racial policing. In the early 1930s, bus drivers enforced the color line with brute force. They forbade Black women from boarding the bus, harassed them verbally, and ejected them in unfamiliar locations. By the mid-1930s, after the NAACP lost its case against Pennsylvania Greyhound, the bus industry became even bolder and more brazen in its treatment of Black women passengers. As bus traveled surged, so did violence. While the NAACP encouraged Black women to persist in their resistance, they underestimated the intentions of the bus industry, not understanding the culture of violence that undergirded buses. Before World War II, police officers and bus drivers arrested seventeen Black women, mostly poor Southern migrants. By the time the nation entered the war, this type of violence and state action had become normalized, and Black male soldiers would be on the receiving end of this treatment.

But some Black women bus passengers took the extra step to hire lawyers and file lawsuits. Chapters 3 and 4 investigate the complexity of Black women's litigiousness against the increasingly powerful and violent bus industry. Black women's lawsuits transformed the bus industry, shaped American law, and provided Black and white lawyers and the NAACP a road map to litigate cases against bus companies for both segregation and personal injury.

Part II Taking Bus Companies to Court

The Indiana Law on racial discrimination is clear. It does not tolerate discrimination. Ignoring the fact that one of the principals in this case is a white man and the other a Negro woman, it must be viewed solely as an aggravated attack by a strong man upon a woman who was both weak and ill. She was both injured and humiliated.

—Judge Fred Pickett, Richmond, Indiana, 1927

According to the evidence plaintiff is well thought of by the school authorities of the parish in which she teaches. She otherwise seems to enjoy a good reputation, and no doubt this unfortunate incident caused her considerable embarrassment, humiliation, and mental suffering.

—Judge Samuel LeBlanc, Baton Rouge, Louisiana, 1942

3 Suing for Front Seats

Migrant Women's Lawsuits in the Jim Crow North

In October 1929, Paulina Stevens, a thirty-six-year-old Black woman in Detroit, purchased a Greyhound bus ticket to travel to Lima, Ohio, a city that was 150 miles away. A native of Georgia, Stevens had migrated to Michigan, where she married a white man who labored as a checker in a nightclub, while she managed boarders in their Black Bottom home.[1] Stevens's bus ticket did not specify a seat number, prompting her to select a seat in the third row. But the white driver forced her to move to the rear. During the trip, it began to rain, and water flooded into the back of the bus, soaking Stevens's clothes. When she returned to her home in Detroit, she was severely ill. Incensed at these conditions, Stevens hired W. Hayes McKinney, a prominent Black attorney in Detroit who was also president of the local chapter of the National Association for the Advancement of Colored People (NAACP). Stevens sued the Greyhound Bus Company for $500 in damages. In a municipal court in Detroit, Judge Jesse Drake sided with Stevens and awarded her $100 in damages.[2] Greyhound was displeased with the verdict and filed an appeal. The case was appealed to the Washtenaw County Circuit Court, where it was presided over by noted Michigan judge George W. Sample, who had a record of supporting civil rights causes.[3] In his ruling, Judge Sample affirmed the lower court's decision and increased Paulina Stevens's award by $250, giving her a grand total of $350 in damages against Greyhound. Judge Sample used this case as an opportunity to weigh in on the current state of race relations, stating that Paulina Stevens was a descendent of slaves and that her ancestors were brought to the United States against their will, and that individual states had ratified the Thirteenth, Fourteenth, and Fifteenth Amendments to the US Constitution, which guaranteed that white citizens could not take away her rights. Finally, Judge Sample warned that the socialist Bolshevik government in Russia was making appeals to African Americans, and it was important for the US government to affirm the rights of Black citizens.[4] He was tempted to award her as much as $1,000.[5]

Stevens v. Greyhound is marked by notes of predictability alongside surprising revelations. Paulina Stevens's experiences on a Greyhound bus were not at all unusual, as she was merely one of thousands of Black women customers who experienced this treatment in the interwar era. During this period, the Greyhound Management Company routinely instructed its bus drivers, ticket agents, and managers to force Black women passengers into the back of the bus. And since the hardware on these buses was often rickety, it meant that passengers—particularly those in the back of the bus—were vulnerable to rain, snow, and wind, often resulting in illness. Greyhound uniformly practiced racial segregation, even though Michigan and Ohio were states with civil rights statutes that banned discrimination in public accommodations.

But other aspects of Paulina Stevens's lawsuit do not map neatly onto the cultural memories of bus segregation in the United States. Stevens sued against bus segregation in Detroit, Michigan, not Montgomery, Alabama. Unlike Rosa Parks, she was not a seasoned political activist.[6] A working-class migrant whose formal education stopped at the third grade, she lived on the edges of poverty and was not connected to elite social circles or political causes in Detroit. Yet Paulina Stevens *knew* that her treatment on Greyhound was not only wrong but likely illegal. Northern and Midwestern states, including Michigan, all had civil rights statutes, which stated that the right to public accommodation could not be abridged by race.[7] Equally surprising, not one but two white judges in Michigan sided with her over Greyhound. And Judge Sample expressed not only a remarkable degree of sympathy to the plight of African Americans at the apex of Jim Crow segregation but also disappointment with the current state of race relations in the United States. He rightly pointed out that the Reconstruction amendments to the Constitution guaranteed Paulina Stevens due process and citizenship rights and also noted that her ancestors had been forcibly transported to the United States. But he tempered his sympathy for Stevens with a dose of caution. Judge Sample's fears about a Black-socialist alliance mirrored broader patterns of white anxiety in the United States in this period. Cumulatively, these circumstances worked in Stevens's favor, resulting in a victorious day in court, damages for her injuries, and a recognition that Greyhound was wrong to mistreat a customer.

After Stevens's verdict was handed down, she might have disappeared from public consciousness. During the 1930s, her husband died, and she slipped into poverty, supporting herself as a maid in Detroit and renting a room in the Fischer Lodge flophouse.[8] But African Americans did not forget her lawsuit. The three major Black weeklies—the *Baltimore Afro-American*, the *Chicago Defender*, and the *Pittsburgh Courier*—all covered the Paulina Stevens case and updated readers on its progress. The historian Margaret Burnham argues that Black newspapers in this era were important because they publicized African Americans' traumatic episodes to empathetic readers across the country and animated Black visions for justice.[9] For African American women, reading about the details of Paulina Stevens's successful lawsuit against Greyhound likely inspired them to consider a potential course of legal action when they experienced similar forms of bus discrimination.

The Stevens case also resonated with NAACP leaders. One year after her verdict was announced, Roy Wilkins, the newly minted assistant secretary, wrote to Louis C. Blount, the president of Detroit's local chapter, requesting the details of her case. In his letter, Wilkins referred to a "colored woman in Detroit" who sued Greyhound for violating Michigan's civil rights law and the illness that resulted from her rear seat on the bus. Wilkins correctly recalled the award that Stevens received, first $150, then ultimately $350. Wilkins ended his letter by noting that any information he could provide would be useful in "fighting [bus] discrimination" where racial segregation was illegal.[10] Roy Wilkins's letter demonstrates a central fact about bus segregation lawsuits in the Midwest: Working-class Black women, often Southern migrants, initiated them on their own accord. It was *their* labor—hiring lawyers, appearing in court, and suing bus companies—that educated both NAACP leaders and ordinary African Americans about possible avenues to contest racial segregation and hold bus companies accountable for the physical and emotional toll of such ill treatment.

Beginning in the late 1920s, Black women, mostly Southern migrants, filed lawsuits against bus companies to test the boundaries of citizenship rights in the Jim Crow North and critique the racist and violent practices embedded in the Midwestern bus industry. I term this action "migrant citizenship." Drawing on their migrant-based survival skills and indigenous legal knowledge, Black women contested the discrimination they experienced on buses by knocking on the doors of lawyer's offices and entering courtrooms to testify about their experiences. Black women witnessed firsthand how the Midwestern bus industry modeled itself on the Jim Crow South, and they narrated these experiences in court. Utilizing the services of mostly Black attorneys, Black women educated the civil rights community about the effective uses of the law to uphold civil rights statutes, secure damages, and punish bus companies. Black men also took bus companies to court in the Jim Crow North, experiencing similar victories

TABLE 3.1 Black women's bus lawsuits in the Midwest and the North, 1927–1942

Year	*First name*	*Last name*	*Occupation*	*State*	*Bus line*	*Outcome*	*Amount*	*Incident*	*Attorney*	*Attorney's race*	*Judge*
1927	Laura	Fischer	Unknown	IN	Greyhound	**Victory**	$500	Assault	C. R. Richardson	Black	Fred Pickett
1927	Helen	Dorsey	Probation officer	IN	Blue Goose	Unknown	$500	Denial	R. D. O'Hara	Black	Unknown
1930	Paulina	Stevens	Boarding-house	MI	Greyhound	**Victory**	$350	Segregation	W. Hayes McKinney	Black	George W. Sample
1931	D'Lallah	McIntyre	Unknown	OH	Greyhound	Unknown	Unknown	Comfort	James C. Thomas	Black	Unknown
1932	Elemenoire	Austin	Teacher	OH	Greyhound	Unknown	$20,000	Discrimination	Chester Gillespie	Black	Unknown
1932	Iola	Ellis	Housewife	OH	Greyhound	Unknown	$20,000	Discrimination	Chester Gillespie	Black	Unknown
1934	Jane	Hunter	Phyllis Wheatley YWCA president	OH	Greyhound	Unknown	$2,500	Comfort	Norman McGhee	Black	Unknown
1935	Zena	Higgins	Minister	KS	Southern Kansas Stage Lines	**Victory**	$500	Segregation	James K. Cubbison	White	Johnston
1935	Maude	Lauther	Unknown	NY	Eastern Greyhound	**Victory**	$150	Segregation	Unknown	Unknown	Unknown
1935	Willetta	Brown	Unknown	OH	Greyhound	**Victory**	$250	Comfort	Chester Gillespie	Black	David Moylan
1935	Callie	Stevens	Maid	IL	Safeway Bus Company	**Victory**	$60	Segregation	William H. Temple/Irvin C. Mollinson	Black	Francis Borelli

1937	Lena	Jones	Maid	OH	Youngstown Municipal Railway Company	**Victory**	$800	Injury	Peter B. Betras	White	J. Roberts
1937	Alice	Prince	Teacher	MA	Eastern Greyhound	Unknown	Unknown	Segregation	Irwin T. Dorch	Black	Unknown
1939	Gertrude	Herndon	Unknown	OH	Greyhound	Unknown	$50,000	Segregation	Alexander H. Martin	Black	Unknown
1939	Emma	Means	Unknown	PA	Pennsylvania Greyhound	Unknown	$50,000	—	Harry O. Levin	White	Unknown
1939	Esther	Carroll	Unknown	PA	Pennsylvania Greyhound	Unknown	$10,000	Personal injury	Harry O. Levin	White	Unknown
1941	Clara	Wilson	Unknown	IL	Greyhound	Unknown	Unknown	Segregation	Richard E. Westbrooks	Black	Unknown
1941	Sarah	Love	Housewife	MI	Greyhound	**Victory**	$250	Humiliation	John M. Morris	Black	Ernest A. O'Brien
1942	Melba	Goss	Clerk	OH	Greyhound	Unknown	Unknown	Segregation	Walter W. Harris	Black	Unknown

Sources: "Bus Driver Faces Trial After Row with Negro Woman," *Richmond Palladium*, November 21, 1927, 1; "Bus Discrimination Given Setback by Indiana Judges," *Chicago Defender*, December 3, 1927, 2; "Seeks $500 Damages for Bus Discrimination," *Chicago Defender*, December 31, 1927, 4; "Greyhound Company Loses Bus Segregation Suit," *Baltimore Afro-American*, February 22, 1930, 1; "NAACP Lawyers Win Signal Victory," *Pittsburgh Courier*, April 6, 1935, 1; "Woman Sues Bus Line; Wins Damages for Jim Crow; Jury Gives Award in Court," *Chicago Defender*, March 30, 1935, 1; "Bus Co. Sued," *Cleveland Call and Post*, January 26, 1935, 1; "Greyhound Lines Pay Damages of $250 Hastily," *Atlanta Daily World*, June 10, 1935, 1; "Two Win Damage Suits in Bus Company Jim Crow Cases," *Baltimore Afro-American*, April 20, 1935, 10; *Jones*, 1937 WL 2366; "Discrimination Charged in Proposed Suit Against Greyhound Bus," *New York Amsterdam News*, December 16, 1931, 2; "Two Women Sue Greyhound Lines for Segregation," *Chicago Defender*, January 9, 1932, 4; "Jane Hunter Sues Bus Company for Insult," *Atlanta Daily World*, June 1, 1934, 2; "Denied Bus Seat, Sues," *New York Amsterdam News*, October 9, 1937, 24; "Woman Sues Bus Line for $20,000 for Maltreatment," *Chicago Defender*, November 6, 937, 5; "Seeks $50,000 from Bus Lines," *Atlanta Daily World*, April 2, 1939, 1; "50,000 J.C. Suit Faces Bus Line," *Baltimore Afro-American*, September 2, 1939, 24; "To Sue Bus Company for Jim Crow Transit," *Chicago Defender*, May 31, 1941, 9; "Bus Company Faces Suit for $10,000," *Baltimore Afro-American*, December 23, 1939, 24; "Woman Awarded $250 in Damages for Humiliation While Riding on Bus," *Detroit Tribune*, August 2, 1941, 1.

as well as defeats. But taken together, Black women outnumbered Black men in both the number of lawsuits that were filed and the visibility of their cases in the Black press.[11] Black women composed a disproportionate number of litigants in the Jim Crow North because they rode buses more frequently as they performed the critical labor of visiting the families they had left as a result of the Great Migration. In filing these lawsuits, Black women laid the foundation for future legal challenges to segregation and inspired African Americans across the nation to protest these practices as bus travel surged in popularity.

Black Migration to the Jim Crow North

Black women filed their lawsuits in Northern and Midwestern courts in the era of the Great Migration. Between 1910 and 1950, nearly three million Black Southerners streamed into the region's major cities, including Chicago, Cleveland, Detroit, Indianapolis, New York, Philadelphia, and Pittsburgh. Black Southern migrants sought economic opportunities, full citizenship rights, and safety from violence, but these dreams were soon dashed. Systems of structural racism in the Jim Crow North—palpable in education, labor, and leisure—abounded. These cities were already reeling with ethnic tensions marked by the arrival of twenty-six million immigrants from Southern and Eastern Europe, who had settled there between the 1890s and 1924. Anti-immigrant hostility only exacerbated the stark racism that Black Southern migrants faced. In the Red Summer of 1919, over three hundred race riots had erupted in cities across the country, including Chicago, East St. Louis, and Washington, DC. These dramatic days-long episodes existed alongside everyday patterns of violence, manifest in interracial police brutality and quotidian acts of cruelty. The bright promises of high paid industrial employment were dimmed by the reality that most Black workers—men and women—were confined to the lowest rungs of the economic ladder in the service economy, laboring as menial workers, cooks, maids, and laundresses. Certainly, these positions paid higher wages than most agricultural jobs in the Jim Crow South, but urban life was expensive. And some Northern and Midwestern cities practiced a system of de facto segregation, forcing African Americans to use separate entrances and seating areas at movie theaters and department stores. Housing conditions were abysmal as African Americans crowded into tenement apartments in poor neighborhoods with few municipal services, including sewage, power, and electricity. White Americans banned African Americans from moving into better neighborhoods, fearful that their housing prices would decline.[12] In the streets, white police officers surveilled and attacked African Americans and overpoliced their everyday activities. White newspapers in Northern and Midwestern cities teemed with narratives about Black criminality, discussing how Black migrants were responsible for murder, theft, rape, and other crimes.[13] These verbal attacks were also gendered in that many institutions in the Jim Crow North—including the press and the police—linked African American women with prostitution and deviancy, always downplaying the lived realities of sexual assault and rape.[14]

Not only did African American women find the North and Midwest to be sites of anti-Black racism, but they also encountered intraracial tensions. These cities were home to older Black communities, whose roots stretched back to the eighteenth and nineteenth centuries. Black residents had worked hard to establish reputations of respectability, and some had prospered financially. For these elite Black urbanites, the arrival of poor Southern migrants disrupted their long-standing efforts to cultivate reputations of dignity and decorum. These African Americans were especially condescending about foodways, spirituality, and the idiosyncratic culture of the rural South. Established Black residents responded to the arrival of Black Southern migrants by spearheading programming centered around morality and racial uplift. The Black elite encouraged African American women to wear certain types of clothing, avoid participating in underground economies, attend mainstream churches, and comport themselves with dignity.[15]

It was in this fraught context of the Jim Crow North that Black migrant women encountered a color line on the bus. As service workers, they earned very little money and spent their hard-earned wages on bus tickets to visit family and friends. Not only did most Black women come from a context of economic precarity, but conflicts over bus segregation put them in very dangerous situations, in which they were subject to abuse from bus drivers, police officers, and white passengers. The reason why so many Black women resisted their mistreatment can be traced to their migrant-based survival skills. They had already made the difficult decision to leave the South and venture into new cities with few networks, resources, or systems of support. For many migrants, the Black press was their lifeline, offering information about Black life in the North. Many of these newspapers provided insights not only about Black urban life but also about Black legal life, giving African American readers a glimpse into the legal world.[16] It was Black women's determination to forge a new life in the Jim Crow North, bolstered by their curiosity about their legal rights in their new states of residency, that gave them the courage to knock on the doors of African American lawyers and bring bus companies to court.

Black Migrant Lawyers in the Jim Crow North

As Black Southerners streamed into Northern and Midwestern cities, they forged an important client base for Black lawyers. Among the ranks of Black professionals—including pharmacists, physicians, and dentists—lawyers represented the smallest constituency. There were few Black law schools at the time. While many African American law schools had opened in the era of Reconstruction, most did not last into the twentieth century.[17] In the 1920s and 1930s, there was only one noteworthy Black law school, Howard University School of Law, which had been founded in Washington, DC, in 1867. Some white law schools—including Harvard, Northwestern, the University of Iowa, the University of Michigan, and the University of Pennsylvania—admitted Black students.[18] Not only were there fewer opportunities for aspiring Black professionals to pursue a career in law, but in a racist society predicated on an unjust legal system, African Americans were understandably reluctant to seek the counsel of a Black attorney.[19] But on the other hand, African Americans had a rich legal tradition stretching back to the eighteenth century, where they had waged lawsuits for freedom, property, and a host of civil rights matters, including the right to access education, transportation, and public accommodations on an equal basis.[20] Beyond explicit civil rights struggles, poor Black Southerners were familiar with the law, utilizing it in their churches, fraternal orders, efforts to receive compensation for lost wages, and disputes over property.[21] When Black women migrated to the North, they packed this indigenous legal knowledge in their suitcases, later deploying it in their lawsuits against the bus industry.

By the 1920s, the Black legal profession was poised at a crossroads, typified by an increase in professional standards alongside rising opportunities for Black lawyers. In 1923, the American Bar Association and the American Association of Law Schools increased the requirements for law school admission, which led to an overall decline in the number of law school students and an especially marked decrease in Black student admissions.[22] In 1930, there were only 1,230 Black lawyers in the United States, compared with 159,173 white lawyers. These Black lawyers were not evenly dispersed; the states with the largest number of African American lawyers included New York, Illinois, and Ohio, all key destinations for Black Southern migrants. In 1936, the distinguished Black attorney and future NAACP lawyer

Charles Hamilton Houston wrote an article titled "The Need for Negro Lawyers," which was published in the *Journal of Negro Education*. Houston presented these grim statistics but tempered them with a few conclusions. He noted the paucity of Black lawyers in the Deep South, observing that African American lawyers were much more heavily concentrated in Northern and Midwestern states. He issued a call for more Black lawyers to be on the front lines of civil rights matters, arguing that the "great work of the Negro lawyer in the next generation" should occur in the South, where they will "wage their fight for true equality before the law."[23] But what Houston failed to recognize is that Black lawyers in the North and Midwest also filed important lawsuits on a range of civil rights matters, which sharpened their legal skills and inspired their future campaigns for dismantling racial segregation in the South.

Despite the demographic challenges of the Black legal profession, the Great Migration marked a golden opportunity for African American lawyers, giving these attorneys a cohort of clients and a compelling list of civil rights causes.[24] Most, but not all, of these Black lawyers were Southern migrants themselves. In the 1920s and 1930s, courtrooms began to fill with Black plaintiffs and their attorneys, forcing states in the Midwest and the North to grapple with the enforcement of their civil rights statutes. By trying these transportation segregation cases, Black lawyers learned about the ways that they could apply state civil rights statutes to their advantage. This strategic timing in the 1920s—typified by the advent of commercial and municipal bus companies, the migration of African Americans into Northern and Midwestern cities, and the eagerness of Black attorneys—led to many of the first lawsuits against bus segregation in the Midwest and the North. And it was most often African American women migrants who initiated these cases. Even though many of these Black lawyers were affiliated with the local chapters of the NAACP, most city branches lacked the resources to wage these cases. These lawsuits only occurred because African American women brought these injustices to the attention of Black attorneys and hired them. For these Black lawyers, bus segregation cases mapped onto their larger canvas of civil rights litigation. These lawyers viewed bus segregation cases as part of the broader struggle for Black electoral representation, the dismantling of Jim Crow practices in the North, and ultimately a legal strategy to overturn the Southern doctrine of racial segregation.[25]

The legal system in the Jim Crow North was one of complexity and contradiction. Every Northern and Midwestern state where African Americans migrated had a civil rights statute, which banned discrimination in public

TABLE 3.2 State civil rights statutes

State	*Date statutes enacted*
Iowa	1857, 1873, 1884
Washington, DC	1863
Massachusetts	1865, 1866, 1885
Pennsylvania	1867, 1881
New York	1873, 1881
Kansas	1874
Connecticut	1884
New Jersey	1884
Ohio	1884
Colorado	1885
Illinois	1885
Indiana	1885
Michigan	1885
Minnesota	1885
Nebraska	1885
Rhode Island	1885

Source: F. Johnson, *Development of State Legislation Concerning the Free Negro.*

accommodations. Formal racial segregation was illegal, and African Americans were able to vote without any restrictions. Some of these states, especially in the Midwest, had a proud heritage of abolition, often pointing to their role in the Underground Railroad and a strong record of Civil War military service. It is possible that some white judges and lawyers were aware of their state's civil rights history and viewed the law as an instrument to distinguish the North from the South. With a few exceptions, African American women turned to Black attorneys for legal counsel, and that began with Laura Fischer.

Bus Discrimination Given Setback: The Earliest Lawsuits

On Saturday, November 19, 1927, Laura Fischer, a twenty-one-year-old Black woman, walked to the Greyhound Bus Station in Richmond, Indiana, to board her afternoon bus. A native of Cartersville, Georgia, Fischer had recently migrated to Cincinnati, where she roomed with other Southern migrants.[26] When Fischer boarded the bus, she slipped into a seat near the front. The driver was Glen Branoski, an immigrant from Poland. Like some bus drivers, he had formerly operated a taxi. Branoski demanded that Fischer move to the back of the bus. Fischer protested, stating that her ticket allowed her to sit anywhere on the bus, and that the rear seats were unheated. Branoski swiftly ejected her from the bus.[27] When Fischer attempted to reboard, he grabbed her and threw her onto the sidewalk. Branoski's violent behavior demonstrated how bus drivers—even in the earliest days of the industry—were quick to assault Black women passengers. By this time, as many as 150 people had gathered to witness the altercation. Branoski called the police, informing them that Greyhound followed the Jim Crow law. But the white officers informed him that discrimination was illegal in Indiana. Furious, Glen Branoski tore up Laura Fischer's ticket and drove off.[28]

At this moment, Laura Fischer was trapped in a vulnerable position. Visibly shaken from the encounter, she managed to escape the crowd. A woman of little economic means, Fischer had a seventh-grade education, was far from her family, and bore the scars of white supremacy. Even though newspaper articles referred to her as married, she was likely estranged from her husband, a common occurrence in the Great Migration.[29] But as a new resident of the Midwest, she was armed with one crucial piece of information: The law was on her side. Fischer had already made one momentous decision in her life: to leave her family in Cartersville, Georgia, and forge a new life in the unfamiliar city of Cincinnati, Ohio. While the sources do not speak to her subjectivities, it is likely that she sought to live in a place where she was not subject to the daily fears of racial and sexual violence and everyday humiliations of racial segregation. Fischer stayed in Richmond for the weekend and contacted the eminent Black attorney Cornelius Roscoe "C. R." Richardson, who agreed to represent her in a lawsuit against Greyhound. Richardson was a pillar of Richmond's Black community. A graduate of Howard University School of Law, he was a staunch member of the Republican Party, was a prominent Elk, and had a thriving law practice.[30]

While Laura Fischer secured legal counsel, the Richmond police continued to pursue her case. When Glen Branoski returned to the city, police officers arrested him and took him to jail, where his bail was set at $500.[31] A few weeks later, Fischer and her attorney walked into the city court in Richmond, where Judge Fred Pickett presided over the case. During the trial, both sides sparred over the legality of racial segregation on buses in Indiana. C. R. Richardson emphasized Indiana's civil rights statute and called Laura Fischer to the stand, where she testified about the details of her assault. Glen Branoski appeared in court with his lawyer, an Italian immigrant named Anvedeo Vioni.[32] He pled guilty to the assault and battery but declined to testify, insisting that Greyhound had sanctioned these segregation practices.[33] After hearing from both sides, Judge Pickett sided with Laura

Fischer. He held that Indiana did not "tolerate" discrimination. Focusing on Fischer's sex, he insisted that the case must be viewed "solely as an aggravated, unprovoked attack by a strong man upon a woman who was both weak and ill." Judge Pickett declared that his court considered violence against women to be a "serious offense," and ordered that Branoski pay a $25 fine and serve fifty days in jail for assault and battery.[34] This decision revealed prevailing cultural assumptions about the weakness and frailty of women's bodies. While judges were quick to denounce violence against white women, it was less common but not unprecedented for Black women to be accorded these protections.[35] In this ruling, Judge Pickett placed his court firmly on the side of Black equality in Indiana.[36]

But in another surprising turn, Fischer's attorney, C. R. Richardson, conferred with Branoski's lawyer, Anvedeo Vioni. Together, the opposing counsels asked Judge Pickett to reduce Branoski's sentence. Judge Pickett consented and lowered Bronoski's jail time from fifty days to twenty. Richardson noted that he and his client did not ask for Branoski's "severe penalty" and merely sought a "vindication of equal rights of Race passengers with white passengers on public conveyances."[37] In practical terms, this meant that the doctrine of racial segregation was illegal, both in the state of Indiana and as a policy for the Greyhound Bus Company in that state. Additionally, the Greyhound Bus Company agreed to pay Laura Fischer $500 in settlement.[38]

Laura Fischer's lawsuit marked the very first time that a bus company in the United States ever compensated a passenger for racial violence and represented one of the very rare instances when a white bus driver was punished with jail time. Fischer won her case because she encountered a sympathetic white judge, she had excellent legal counsel, and the law was on her side. In 1927, Greyhound was still a relatively new company and might not have yet learned how to adequately dismiss these types of cases.

The Fischer case seemed to set many promising precedents, whether it was compensation for Black plaintiffs, punishment for white drivers, or accountability for bus companies. Journalists in both the Black and white press filed stories, circulating news about Laura Fischer's victory to residents throughout the Midwest. Black newspapers in this era published stories about bus discrimination across the country.[39] For African American women, reading about the details of Laura Fischer's successful lawsuit against Greyhound likely inspired them to consider a potential course of legal action when they experienced similar forms of bus discrimination. While the Fischer case ended in defeat for Greyhound, the lawsuit taught the fledgling bus company that it needed to enact stricter provisions with their drivers and contest, rather than settle, future cases.

The same month that the Fischer verdict was handed down, Helen M. Dorsey, a resident of Evansville, Indiana, had another conflict on a bus, but the circumstances were different. A recent widow, Dorsey worked as a probation officer in the public schools while she raised her son and daughter. Even though Dorsey was a Southern migrant, she had more education and resources than most Black women in the state. In 1927, she learned that she had to return to her hometown of Louisville, Kentucky, to attend to an important financial matter, which might have been related to the estate of her late husband. This was not unusual, as many migrants often had to return to the South to deal with property.[40] Since this trip involved legal paperwork, Dorsey called the Blue Goose Bus Company and reserved two seats: one for herself and another for her attorney, Rudolph D. "R. D." O'Hara, a recent veteran of World War I and an activist in Republican politics.[41] When the bus driver slowed to pull up to the appointed stop, he noticed that his incoming passengers were Black. The driver slammed his foot on the gas and sped away. Not only was this humiliating for a paying customer to be denied access for a trip she had already purchased, but in missing this visit to Kentucky, Helen Dorsey was unable to be present for these financial matters. Dorsey instructed R. D. O'Hara to sue Blue Goose for $500 in damages, but the outcome of her case is unknown.[42]

In this fluid legal climate, Black women in the Midwest continued to file lawsuits against bus segregation. In October 1929, Paulina Stevens sued Greyhound for segregation and illness on her trip from Detroit to Ohio, ultimately securing a settlement of $350 in damages. Paulina Stevens's lawsuit demonstrates the profound differences that migration made in her life. When she moved from Georgia to Michigan, her citizenship rights changed. She was able to enjoy an interracial marriage to her husband, Fred Stevens, sue in court against Greyhound, and receive two decisions in her favor, both from white judges.[43] In fact, Judge George W. Sample used her case as an opportunity to discuss race relations, describing the oppressions that African Americans had endured since slavery. While it is possible that she might have been able to sue in the South, she would have had to restrict her case to the area of personal injury and not racial segregation.[44]

But other Black women did not receive these same legal outcomes. In December 1931, Mrs. D'Lallah McIntryre of New York City booked a Greyhound Bus trip to visit Chicago, her former home. Initially, the trip was pleasant and uneventful. But all of that ended when the bus wheeled into

Massillon, Ohio, a small town fifty miles from Cleveland. McIntyre walked into the Greyhound restaurant and sat at a table, expecting to be served. Instead, the waitresses avoided her and denied her service. When she requested to wash her hands and order a glass of water, the proprietor of the establishment threatened to throw her out and forbade her from using the restroom. When McIntyre reported this behavior to the bus driver, he shrugged it off as "unfortunate" but attributed it to the provincialism of the small town.[45] When she returned to New York City, McIntyre hired a Black lawyer, James C. Thomas, to sue Greyhound.[46] Thomas described McIntyre's case as "clean cut."[47] The outcome of McIntyre's case is unknown, but its lack of coverage in the Black press suggests that either D'Lallah McIntyre was unable to secure damages against Greyhound or that she and her attorney negotiated a private settlement.

Cumulatively, these four early cases against bus segregation reveal a few patterns. First, the lawsuits of Laura Fischer and Paulina Stevens prompted three white judges to weigh in on race relations in the United States and deliver sympathetic opinions for these women. But these decisions were not uniform. Judge George Sample in Ann Arbor, Michigan, pointed to Paulina Stevens's race, while in Richmond, Indiana, Judge Fred Pickett highlighted Laura Fischer's sex. Three out of these four cases were aimed at the Greyhound Bus Company, which signaled the outsized role that Greyhound would play in these discrimination cases. And even though Black women likely lost two of these cases, the enthusiasm on the part of white judges to punish white bus companies and even white bus drivers signaled that Black women in the Jim Crow North might experience favorable outcomes. And it would be Black women migrants in Cleveland, Ohio, who would become the next cohort of passengers to take Greyhound to court.

Cleveland Connections: Migrant Women and Greyhound

By the early 1930s, Cleveland became the epicenter of both the bus industry and bus lawsuits. This was not a coincidence. In 1931, the Greyhound Management Company had relocated from Chicago to Cleveland. Greyhound had grown at a rapid pace. From its humble roots in Hibbing, Minnesota, as a bus line transporting white workers to mining camps, Greyhound was now a publicly traded company with two thousand employees scattered across the United States and Canada.[48] In February 1932, the Greyhound Management Company dedicated its brand-new headquarters in downtown Cleveland. Located at the corner of Ninth and Superior Avenues, this

Greyhound dedicated its gleaming and light-filled terminal on Ninth and Superior Avenues in Cleveland, Ohio, in February 1931. This bus terminal resembled many urban train stations. *Source*: "Ample Space, Light and Comfort Facilities Are Provided in Cleveland's New Terminal," *Bus Transportation*, March 1932, 113.

sprawling terminal was twelve thousand square feet, fitted with terrazzo floors, marble-paneled walls, and large windows. The ground floor housed a lunch and soda counter, stores selling cigars and clothing, a barber shop, and a telegraph office. The terminal was large enough to accommodate twelve buses at one time. Executives in the Greyhound Management Company were housed in offices on the second floor. There was so much excitement about this new building that forty thousand residents of Cleveland streamed inside to inspect Greyhound's brand-new terminal on the first day.[49] It is likely that African Americans made up some of these visitors, eager to ride buses to sustain their family bonds in an era of mass migration.

Not only was Cleveland home to Greyhound's new headquarters, but it was also a destination for the first Great Migration. Between 1915 and 1930, approximately sixty thousand African American women and men left their homes in Alabama, Georgia, Florida, Mississippi, Tennessee, and Texas and streamed into the city, eager to labor in railroads, steel, oil, paint, and tires.[50] Black women migrants immediately saw promise in Cleveland's booming economy in the 1920s. In Mobile, Alabama, a Black woman earned less than three dollars a week as a maid, while in Cleveland, weekly wages were as high as seven dollars, demonstrating the profound difference that migration made.[51] Migrants primarily settled in a Black neighborhood between Central and Euclid Avenues, which was only a few miles from Greyhound's new headquarters.[52] The city's Black population was large enough to sustain two newspapers—the *Cleveland Gazette* and the *Cleveland Call and Post*. For these Black residents of Cleveland, Greyhound became their local company. And because these migrants had roots that stretched across the Deep South, interstate buses were a necessity. As Black women in Cleveland moved to this migrant neighborhood, joined social networks, read the newspaper, and purchased Greyhound bus tickets, they began to share critical knowledge and experiences about bus discrimination and potential legal avenues to contest it. Migrant women made bus discrimination lawsuits central to their political culture in Cleveland.

In April 1931, two clubwomen in Cleveland visited the Greyhound headquarters to purchase round-trip bus tickets to visit Los Angeles, California, to attend a meeting of the National Association of Colored Women (NACW).[53] Both were in their late thirties and active in social circles. Iola Wimbs Ellis was a native of Alabama, who had studied at Tuskegee and lived in Tennessee, where she taught agriculture in public schools, before migrating to Cleveland with her husband.[54] She was accompanied by Elemenoire Austin, a thirty-seven-year-old woman who was a native of Mississippi.[55] Austin and Ellis lived only a few houses down from each other on East Eighty-Seventh Street. These women were both active members of the NACW. By 1931, as all Americans were reeling from the Great Depression, Austin and Ellis opted for travel to California on a Greyhound bus. As Cleveland residents, Greyhound was their local company. Both paid over eighty dollars for their tickets. But their visions for the excellent customer service Greyhound promised in its glossy advertisements were dashed once they boarded the bus. In the early 1930s, a cross-country bus trip involved many stops and took multiple days. Greyhound agents and employees denied Ellis and Austin food and water at rest stops, did not permit them to use the restrooms, forced them to stand in the rain and cold, and referred to them as "N***** women."[56]

When Austin and Ellis returned to Cleveland, they immediately contacted Chester K. Gillespie, a Black attorney in the city. In private practice since 1920, Gillespie was active in the city's NAACP chapter and had a reputation for championing many civil rights causes. The legal scholar J. Clay Smith Jr. calls Gillespie "one of Cleveland's most aggressive black civil rights lawyers."[57] Gillespie saw promise in this case and agreed to represent Austin and Ellis and sue Greyhound for $20,000.[58] After a year of paperwork, the district court heard the case.[59] The outcome of this case is unknown, which suggests that the lawsuit was either unsuccessful or settled out of court.

But this would not be the first time that Black women in Cleveland would take Greyhound to court for similar types of discrimination. A few years later in June 1934, Jane Hunter, a distinguished clubwoman and the president of Cleveland's Phyllis Wheatley Young Women's Christian Association (YWCA), was traveling on a Greyhound bus from Louisville, Kentucky, back to her home. Hunter was accompanied by a white woman, who might have been a fellow YWCA worker. During the trip, the bus stopped in Wilmington, Kentucky, where Hunter tried to eat in the restaurant but was refused service. The restaurant manager told her that they only served bus passengers. Hunter's white companion demanded that the manager accommodate her, but he would not budge. When she returned to Cleveland, Jane Hunter met with her attorney, Norman McGhee, and filed a lawsuit against Greyhound for damages of $2,500.[60] There are few notable facts in this case. Jane Hunter was a prominent figure, prompting Black newspapers to cover her case widely in the press. Reporters expressed indignation that such a distinguished woman could be denied service in a restaurant. An article in the *Atlanta Daily World* commented that Hunter was suing for a "trivial" amount considering that she was a woman who was accustomed to the "finest hostelries in the country."[61] She was likely inspired to sue Greyhound because she had been a Cleveland resident since 1905 and was aware of Greyhound's presence as well as Black women's protest culture against bus discrimination. Hunter was the only known Black woman to have sued Greyhound as an attorney. In 1925, Hunter had graduated from the Cleveland Law School and was admitted to the Ohio bar. As a lawyer, Hunter held specialized knowledge about the law and legal procedure. But the outcome of this case is unknown, which makes it likely that Jane Hunter was not successful. Even though Kentucky never passed laws that formalized racial segregation on its buses or inside its restaurants, no Black woman ever successfully challenged these practices in the state.

Only one year later, Willetta Brown became the next Black woman in Cleveland to take Greyhound to court. A native of Tennessee, she had migrated to Cleveland, settling in a house on Kinsman Road in the city's Black neighborhood.[62] In October 1934, her mother died, prompting her to book a trip back to Tennessee for the funeral. Brown visited the Greyhound headquarters to book her trip, where the agent assured her that she would be able to enjoy the full suite of Greyhound services, including access to restrooms and refreshments. But Brown found that the trip was less than ideal. When the bus wheeled into Lexington, Kentucky, for a rest stop, she was denied service in the restaurant. Furthermore, at two o'clock in the morning, a white male passenger assaulted her. When Brown reported this behavior to the bus driver, he hurled a racial epithet at her, threatening to rip up her ticket and eject her from the bus.[63]

While the evidence is not explicit here, the fact that a white passenger assaulted her at two in the morning suggests that the attack might have been sexual in nature. As a Southern migrant, Willetta Brown might have been hesitant to disclose these intimate details for fear they would undermine her claims to respectability.[64] African American women were thought to be oversexualized in American culture in both the Jim Crow North and the Jim Crow South, making it nearly impossible for Black women to hold civilian white men accountable for sexual assault and rape. The *Cleveland Call and Post*, the Black newspaper that reported the incident, might have felt pressure to conceal the sexual aspects of Brown's case for fear of compromising her sympathy as a victim.[65]

Willetta Brown's experiences on Greyhound—denial of service, assault by a white male passenger, and abuse at the hands of the white bus driver—convinced her that she needed to sue. When she returned to Cleveland, she met with Chester Gillespie, the same attorney who had represented Iola Ellis and Elemenoire Austin in their lawsuit against Greyhound. Willetta Brown sued the Pennsylvania Greyhound Lines for $2,500, and her case traveled to the Municipal Court of Cleveland. Chester Gillespie put Greyhound on the defensive, accusing the company of deliberately denying African American passengers services on their buses. Brown testified that when she purchased her ticket, the agent told her that Greyhound did not advertise in Black newspapers and was not interested in seeking Black patronage. Both Brown and Gillespie used that narrative as evidence that Greyhound had not treated her as a proper customer. This was a stunning admission by the agent. Even though Greyhound had woven white supremacy into the fabric of its company culture, in its encounters with civil rights organizations it always claimed to desire Black patrons.[66]

The white judge, David Moylan, found for Willetta Brown and ordered the Greyhound Management Company to pay her $250 in damages.[67] Not only did Brown have a compelling case against Greyhound, but Moylan's personal circumstances might have affected his judgment. A former railroad switchman, Moylan had lost both of his arms in railroad accidents. Following this trauma, he studied the law, was elected to the Cleveland City Council, and became a judge in municipal court.[68] Moylan's injuries from the railroad industry might have given him a dose of sympathy toward Brown. The fact that Greyhound had its headquarters in Cleveland might also have persuaded Moylan to punish the company. But regardless of his motivation, Judge Moylan decided that Willetta Brown deserved damages from Greyhound and ordered the company to pay her a settlement.

In a surprising turn of events, Greyhound refused to pay Brown her settlement. Gillespie contacted Greyhound and left a threatening message, saying that if the company did not pay the money owed to Willetta Brown, he would ask a court bailiff to install a sign on one of its packed buses, announcing that it did not desire Black customers.[69] Gillespie's bold warning evinced his weariness with Greyhound as a company that routinely discriminated against Black women passengers, not only in Cleveland but across the country.

Other Victories

Even though Cleveland played an outsized role in lawsuits against Greyhound, Black women in this period also achieved legal victories in Chicago and New York. These lawsuits demonstrate not only Black women litigants' compelling evidence of discrimination but also the time and money that bus companies spent on evading responsibility for this discrimination. In 1935, Maude Lauther, a resident of New York City, booked a trip on the Eastern Greyhound Lines of New England. The white driver ordered her to take a seat in the rear. Lauther sued the Eastern Greyhound Lines of New England, and a judge ruled in her favor.[70] But the woman whose lawsuit cost the bus industry thousands of dollars was Callie Stevens. A native of Texas, Callie Stevens was widowed at a young age. In search of better prospects, she migrated to Chicago in her twenties, where she rented an apartment on South Michigan Avenue and secured a job as a maid for the electric railroad.[71] In May 1933, Stevens purchased a ticket on the Safeway Bus Line to travel to New York City. Even though Stevens had a ticket that specifically listed her seat number, the white bus driver refused to honor it, demanding that she move to the back of the bus. Stevens had to ride over seven hundred miles on a seat that was located above the wheel and did not recline. Within three days of her return to Chicago, she met with attorneys Irvin C. Mollinson and William H. Temple to defend her in a jury trial.[72] Both Mollinson and Temple were part of the NAACP's legal redress committee, where, over the years, they had represented African Americans in their fight to eat in restaurants, sit in any bus seat, or seek refuge from Southern racial violence in Chicago.[73] The Safeway Bus Company hired a white law firm to challenge Stevens's lawsuit. For two years, the legal teams engaged in the allegations of the complaint. Safeway continually pressed for the case to settle out of court, but Stevens refused. Finally, in March 1935, the case traveled to the Municipal Court of Chicago, presided over by Judge Francis Borelli. It was clear that the Safeway Bus Company took this lawsuit seriously because it appointed five lawyers to litigate the case against Callie Stevens. Coincidentally, four of these attorneys were stockholders in Safeway.

In court proceedings, Callie Stevens's legal team effectively questioned bus company officials, pushing them to acknowledge the company's racist practices. For example, when Temple asked Safeway's president, Paul Dilmar, about how the bus line handled Black customers, he succeeded in capturing a crucial piece of testimony: The Safeway Bus Company always put Black passengers over the rear axle or in seats that did not recline. Dilmar admitted that this policy "was a matter of discrimination on account of color." Similarly, another white witness acknowledged that the company instituted this policy because the wives of white male passengers objected to riding alongside Black passengers for more than a thousand miles. This testimony demonstrated that the Safeway Bus Company, like most lines in the bus industry, was deliberate in working to please white women customers at the expense of Black women's comfort.[74]

After hearing from both sides, the jury entered a verdict in favor of Callie Stevens, finding that it was illegal to discriminate against Stevens in Illinois because of the civil rights statute.[75] The jury awarded Stevens $60 in damages. Even though this was a negligible amount of money, Black activists celebrated the victory. A jury had sided with Stevens over the bus company. The $60 that Stevens was awarded was merely symbolic; it was far more significant that the Safeway Bus Company had paid five lawyers to litigate the case over a period of two years, brought in a range of witnesses to defend the company, and then was forced to acknowledge the bus line's complicity in racist company policies. The Safeway Bus Company lost far more money in the litigation than in the settlement. The *Pittsburgh Courier* termed the company's fight a "stubborn" one and noted that some members of the jury wanted to award Stevens as much as $300 in damages. At this point in time, the Chicago branch of the NAACP had received over fifty complaints about discrimination on buses, and Callie Stevens's case marked the very first time that a judge in the city awarded any Black passenger damages.[76] Collectively, the successful lawsuits of Willetta Brown, Maude Lauther, and Callie Stevens demonstrate that Black women formed a crucial constituency of bus passengers in this period but were unwilling to accept that racial discrimination was inevitable.

In addition to suing for segregation and unequal treatment, African American women also waged a few personal injury lawsuits against bus lines. In Youngstown, Ohio, Lena Jones sued the municipal bus company for injuries she sustained. In July 1934, Jones, a twenty-one-year-old migrant from Tennessee who labored as a bar maid in a tavern, boarded a bus in downtown Youngstown.[77] There were several children on the bus who had recently been to the park and were eating bananas. When Jones stepped into the aisle to depart from the bus, she slipped on a banana peel. The bus driver rushed to assist her and noticed that the floor was slippery from the banana peels. Jones sued the bus company for negligence. She hired a white lawyer, who brought in two Black witnesses to corroborate Jones's story, and the jury and judge awarded her $800 in damages.[78] The bus company contested the case, and it traveled to the court of appeals in Ohio. Judge J. Roberts concurred with the lower court, ruling that the bus driver should have been aware of the slippery conditions and exercised care to protect bus passengers.[79] Lena Jones was one of the few African American women living in the Midwest who hired a white attorney to represent her.

The other major personal injury lawsuit in this period was initiated by Zena Higgins, who demonstrated that racial exclusion could lead to health problems. In January 1931, Higgins, a minister, and her husband, B. R. Higgins, arranged a bus trip from Ottawa, Kansas, to their home in Kansas City, Missouri. At 7:30 p.m., they walked into the ticket office of the Southern Kansas Stage Lines and purchased their tickets for a 9 p.m. bus. Given the departure time, they walked into the waiting room, which was part of the North American Hotel Ottawa. They soon discovered that the hotel banned African Americans, forcing them outside into howling wind, a snowstorm, and bitter temperatures. To keep warm and prevent frostbite, the couple paced outside for ninety minutes. When their bus pulled up, they reported their experience to the driver, who replied that it was "not an uncommon thing." During the ride, the cold weather caught up with Zena Higgins as she developed a sore throat, body aches, and chills. Over the next few weeks, she developed a case of bronchial pneumonia and pleurisy. Livid, Higgins hired James K. Cubbison, a white lawyer, and sued the Southern Kansas Stage Lines, asking for $27 in doctor's fees and $473 for expenses incurred as a result of her illness.[80] She also contacted the national office of the NAACP and explained her situation.[81] In court, Higgins made a compelling case, and the jury awarded her $500 for the lack of accommodation and medical expenses incurred.[82] Angered that Zena Higgins had received a settlement, the Southern Kansas Stage Lines appealed the decision, and in April 1935, the Supreme Court of Kansas heard the case and affirmed the decision of the lower court. In demonstrating the health effects of racial segregation, Zena Higgins won her case.[83] Presumably, her husband had similar complaints, but it was Zena Higgins who initiated the lawsuit, testified about the ways that racial segregation had negatively affected her health, and served as the public face of this lawsuit, both at the trial and at the appeal. She had a solid case precisely because Kansas had a civil rights law, which had been enacted in 1874.[84]

All of these lawsuits focused on a unique set of circumstances, and there are a few theories why white judges in Illinois, Kansas, New York, and Ohio sided with Black women litigants during this period. First, in the late 1920s and early 1930s, the future of automobility was uncertain. It was not until 1935 that bus travel eclipsed the popularity of train travel in the United States. In this early period, the stakes around buses were lower. Second, these judges and juries honored the civil rights statutes of their states, which had been passed in the 1870s and 1880s and were still being enforced. These judges did not simply render decisions in favor of Black women plaintiffs; rather, a few sensed that these cases held major implications for race relations, prompting them to issue opinions that stretched far beyond the legality of bus segregation. Judge Pickett in Indiana and Judge Sample in Michigan both ruled in favor of Black women and commented on the state of race relations. In handing down these verdicts, it is possible that these judges wished to distinguish themselves and their states from their counterparts in the US South. By upholding—not denigrating—the legal rights of African Americans, these white judges helped to cultivate an image of the Midwest as a region that respected the letter of the law. Even though historians rightly critique the racism and inequalities that existed in the Jim Crow North, these examples of Black women's victorious lawsuits demonstrate that there were concrete legal differences between Cleveland, Ohio, and Cleveland, Tennessee.[85] But as more Black women began to board buses in the Great Depression and the Great Migration, these rides became even more violent.

Violence Surges: Losing in the Jim Crow North

While these cases represent a burst of success, these victories were short-lived. As Black women continued to challenge the legality of racial segregation on buses, most white judges in the Midwest stopped siding with them. There are a few reasons that explain this shift. First, bus companies, especially Greyhound, learned important lessons from these early lawsuits and began to produce public documents to evade claims of discrimination. After the local press in Indiana belittled bus driver Glen Branoski's Polish heritage, Greyhound wrote a new manual for its bus drivers, in which they insisted that all drivers be US citizens and receive extensive training in courtesy and customer service. By publishing such deliberate text that publicly constructed white bus drivers as well-trained and courteous figures, Greyhound explicitly refuted Black women's claims against bus driver violence. In court, bus drivers could now point to the extensive training that they received, quash the accusations that they were illegal aliens, and invalidate the testimony of Black women customers with the absolute power of the bus driver and his increasingly respected bus company.[86]

Greyhound also broadened its public relations image in the Black community. Since its inception, African Americans had ridden Greyhound buses out of necessity. Over the years, Black communities had chartered Greyhound buses for sporting events and church gatherings.[87] There is no evidence that Greyhound ever denied these requests. But as bus violence surged, African Americans searched for an alternative transportation solution. While Black enthusiasm for Greyhound waned, the company publicly solicited business from the NAACP as a strategy to evade claims that they discriminated against Black passengers. In 1936, a Greyhound ticket agent visited the NAACP headquarters, requesting to secure a contract to transport members to its biennial conference. NAACP officials publicly rebuffed this offer, citing the intolerance of the company and its explicit patterns of segregation. But this gesture only strengthened Greyhound's claim that it desired Black riders.[88] By the mid-1930s, Greyhound became the preeminent bus company in the United States, and it was clear that buses were providing a real service to Americans during the Great Depression. Additionally, race relations in Northern cities worsened, typified by an increase in police violence. As anti-Black bus violence proliferated, it became more normalized in American culture, and white judges no longer expressed the same level of outrage. All of these circumstances help to explain why Black women began to lose their lawsuits in the Jim Crow North.

African Americans' citizenship rights in the Jim Crow North also evolved in the 1930s. First, in response to the crisis of the Great Depression and fueled by a rising tide of militancy, African Americans began to stage "Don't Buy Where You Can't Work" campaigns in cities throughout the Jim Crow

North, including Cleveland, Chicago, Detroit, and New York.[89] These movements evinced new strains of Black militancy, pressing for employment in stores with Black patrons. This type of activism around consumption likely put the bus industry on edge and also pushed white judges to quell Black rights. Additionally, with the advent of New Deal programs, some African Americans were able to benefit from government initiatives, whether it was a labor program, a housing project, an arts event, or a school. It is also possible that white judges felt as though Black civil rights and their relationship to the state were changing at a rapid pace, and this might have influenced their unwillingness to offer significant decisions toward Black civil rights. Finally, the Great Migration had resulted in major Black political constituencies in the Jim Crow North, typified by the election of African Americans to city councils, school boards, state government, and the US House of Representatives. By the 1936 election, many African Americans had switched to the Democratic Party and formed a constituency in the administration of Franklin D. Roosevelt. It is possible that white judges in these cities resented the newfound political influence of Black voters and decided to render decisions that favored bus companies over Black passengers.

The success of Black women's seven lawsuits in the late 1920s and early 1930s inspired other Black women to bring bus discrimination to court, but they did not experience the same legal victories. In the late 1930s, six Black women sued Greyhound for segregation and injury on interstate buses, and it is likely that all of these cases resulted in defeat.[90] In most of these lawsuits, migrant women experienced segregation and racial violence in the Jim Crow South and were unable to rely on state civil rights statutes. But these lawsuits also demonstrate that bus violence against Black women passengers had escalated. During this period, police officers in Missouri detained a Black woman passenger in jail for six hours, bus drivers knocked a Black woman passenger unconscious for the duration of her journey, and many Black women experienced quotidian patterns of violence. Focusing on the story of one passenger—Gertrude Herndon—demonstrates the escalating brutality of Greyhound, its bus drivers, and the overall culture of bus violence.

In 1939, Gertrude Herndon, a resident of Cleveland, Ohio, purchased a ticket to travel to Alabama. When she changed buses in Birmingham, the white bus driver denied her a seat on the bus and refused to reimburse her for her ticket. Adding to her stress level, a white male passenger who weighed over 250 pounds intervened, telling the driver to eject her from the bus. When she protested, the man punched her, and she fell to the floor. He continued to assault her, kicking her face, head, and body. Herndon stated that the bus driver "encouraged" this attack and cheered the passenger on. Her screams were so loud that another company employee arrived and told Herndon to be quiet. Police officers swiftly arrested Herndon and denied her access to a lawyer, charging her with disorderly conduct. Since she could not pay the court fees, she was sentenced to thirty days in an Alabama workhouse. According to Herndon, the Greyhound Bus Company had insisted on these charges to intimidate her from suing the company.[91] Herndon, a victim of racial and possibly sexual violence in the Jim Crow South, had gone from being a bus customer to being a criminal. The evidence of her assault was irrefutable. When Herndon returned to her home in Cleveland, she was still recovering from the injuries she sustained.[92] She also met with Black attorney Alexander H. Martin and filed a $50,000 lawsuit against the Greyhound Management Company.[93] The front page of the Black newspaper the *Cleveland Call and Post* declared, "Seeks $50,000 from Bus Lines." The outcome of Gertrude Herndon's lawsuit is unknown, and the lack of press coverage suggests that she was not successful in court.

While Black women took the bus industry to court, other African Americans tried to pass national legislation. In 1934, Arthur Mitchell beat Oscar DePriest in Illinois's First Congressional District, becoming the first African American Democrat elected to Congress. In 1937, Mitchell traveled to Hot Springs, Arkansas, for a vacation and was banned from a Pullman car, prompting his lawsuit.[94] While he contested the charges in court, he also introduced a bill banning interstate transportation segregation in Congress three times—in 1938, 1939, and 1941—but there was never any legislative progress.[95]

Cease and Desist

By the late 1930s, African American women in the Jim Crow North began to employ a more aggressive legal strategy. The final two cases demonstrate that Black women and their attorneys were eager to try new legal tactics. In fall 1940, Sarah M. Love, a forty-year-old resident of Jackson, Michigan, was experiencing many life changes. A native of Louisiana, she had migrated to Flint, Michigan, in the 1920s. Her husband had labored in the automobile industry while she worked as a maid. In the 1930s, the couple divorced, she married her second husband, and they settled in the nearby city of Jackson.[96] In October 1940, an automobile accident killed her brother, who was living in Chicago. As his next of kin, Love booked a Greyhound ticket from Michigan to Chicago so that she could identify the body. On the way, the bus stopped in Kalamazoo, Michigan. This rest stop was home to the Crystal Café. Love walked into the café and ordered a beef sandwich. The waiter took a very long time processing her order. When he finally did serve her, he offered her the sandwich with his bare hands, with no plates, napkins, or wrapper. She rejected this insulting sandwich and left the café. When she reboarded the bus, the driver interrogated her, demanding that she pay for the sandwich. She refused and told him that she would report his behavior. The driver returned with three police officers, and they arrested Love. She was detained at the police station for several hours, until the chief of police arrived and faulted the bus driver. Love caught another bus to Chicago and had to pay extra money to have her brother's body held at the morgue.[97]

The bus driver who called the police on Sarah Love was Manfred Burleigh. A native of Missouri, he had held various executive positions at Greyhound, including president of the Ohio Greyhound Lines, regional manager of the Central Greyhound Lines, and general manager of the Canadian Greyhound Lines.[98] He later founded an airline company affiliated with Greyhound. It is unclear why Burleigh—a prominent executive at Greyhound—was Sarah Love's bus driver that day. It is possible that he was not the bus driver but in fact the regional manager who crafted the bus policies. The clear violation here was that he had instructed Michigan police officers to arrest Love. This was not necessarily unusual. That year alone, officers had arrested at least five Black women on buses in the South. But Love's case was in *Michigan*, a state with a civil rights law. Her arrest threatened to demonstrate no legal difference between Michigan and Mississippi in the eyes of the violent bus industry. Sarah Love and her attorneys were determined to prove otherwise.

When she returned to Michigan, Love engaged in a flurry of legal activity. She met with the city prosecutor in Detroit, who advised her to contact the NAACP and the bus company. Love first wrote to the Greyhound Management Company in Cleveland, recounting her experience. Greyhound's traffic manager, Lawrence H. Ristow, promised to conduct an investigation, but it never materialized.[99] Love also wrote to the NAACP's national office in New York City, and her letter reached the desk of Thurgood Marshall, who was working with the Legal Defense Fund. Upon reading her account, Marshall expressed sympathy with the harrowing details of her incident and was confident that she might be able to score a legal victory against

Greyhound. Marshall rightly noted that "the Greyhound Bus Company is just about 100 percent anti-Negro all over the country." While Greyhound was a consistent offender, Marshall observed that the company was "clever enough to usually protect themselves against legal action." After receiving hundreds of letters describing bus discrimination, Marshall remarked that Greyhound was eager to accept Black dollars but, at the same time, worked to "embarrass" and "discriminate" against Black passengers at every turn. Marshall believed that Sarah Love's lawsuit would be a healing balm to African Americans across the country who had "suffered rudeness and discrimination" from Greyhound lines.[100]

After hearing Thurgood Marshall's enthusiasm about her case, Love met with John M. Morris, a Black attorney in Detroit.[101] Morris helped Love file a lawsuit against the Central Greyhound Lines for a total of $10,000. Love's case was scheduled to be heard in the municipal court but was then moved to the Eastern District of Michigan, a federal court, where it was presided over by Judge Ernest A. O'Brien. In the court proceedings, Love testified about the death of her brother in an automobile accident, her work to recover the body in the morgue, and the added expense of lateness. Greyhound's attorneys called six witnesses, including the bus driver, the waiter, and one of the police officers who arrested Love.

A jury returned a verdict in favor of Love, awarding her $250 for the humiliation that she suffered.[102] Here, a key element of the trial was the localism. For white residents of Michigan, the Sarah Love case was one that they could relate to on a deep level. First and foremost, her brother had been killed in an automobile accident, and Michigan was the capital of automobility. Next, she was explicitly denied service in an eating establishment. Hearing these visceral details—the beef sandwich with no wrapper and the hostility on the part of the driver—conveyed to white Michiganders that her exclusion at the Crystal Café was a matter of racial discrimination. Finally, the fact that a white police officer in Michigan chided the bus driver signaled that the bus company had overreached its practices of racial segregation and intolerance. The Love case marked another victory for Black women in Michigan. By convincing a jury in a federal court that Greyhound had committed major errors in discriminating against a Black woman passenger, Sarah Love secured a decisive legal win against Greyhound. If Love had still been living in Louisiana, she never would have received this verdict.

Only a few days after Sarah Love won her case, Melba Goss, a resident of Ohio, contemplated another legal battle. A native of Somerset, Kentucky, she had moved to Lockland, a city near Cincinnati, where she worked as a clerk. Through her job, Goss had gained important legal knowledge.[103] In September 1942, Goss had purchased a ticket to travel on the Southeastern Greyhound Lines to visit her family in Somerset. While on the bus, the driver told her that, as a Black passenger, she either had to sit in the back or alight. Goss refused to move, and the driver evicted her from the bus. At one o'clock in the morning, Melba Goss was forced to have her ticket refunded. Since she was unable to complete her journey, Goss, like many Black women who came before her, made the decision to sue Southeastern Greyhound Lines, Incorporated. She hired Myron Bush and Walter W. Harris, two Black attorneys in Cincinnati.[104]

But Melba Goss took a decidedly different approach in her lawsuit against Greyhound. Not only did she argue that Southeastern Greyhound's practices violated Ohio civil rights law, but she ordered the company to cease and desist, charging that their policies of discrimination were ultra vires to their articles of incorporation. Goss stated that she was filing this case on behalf of all African Americans in Ohio, charging that Greyhound had engaged in flagrant practices of racial discrimination. Goss stated that "the shareholders, directors and officers of said corporation have conspired to defeat the purposes of the corporation as contained in their franchise, by not only violating the laws of this state but by condoning, ratifying, and participating in acts not authorized by said franchise articles of incorporation or by-laws, and by conspiring with other operators of buses which are common carriers, for the same purpose that they by this conspiracy do practice this custom against Negro citizens because of race, creed, or color, and thereby go beyond the legal purposes of their existence."[105]

In this lawsuit, Melba Goss evinced a complex understanding of Greyhound as a corporation. It was not merely a bus line. It was composed of shareholders in the corporate stock, had a board of directors, and employed white male executives who crafted the company's policies. The company had violated its articles of incorporation by enforcing policies of discrimination against its Black passengers. Goss argued that Southeastern Greyhound should "be ordered and directed to cease and desist from further operation in this state and that they be ordered to terminate their existence through a receivership, and as a corporate entity, be declared null and void."[106] A newspaper article in the *Cleveland Call and Post* called her case "novel."[107]

Melba Goss's petition against Greyhound demonstrated that Black women now understood that bus corporations wielded too much power and routinely discriminated in the lives of ordinary African Americans in problematic ways. By filing this petition, Goss showcased a sophisticated understanding of the way that bus corporations operated.[108] As a citizen of Ohio, she was aware that it was illegal for this bus company to insist on racial discrimination. For Melba Goss, her location in Ohio enabled her to have a different relationship with this company because the Greyhound Management Company was based in the state.[109]

The outcome of Melba Gross's case is unknown, but her insistence that Greyhound be dissolved demonstrates that Black women litigants had raised the stakes in their lawsuits against the bus industry. Rather than merely asking for damages for their inconveniences, Black women and their attorneys had taken a more aggressive stance, arguing that Greyhound was a dangerous company and needed severe legal consequences to curb the unrelenting abuse that Black passengers experienced.

Recovering Migrant Women's Citizenship

Between 1927 and 1942, at least nineteen African American women migrants in the Jim Crow North filed lawsuits against the bus industry, and the majority of cases centered on bus segregation. With a few exceptions, most of these cases were aimed at Greyhound. These lawsuits reveal a few key patterns. First, as soon as Black women boarded buses in the late 1920s, they sued for discrimination and scored a few legal victories. While African American women did not receive very much money in damages, their cases inspired Black women across the country to wage similar types of lawsuits. But by the mid-1930s, as Greyhound solidified its corporate power and responded to Black women's resistance by policing and overpolicing their passengers, these lawsuits lost their potency in the eyes of the law. Greyhound shrewdly evaded all claims of responsibility, blaming any and all violence on both the racist attitudes of the Jim Crow South and the deviancy of Black women passengers. Of course, this Midwestern company embodied these attitudes from the outset and trained its drivers to police Black women as deviant passengers.

African American women's lawsuits against bus segregation in the Jim Crow North illuminate a new narrative about the Great Migration. These handful of cases demonstrate that despite the difficulties of migration, over a dozen African American women were able to successfully sue these bus companies, and some received legal victories. Even though these cases might have been largely lost to history until now, many readers of the Black press were aware of these lawsuits, and they inspired this burst of litigiousness against bus segregation into the 1960s.

Importantly, these lawsuits in the North inspired lawsuits in the South. But while Black women like Laura Fischer, Paulina Stevens, and Sarah Love were able to make race explicit in their cases, legally savvy Black women in the Jim Crow South had to conceal the racial implications of their lawsuits and sue for personal injury and torts. Chapter 4 explores Black women's lawsuits in the South in the same period, revealing how the system of Jim Crow white supremacy shaped both legal strategies and legal outcomes.

4 A Measure of Justice

Subversive Legal Strategies in the Jim Crow South

On a very early Monday morning in May 1938, Olivia Shankle, a thirty-one-year-old teacher in Louisiana, boarded a Tri-State bus. Shankle was traveling from her home in Lake Charles to DeRidder, a town about forty miles away. During the week, Shankle taught in the local school in DeRidder, but spent the weekends with her husband, Everett Shankle.[1] Since she had been making this journey every week for twelve years, she had requested that the driver make a stop near her school. As the bus neared the school, Shankle pushed the buzzer but quickly discovered that it was broken. She called out to the white bus driver, Sam Brickley, but he ignored her. A white woman who was sitting near the front repeated Olivia Shankle's request, but Brickley refused to stop. When the bus pulled into the station, Shankle walked to retrieve her luggage and asked Brickley if there was a new management policy that prevented her from requesting a stop. Brickley snapped at Shankle to "shut her mouth," and she protested, stating that this line of questioning fell within her legal right. Brickley then curled his fingers into a fist and punched Shankle in the face. His force was so great that she collapsed onto the cement pavement of the bus station. This assault left her with a black eye and a permanent ringing in her ears. When Shankle recovered from her injuries, she hired the white law firm of Plauche & Stockwell to sue the Tri-State Transit Company of Louisiana for $5,000 in damages and another $5,000 for humiliation and mental suffering. Not only did Olivia Shankle seek to recover damages, but her husband, Everett Shankle, also sued for the medical expenses to treat his wife, as well as the mental strain on their marriage.

In court, Olivia Shankle appeared alongside representatives from the Tri-State Transit Company and the white driver, speaking to a jury likely composed of white men.[2] In her testimony, Shankle shrewdly emphasized four aspects of her case to make it compelling for the white members of the jury: her physical frailty, her professional job, her respectability, and the kindness of the fellow white passengers on the bus. By appearing in court, jurors were able to visualize this conflict: Olivia Shankle was a very petite woman who weighed only 110 pounds, while the bus driver, Sam Brickley, was a much larger and more physically imposing person. And they were able to hear Olivia Shankle narrate her version of the events that transpired. Shankle testified how this ordinary bus trip to work had escalated into a horrifying event. She told the jury that she had been employed as a teacher for twelve years in the Beauregard Parish and held an esteemed reputation from the school administration and parents. Throughout the bus ride, she had expressed respect and decorum toward the bus driver. In fact, Shankle acknowledged that a fellow white passenger had come to her aid and implored the bus driver to stop the bus. Despite the courtesy she had extended to the driver, he assaulted her brutally. Not only did she need to seek medical attention for this attack, but the damage to her left eardrum undermined her future earnings as a teacher. After Olivia testified, Everett Shankle took the stand and offered intimate details about his marriage, stating that his wife's injuries had caused considerable strain on their companionship. At no point in these court proceedings did Olivia and Everett Shankle broach the issues of race or racial segregation.[3]

After hearing from both sides, the jury awarded Olivia Shankle $250 and Everett Shankle $48. There was a quiet revolution in this verdict. Even though the ruling did not touch the issue of racial segregation, white citizens in Louisiana implicitly weighed in on politically charged matters in Jim Crow Louisiana. Not only did the jury acknowledge that a white bus driver had assaulted Olivia Shankle and caused her bodily harm, but they also recognized that this abuse had affected her marriage. Olivia Shankle was not very far removed from slavery. Her own mother was born in Louisiana in 1865, just as the Civil War ended, and her parents were the first generation of Black Louisianians to enjoy the right of legal marriage.[4]

Both Olivia Shankle and the Tri-State Transit Company were disappointed with the court's ruling, and each party appealed the decision. Olivia and Everett Shankle sought an increase in damages, while the Tri-State Transit Company sued to reverse the outcome. On appeal, the case traveled to the First Circuit Court of Appeals of Louisiana, presided over by Judge Samuel A. LeBlanc. Judge LeBlanc issued a ruling in which he sided with the Shankles. Judge LeBlanc held that Sam Brickley's "attack" on Olivia Shankle was inappropriate. He acknowledged that while Shankle's reactions may have been "irritating," he emphasized the power imbalance between a Black woman and the white Southern bus driver. He also highlighted Shankle's respectability, describing her as a woman of "good reputation," and lamented that this incident had caused her "considerable embarrassment, humiliation, and mental suffering." Judge LeBlanc concluded that "these facts under our law would not justify an assault" and ruled that Shankle's damages should be doubled, granting her $500 in damages. The other judges, John Hugo Dore and Charles Ellis Ott, concurred with his ruling. In fact, Judge Dore had written opinions in two other appellate cases brought by African American women against white bus companies.[5] Olivia Shankle was not an aberration. She was merely one of more than a dozen Black women who sued white bus companies in the South before the postwar Black freedom struggle.

Shankle v. Tri-State Transit Company was both revolutionary and repressive at the same time. In the 1930s, deep in rural Jim Crow Louisiana, a white judge denounced a white bus driver who assaulted a Black woman and awarded her compensation for her physical injuries and mental anguish. Judge LeBlanc's ruling respected Olivia Shankle as a person while preserving the oppressive structures of segregation—manifest in education, transportation, and labor—that shaped the everyday circumstances of her life. Because of Louisiana's segregation laws, Olivia Shankle had to travel a significant distance each week to teach in an all-Black school. The scarcity of teaching jobs for Black women meant that she and her husband had to spend the work week apart. And her placement in the back of the Tri-State bus meant that she had limited contact with the driver to communicate her stops. And yet Olivia Shankle was incensed enough about her assault that she exercised one of the very few rights African Americans retained in Jim Crow Louisiana: the right to sue in court.

Before thousands of Southern Black women marched with their feet against bus segregation and racial violence, they walked into courthouses in the Jim Crow South and filed sixteen lawsuits against major bus companies and smaller city-based bus lines.

In the Jim Crow South, where most African Americans could not vote in elections or experience formal representation at the state or federal level, lawsuits represented one of Black women's most potent weapons against bus discrimination and racial violence. But Black women did not score immediate victories against bus discrimination in the Jim Crow South. In fact, their earliest cases ended in resounding defeats. It was only through trial and error that Black women successfully navigated the contours of justice in the Southern bar. Initially, Black women and the civil rights community contested racial segregation on buses. After a string of failed cases, the civil rights community abandoned bus segregation lawsuits in the South, casting them off as hopeless. But Black women living in the trenches of the Jim

TABLE 4.1 Black women's bus lawsuits in the South before World War II

Year	*First name*	*Last name*	*Occupation*	*State*	*Incident*	*Outcome*	*Amount*	*Attorney*	*Attorney's race*	*Judge*	*Court*
1931	Lucille	Brumfield	Teacher	KY	Segregation	Defeat	Unknown	John W. Rowe	Black/ White	Richardson	Court of Appeals of Kentucky
1932	Mamie	Kinchlow	Unknown	VA	Segregation	Defeat	$10,000	Henry Lincoln Johnson Jr.	Black	C. J. Martin	District Court for DC
1932	Sadie	Patillo	Teacher	TX	*Segregation	**Victory**	$10	William R. Blain	White	Frank Lee Hawkins	Court of Criminal Appeals of Texas
1934	Isabella	Smith	Seamstress	MD	Segregation	Defeat	Unknown	Raymond Alexander Pace	Black	Unknown	Unknown
1935	Ollie	Johnson	Laundress	LA	Injury	**Victory**	$4,150	Norman Coon	White	Robert M. Taliaferro	Court of Appeals of Louisiana, 2nd Circuit
1937	Helen	Willis	Pharmacist	VA	*Segregation	**Victory**	Unknown	John C. Carter	Black	Henry C. Leigh	Corporation Court of Virginia, Danville
1937	Jessie Lee	Garner	Cook	MS	*Segregation	**Victory**	$1,000	Jaap & Higgins/ Louise Melton	White	George H. Ethridge	Supreme Court of Mississippi, Division B
1937	Marie	Peterson	Teacher	TN	Luggage	**Victory**	$32.50	A. A. Latting	Black	Unknown	Tennessee Court of Appeals
1938	Ellen	Harris	Cook	NC	*Segregation	**Victory**	Unknown	C. J. Gates/ Edward R. Avant	Black	J. Clarkson	Supreme Court of North Carolina
1938	Della	Martin	Mother	MS	Injury	**Victory**	$1,925	J. Paul White/ Dick C. McCool	White	Virgil A. Griffith	Supreme Court of Mississippi, Division B

1939	Alma	Porter	Cook	AK	Injury	**Victory**	$2,500	Richardson & Richardson	White	J. Seaborn Holt	Supreme Court of Arkansas
1939	Lou	Owens	Managed boarders	LA	Injury	Defeat	Unknown	J. D. Barksdale	White	Hamiter	Court of Appeals of Louisiana, 2nd Circuit
1939	Linnie	Eaddy	Cleaner	SC	Segregation	**Victory**	$500	McEachin & Townsend	Unknown	C. T. Graydon	Supreme Court of South Carolina
1939	Leathy	Hughes	Cook	LA	Injury	Defeat	Unknown	Taylor Porter	White	Samuel A. LeBlanc	Court of Appeals of Louisiana, 1st Circuit
1940	Jennie Bibbs	Didlick	Teacher	KY	Segregation	**Victory**	$200	Joseph N. Elliott	White	Austin D. Adams	Fayette Circuit Court
1941	Rosa	Valdry	Maid	LA	Injury	Defeat	Unknown	Taylor Porter	White	John H. Dore	Court of Appeals of Louisiana, 1st Circuit
1942	Olivia	Shankle	Teacher	LA	Violence	**Victory**	$500	Plauche & Stockwell	White	Samuel A. LeBlanc	Court of Appeals of Louisiana, 1st Circuit
1943	Fannie	Grant	Laundress	LA	Injury	**Victory**	$753	Brumfield & Major	White	John H. Dore	Court of Appeals of Louisiana, 1st Circuit

*Segregation: These decisions faulted the bus lines for NOT enforcing racial segregation.

Sources: *Brumfield*, 240 Ky. 1; *Kinchlow*, 66 App. D.C. 382; "Pennsylvania Woman Sues Greyhound Bus Line for Jim Crow," *Baltimore Afro-American*, October 6, 1934, 1; *Patillo*, 120 Tex.Crim. 568; *Dixie Gas & Fuel Co.*, 47 S.W.2d 457; *State*, 213 N.C. 758; *Mississippi Power & Light Co.*, 179 Miss. 588; *Johnson*, 164 So. 456; "Helen Willis Bus Ride Is Within Law," *Danville Register and Bee*, January 14, 1937, 1; *Tri-State Transit Co.*, 181 Miss. 388; *Missouri Pacific Transp. Co.*, 199 Ark. 225; *Eaddy*, 191 S.C. 538; *Didlick v. Southern Greyhound Company*, November 22, 1940; *Grant*, 15 So.2d 123; *McFarland*, 11 So.2d 19; *Owens*, 191 So. 581; *Valdry*, 5 So.2d 173; *Fry*, 142 Tex. 589.

Crow South did not give up. They persisted in their ongoing culture of litigiousness by suing bus companies in tort. While these cases did not have explicit implications for civil rights law, they affirmed the humanity of Black passengers and put bus companies on the defensive, forcing them to pay close attention to these decisions. They also shaped Southern legal precedent, whether it was affirming the rights of poor litigants to legal counsel or demonstrating that the enforcement of racial segregation imposed a burden on both bus companies and drivers. By the start of World War II, Black women's bus cases had shaped both the Southern bar and the bus industry, paving the way for broader rulings on bus segregation. This movement began on the bus but moved to the courthouse.

Litigating a Case in the Jim Crow South

In the 1930s and 1940s, when Southern Black women walked to the courthouse to litigate cases against the bus industry, they brushed past Confederate statues honoring the generals and soldiers who fought to preserve the institution of slavery.[6] Sixty years after the end of the Civil War, Black women had lost many citizenship rights, but they maintained due process and the right to sue in court. During these decades, the Southern legal system had a notoriously poor reputation. In states where African Americans could not cast ballots, serve on juries, be elected to local and state office, or serve in patronage positions, could they expect to receive verdicts in their favor in the courtroom? The answer is much more complicated and nuanced than most historians have appreciated.

In the 1930s and 1940s, most Southern courts held an unsavory reputation in American culture. One of the most iconic cases from this era was the Scottsboro trials in 1931, in which nine African American boys were accused of and convicted for raping two white women on a train in northern Alabama. An all-white jury sentenced these nine boys to death. The US Supreme Court overturned this conviction, but it generated press coverage around the world, becoming a potent symbol of the injustices in the Southern legal system.[7]

While Scottsboro loomed large, the reality is that Southern law was its own institution, somewhat removed from politics in this era. Southern white supremacist politicians may have employed vitriolic rhetoric, but white judges often expressed more restraint on the delicate matter of race relations.[8] These circumstances were only heightened by history. The white judges who heard these cases and the white lawyers who argued them were the descendants of slaveholders and Confederate soldiers, while the Black women plaintiffs who sued the bus industry were only a few generations removed from slavery. While the Southern legal system was undoubtedly a hostile place, and most white judges favored the politics of white supremacy, Black women were nonetheless able to bring cases to court and, on occasion, receive fair and impartial hearings. Even though most scholars have focused on criminal cases, civil cases represented an important site for Black women to receive justice.[9] In the 1930s and 1940s, Black women forced Southern courts to determine the boundaries of citizenship rights in the growing bus industry.

Legal Defeats in the Jim Crow South

In the late 1920s and early 1930s, as bus travel expanded across the country, Black women encountered a range of unpleasant passenger experiences, whether they were forced to move to the back, experienced violence at the hands of a bus driver, or were banned from these vehicles altogether. But region was a decisive factor in shaping legal outcomes. In Midwestern states, such as Illinois, Indiana, Michigan, and Ohio, African American women immediately began to file lawsuits contesting their treatment. Wielding the power of their state civil rights statutes, they challenged the validity of racial segregation and won several important victories in court. The well-publicized lawsuits of Laura Fischer and Paulina Stevens in the late 1920s inspired Black women across the country to take bus companies to court.[10] But these legal victories were tied to region. Fischer and Stevens had firm legal ground and were able to make race and anti-Black racism central to their cases.

The South was different. Racial segregation was the prevailing system, shaping both the law and broader cultural attitudes. As interstate and municipal buses debuted, some states immediately revised their statutes to explicitly include this form of transportation in their laws. For instance, Georgia, Louisiana, Mississippi, and Virginia all revised their statutes in the late 1920s and early 1930s, likely sensing that bus segregation would be important.

It was in this context of prevailing support for racial segregation in the 1920s and 1930s that Black women took bus companies to court in the Jim Crow South and lost. Black women waged these lawsuits with the explicit backing of the National Association for the Advancement of Colored People (NAACP) and other civil rights communities. In 1927, Lucille Brumfield, a

TABLE 4.2 Bus segregation statutes in the Jim Crow South

State	*Bus*	*Year*	*Train*	*Streetcar*	*Waiting room*	*Sleeping car*	*Restaurant*	*Prisoner or nurse*	*Charter*	*Police officer*
Alabama	Yes	1931	Yes	No	Yes	No	No	Yes	No	No
Arkansas	Yes	1937	Yes	Yes	Yes	Yes	No	Yes	No	No
Florida	Yes	N.A.	Yes	Yes	Yes	No	No	Yes	Yes	Yes
Georgia	Yes	1931	Yes	No	No	Yes	No	Yes	Yes	Trains
Kentucky	No	N.A.	Yes	No	No	No	No	Yes	N.A.	N.A.
Louisiana	Yes	1928	Yes	Yes	Yes	No	No	Yes	No	No
Maryland	No	N.A.	Yes	Yes	No	No	No	Yes	No	No
Mississippi	Yes	1930	Yes	Yes	Yes	Yes	No	No	No	No
North Carolina	Yes	1933	Yes	Yes	Yes	No	No	Yes	Yes	No
Oklahoma	Yes	1931	Yes	Yes	Yes	No	No	Yes	No	No
South Carolina	Yes	1937	Yes	Yes	Yes	No	Yes	Yes	No	Yes
Tennessee	No	N.A.	Yes	Yes	No	No	No	Yes	No	No
Texas	Yes	1943	Yes	Yes	Yes	Yes	No	Yes	Yes	No
Virginia	Yes	1930	Yes	Yes	No	No	No	Yes	No	Yes

Source: Murray, *States' Laws on Race and Color*.

teacher in Kentucky, became the first African American in the country to sue a bus company. On Saturday, July 16, 1927, she walked to the Union Bus Station in Lexington, Kentucky, to purchase a ticket on a Consolidated Coach bus for a trip to the nearby city of Danville. When she attempted to board the bus, the driver would not give her a seat despite the empty seats on the bus. Brumfield was stranded in Lexington longer than she intended. The bus company insisted that it had a reservation system and offered Brumfield a bus at a later hour. She hired two lawyers in Lexington—one Black, one white—and sued Consolidated Coach Corporation for $2,500 for breach of contract, contending that the bus company had discriminated against her as a Black woman.

Lucille Brumfield's lawsuit put Consolidated Coach on edge. After conversing with the Kentucky Commission on Interracial Cooperation, the company held a training session at which drivers were educated on avoiding discrimination to prevent more lawsuits.[11] This response demonstrated the company's genuine wariness of lawsuits. But there was little to fear. Lucille Brumfield lost her case in the Fayette Circuit Court in a jury trial. She appealed the decision to the Supreme Court of Kentucky, which affirmed the judgment of the lower court. Brumfield had made a few miscalculations in her lawsuit. She hired a legal team composed of one Black and one white attorney, which might have compromised her case. Additionally, proving racial discrimination was nearly impossible in the Jim Crow South. This was even true in a more racially moderate state like Kentucky, where trains were segregated but buses were not and there was no civil rights statue. Even though Consolidated Coach did work to improve its services toward Black passengers, that was short-lived. By 1929, Greyhound had acquired the Consolidated Coach lines and imposed its business model, racist practices, and bus driver culture on this new company.[12]

Even though Lucille Brumfield's defeat traveled all the way to the state's supreme court and was well publicized in the press, Black women continued to contest bus segregation and lose their cases in the South. Not only did these litigants have harrowing experiences, but they were arrested for defying bus segregation and spent time in jail. These lawsuits typify the escalating violence that bus drivers began to enact on Black women passengers. In 1932, Mamie Kinchlow, a resident of New York City, learned that her mother had died, and she booked a bus trip to Virginia for the funeral. When the bus wheeled into Virginia, the driver forced her and another passenger, Bessie Nelson, to move to the back, and they refused. The next morning in police court, each woman was fined twenty-five dollars for violating Virginia's segregation law and for disorderly conduct.[13] Kinchlow located the funds to pay the fine and traveled back to New York, but Nelson had no money and spent a week doing laundry for a municipal hospital to cover the court costs.[14] Kinchlow hired a Black lawyer, Henry Lincoln Johnson Jr., and sued the People's Rapid Transit Company for $10,000 in the District Court for the District of Columbia. Kinchlow sued on three grounds: breach of contract, wrongful ejection from the bus, and false grounds for imprisonment, claiming that the bus driver did not have the standing to eject her from the bus. Ultimately, the court decided against Kinchlow and in favor of People's Rapid Transit. Mamie Kinchlow appealed the decision, and it stayed with the courts for an agonizing four years before the Court of Appeals for the District of Columbia sustained the original decision, holding that Kinchlow had violated Virginia's segregation statute and that her arrest had been legitimate.[15] The Kinchlow case marked a devastating defeat, one that lingered in the courts for years.[16]

In 1934, Isabella Smith became the third Black woman to contest racial segregation on buses in the Jim Crow South and lose. A widow in her forties, Smith had migrated from Virginia to Philadelphia, where she settled in a Black neighborhood and supported herself as a seamstress.[17] In October 1934, she boarded a Greyhound Bus for a visit with her family. The trip to Virginia was uneventful, but on the return trip in Princess Ann, Maryland, the driver ordered her to move to the back of the bus. Smith refused, prompting the bus driver to threaten her by shouting, "We lynch colored people down here when they don't obey orders given by whites." Smith refused again, and police officers arrested her. She spent a cold night in jail before she was released the next morning. When Smith returned to Philadelphia, she was ill. She hired eminent Black attorney Raymond Alexander Pace to sue the Greyhound Bus Company.[18] An editorial in the *Baltimore Afro-American* praised Isabella Smith for her bravery in both refusing to abide by racial segregation practices and suing the Greyhound Bus Company for a sum of ten thousand dollars. "Mrs. Smith," the editorial stated, "does well to press her suit. Others who are browbeaten should likewise haul the Greyhound Bus Company into court. Nothing else will so soon break up this practice."[19] But it appears that Isabella Smith, like Mamie Kinchlow and Bessie Nelson, was not successful in her petition. By 1934, Greyhound's legal team had become adept at fighting lawsuits in court, and it is likely that they marshaled their legal acumen to dismiss the lawsuit.

Cumulatively, the lawsuits of Lucille Brumfield, Mamie Kinchlow, Bessie Nelson, and Isabella Smith reveal key patterns. These women were inspired to wage lawsuits against the bus companies because they read about the victories of Black women in the Jim Crow North. But white judges in the North and the South held very different views about racial segregation. Even though buses were a new form of technology, racial segregation laws in the South had no room for interpretation. And Mamie Kinchlow, Bessie Nelson, and Isabella Smith had all moved to the North, returning to the South as migrants. It is possible that the Southern bar treated this migration with hostility and considered these women outsiders. Finally, these passengers had hired Black attorneys and framed these cases in a language of civil rights, which likely engendered feelings of racial antagonism in white Southern courtrooms.

It is tempting to view these cases as a civil rights failure. Even though the lawsuits demonstrate that Black women waged an early and robust civil rights movement, they also underscore the strength of segregation laws in the Jim Crow South. These defeats suggested that bus segregation lawsuits were not the best instrument to combat racial discrimination in the South. In the aftermath of these cases, the NAACP continued to express sympathy toward Black women who experienced bus discrimination yet developed a defeatist attitude about dismantling bus segregation through legal strategy.[20]

But Black women in the Jim Crow South were not defeated. These women—hardened by the crushing indignities of life in the Jim Crow South—had no choice but to ride buses. As the victims of discrimination and inequality on buses, Black women continued their longer tradition of suing to contest discrimination. If they wanted to receive justice on the buses, they had to challenge these laws as Southern residents and not overtly work to dismantle the system of segregation. Following these cases that ended in setbacks, African American women began to shift their legal strategy to focus on contesting segregation when the law was not explicit. One of the first people to bring such a case was Sadie Patillo, a teacher in Texas.

A Measure of Justice: Litigating for Segregation

In July 1931, Sadie Patillo, a thirty-two-year-old teacher who lived in Beaumont, Texas, was riding a brand-new bus owned by the Eastern Texas Electric Company. The driver forced her to move to the back and Patillo refused because Texas's segregation statute did not explicitly include the word "bus." Police officers arrested Patillo and fined her ten dollars. She hired William R. Blain, a noted white attorney in the city, to defend her. She eventually appealed the fine to the Texas Court of Criminal Appeals. In this groundbreaking opinion, the court sided with Patillo. Writing for the court, Judge Frank Lee Hawkins stated that Patillo was correct because a bus was not a train. Judge Hawkins noted that the state legislature clearly outlined segregation in "trains, street cars, and interurban cars" and suggested that it might be "equally as desirable to segregate them [the races] when passengers upon buses, in view of the recent development of the use of such vehicles not only upon the streets of our cities, but also upon the highways of the state." Judge Hawkins lamented that the legislature had not yet inserted the word "bus" into its laws about racial segregation.[21] Sadie Patillo won her case, but her legal outcome inspired members of the Texas legislature to segregate buses by the late 1930s.[22] Patillo appears to have waged this lawsuit on her own accord. One month after the Texas Court of Criminal Appeals handed down its decision, NAACP leader Roy Wilkins wrote to the West Publishing Company in Minnesota, asking for a copy of the opinion to be sent to his office. Wilkins's curiosity about this case demonstrates that Black women in the Jim Crow South initiated these lawsuits without consulting leaders at the NAACP.[23] When the decision was announced, the Black press covered the case, alerting African Americans about this victory in the Jim Crow South.[24]

Sadie Patillo's choice of legal counsel epitomized the dramatic twists and turns of race relations in the Jim Crow South. Patillo's lawyer, William R. Blain, had been born in Glynn County, Georgia, in 1870, five years after the Civil War ended. His parents were both avid supporters of the Confederacy. His father, William S. Blain, had volunteered to serve in the Confederate army in May 1861 and fought until surrender in 1865.[25] As an adult, the younger Blain moved from his home in Georgia to the up-and-coming city of Beaumont, Texas. There, he established an enterprising law practice, where he routinely defended people for personal injury. In a span of two years, Blain represented two African American women in their cases against the transportation industry.[26] The fact that the son of a former Confederate soldier would defend the rights of African American women in court demonstrates the sea change that occurred during Reconstruction, the persistence of the courts in the lives of Black Southerners, and new complexities in Southern race relations. Scholars of Southern legal history discuss these legal arrangements between white Southern attorneys and Black plaintiffs, noting that white lawyers, especially those suing for personal injury, were eager to earn money through damages. They often treated their Black clients with respect, believing that Black Southerners held a legal right to sue in court, even though they could not cast ballots or enjoy legal representation.[27] In the aftermath of the Patillo verdict, Black women scored three more victorious lawsuits in which they faulted the companies for not properly enforcing racial segregation, and all of these cases revealed the chaos of the color line on crowded Southern buses.

On a rainy afternoon in 1936, Helen Willis, a pharmacist in Danville, Virginia, boarded a Danville Traction and Power Company bus at Craghead Street, and the driver accepted her ticket. Willis was a 1929 graduate of the Howard University Pharmacy School.[28] In compliance with the Virginia segregation statute, she sat in the last seat in the back. However, when she alighted at Union Street for her job at the pharmacy, police officers arrested her. She was fined five dollars in police court. The Danville Traction and Power Company maintained that during peak rush hour, it operated two separate buses: one for white passengers and one for Black passengers, who were mostly workers at the local tobacco factory. Helen Willis hired a local Black attorney, John C. Carter, to represent her.[29] In January 1937, a trial was held at the Corporation Court of Virginia in Danville. Attorneys for Helen Willis and the Danville Traction and Power Company called a total of eight witnesses, including the bus driver, the president of the bus company, and white passengers. After hearing from both sides, Judge Henry C. Leigh ruled in favor of Helen Willis. Judge Leigh contended that Virginia's statute forbade the Danville Traction and Power Company from running separate buses for Black and white passengers but were expected to practice racial segregation on its buses and streetcars.[30] This was a local case, but it generated a great deal of press coverage. Even though this decision upheld racial segregation, both Black and white newspapers interpreted the case as Helen Willis's civil rights victory. For example, the white-owned *Richmond Times-Dispatch* proclaimed, "Negro Wins 'Jim Crow' Case at Danville," while the Black-owned *Baltimore Afro-American* declared, "Woman Wins J.C. Bus Case." Articles in the Black press especially praised Willis for banishing Danville's whites-only buses, which was a clear violation of segregation's doctrine of "separate but equal."[31]

Two years later, another Black woman passenger successfully forced the courts to grapple with the logistics of enforcing bus segregation. In March 1938, Ellen Harris, a cook in Durham, North Carolina, boarded a crowded bus operated by the Durham Public Service Company and took a seat near the very back. A white couple entered the bus. Besides the bench in the very back of the bus, the only vacant seats were one about halfway down, which the wife took, and one next to Ellen Harris. The man asked

Harris to give up her seat, and she refused to do so. Harris calmly stated that the only way she would relinquish her seat was if her fare was refunded. The driver rejected this offer and told her she would be arrested. "Have me arrested," Harris told the driver.[32] In this moment, Harris rejected the prescriptive role she was required to play in the Jim Crow South. Even in upper South states like North Carolina, Black women were expected to adhere to established cultural conventions of segregation. Even though Harris disputed the seat arrangement in a segregated section, she remained firm and was willing to live with the prospect of a criminal record. As a cook in Durham, Harris was not part of the city's Black elite. And yet in her thoroughly ordinary interactions with a white bus driver, she improvised. The historian Stephen Berrey notes that on the bus, Black Southerners were constantly consumed with the dynamics of moving to accommodate white passengers. Through these three words, Ellen Harris rejected these racial scripts.[33] The bus driver then called the police, who swiftly arrested Harris. She was charged with disorderly conduct. Harris hired two Black lawyers in Durham, Caswell Jerry Gates and Edward R. Avant. Gates was a pioneering lawyer in Durham, while Avant had represented several Black clients in civil rights cases in the state. Following a trial in the Superior Court of North Carolina, a jury of eleven men entered a verdict of guilty.[34] But she appealed her conviction, and the Supreme Court of North Carolina agreed to hear the case.

In May 1938, Harris and her lawyers argued the case in the Supreme Court of North Carolina. The local press tracked the details, sensing the high stakes. An article in the *Durham Herald-Sun* noted that the case "may interpret North Carolina's racial segregation laws as applied to buses."[35] In June 1938, the Supreme Court of North Carolina handed down its decision, ruling in favor of Ellen Harris. Writing for the court, Justice J. Clarkson reversed Harris's conviction, outlining the provisions of segregation on transportation in North Carolina. He noted that according to the provisions, "Any person willfully violating the provisions of this section shall be guilty of a misdemeanor." He continued, noting that in recent years, with the construction of paved roads across the state, buses had become "one of the most important carriers of passengers." He urged the Corporation Commission to formalize bus segregation and construct separate waiting areas and restrooms for the "best welfare of the white and Negro races." He framed racial segregation as a matter of "justice . . . in this racial condition that exists among us—a duty that the State owes to all of its citizens."[36] Here, Judge Clarkson ruled that this case defied the logic of segregation, and he sided with Ellen Harris. He noted that "North Carolina's policy in regard to the Negro is segregation and separation with justice, under the Constitution. It has been the means of promoting a friendly relationship and to a great extent brought peace and good will between the sensible elements of the races in this State. This question of separation and segregation was settled long ago."[37]

The Harris case was widely covered in the Black press and revealed some ambiguous truths about Black women, bus segregation, and the law. First, this case demonstrated that white judges *did* take the complexities of these cases into consideration. Judge Clarkson commended Harris for taking pains to follow the principles of segregation, acknowledging that the system was a fraught one, nor did the white judges punish Harris's bold remark to the bus driver, "Have me arrested." The Harris case was also groundbreaking because she had hired two Black attorneys to represent her, and these two Black men were able to score a victory in the Supreme Court of North Carolina, the highest court in the state. While this case affirmed the logic of racial segregation, it also signaled that African Americans could experience a modicum of justice at the bar, even in the Jim Crow South.

In the aftermath of the ruling, an editorial in the *Carolina Times*, the Black newspaper in Durham, opined that the decision was "more significant than may be realized from the surface." The editorial noted that the decision would "bring respect to the race as a whole and to Negro lawyers as professional men." But the editorial lamented that the Harris case demonstrated the extent to which many African Americans missed the opportunities of legal action because they lacked the financial resources or connections to file lawsuits. There were likely "thousands of unjust court decisions made against poor and ignorant Negroes every year" that were not contested. The editorial concluded that "the reversal of the supreme court ought to build confidence" in Black North Carolinians that there was still a "measure of justice that is beyond the reach of weak officials of the law."[38]

The final case in which Black women were successful for upholding racial segregation occurred in Mississippi, arguably the Southern state with the worst record on race relations. In August 1936, Jessie Lee Garner, a twenty-nine-year-old cook in Jackson, boarded a Mississippi Power & Light Company bus at Sutton's Ice Cream Parlor.[39] At the time, Garner was six months pregnant. On the bus, there was no fabric or metal partition demarcating the Black or white sections, only a small plaque. When she boarded, there was only one other Black passenger. But as the bus filled up, the vehicle became crowded, forcing some white male passengers to stand in the aisles. One of those men walked to the back of the bus and demanded that Jessie Lee Garner relinquish her seat. Garner responded that she was unable to stand because she was pregnant but would be departing the bus shortly on Farish Street. The white passenger responded angrily. He struck her in the mouth and eye, and "knocked her violently to the floor." Garner later testified that she was so injured that she "wasn't in a condition to get off the bus." Fortunately, a white male passenger helped carry her off the bus and transported her to her house and into the care of a doctor. She was bleeding heavily.[40] Garner was unable to work and was confined to her bed from August until November, when she gave birth to a stillborn baby.

Garner hired the prominent white law firm of Jaap & Higgins to sue the Mississippi Power & Light Company. She also retained the counsel of Louise Melton, a local white woman lawyer. Together, her legal team demonstrated a great deal of savviness in presenting her case. First, in their complaint, the lawyers noted that the state of Mississippi had enacted the segregation statutes for the purposes of "preserving the peace and preventing breaches of the peace." Their complaint further stated that Jessie Lee Garner not only experienced a traumatic miscarriage but had to pay medical bills, had to hire a servant to help around the house, and suffered tremendous pain and "mental anguish." During the trial, two physicians testified on her behalf and confirmed that her injuries on the bus that day, specifically the violence from the white male passenger, contributed to her miscarriage. During the hearing, Garner stated that she complied with racial segregation, but that the Mississippi Power & Light Company had poor signage demarcating Black and white sections on the bus. Additionally, her lawyers put W. W. Bean on the stand. Bean worked as the claims adjuster for the Mississippi Power & Light Company, which had only been operating buses in Jackson for the past six months. Bean testified that since buses had first begun to run, Mississippi Power & Light Company had received between four and five complaints that white men had attacked African American women, but the company had chosen to ignore them.[41] This casual admission in the court records demonstrated that buses in Mississippi, not unlike buses in all states, were dangerous places for Black women passengers.

The circuit court of Hinds County, Mississippi, ruled in Garner's favor, finding that the Mississippi Power & Light Company was "liable for the passenger's injuries because it failed to prevent passengers from going from one compartment of the bus to another compartment intended for the separate accommodations for the races." In this ruling, the court coded

Garner's miscarriage as "injuries." Her pregnancy and subsequent miscarriage furnished her a bodily marker of womanhood that race could not erase. The bus company appealed the decision, and in October 1937, the Supreme Court of Mississippi affirmed the judgment of the circuit court and Garner's award of damages of $1,000.[42] In her lawsuit, Garner had insisted that it would have violated the laws of Mississippi for a white man to sit in the segregated section, and she won the largest amount.[43]

In her lawsuit, Jessie Lee Garner followed a precise but delicate script. Presenting herself as a respectable Black woman resident of Mississippi, she described how her injuries prevented her from working as a cook and contributed to the death of her fetus. Moreover, her lawyers framed racial segregation as a logical system that was designed to keep order among "law-abiding, peaceable colored persons." This strategy worked, and Garner's lawsuit affirmed three principles. First, she was able to demonstrate that segregation was a system that was difficult to enforce on a bus, involving the careful and precise calibration between signage and service. Not only did segregation impose a burden on the bus line to install fabric or signage to separate the races, but it also forced bus drivers to ensure that passengers were aware of the racial and spatial configurations on the bus. Next, through her lawsuit, Garner demonstrated that many white men in Mississippi were quick to assault Black women. By testifying about her injuries, she was able to narrate her experiences as a victim of interracial violence, a rare opportunity for Black women in Deep South Mississippi. Finally, in hiring white lawyers and enlisting the testimony of white doctors, Garner subtly defied scientific racism, demonstrating that she was a person whose body was fragile and capable of injury.[44] Jessie Lee Garner won her lawsuit in the Mississippi Supreme Court.

In its ruling, Judge George H. Ethridge, writing for the court, focused entirely on the Mississippi Power & Light Company's failure to comply with segregation. The court noted, for example, that the Mississippi law required bus companies to employ "metal, wood, or cloth" in order to install racial segregation on their vehicles. In this case, the Mississippi Power & Light Company had only installed a flimsy sign. "The object of the law was absolute, complete, and perfect separation," the court noted, "so that there should occur none of the outbreaks and conflicts marring the public peace, and ending, it may be, in bloodshed." But he explicitly stated that the bus company's "failure" to follow the state's mandated practices of racial segregation "was not the proximate cause" of Jessie Lee Garner's injuries. Garner scored a crucial victory in her award of $1,000 and, through this lawsuit, her ability to testify in court and narrate her injuries. For Garner, this amount of money was likely life changing. But while the Supreme Court of Mississippi ruled in favor of Garner, the ruling was narrow, contending that the system of racial segregation could never produce medical or health inequities.[45]

In all four cases, Jessie Lee Garner, Ellen Harris, Sadie Patillo, and Helen Willis won their lawsuits, but these legal verdicts marked a decisive victory for segregation. Sadie Patillo inspired Texas to add the word "bus" to its state segregation statute, Jessie Lee Garner's case faulted the Mississippi Power & Light Company for doing a poor job of enforcing racial segregation, and the cases of Ellen Harris and Helen Willis affirmed the logic of racial segregation. In fact, Ellen Harris's case prompted the chief justice to wax poetic about the benefits of racial segregation. However, Helen Willis was successful in identifying a bus company that explicitly banned Black passengers, prompting this important ruling. Perhaps the most devastating of these decisions was the one rendered for Jessie Lee Garner. Here, the Supreme Court of Mississippi issued a narrow decision that refused to link the system of segregation with health conditions—in this case, the death of a fetus. But Garner's award of $1,000 was a tremendous amount of money and signaled that litigating bus discrimination through tort lawsuits could be a promising legal avenue for Black women in the Jim Crow South.

The "Poor Have Rights": The Quiet Revolution of Torts Lawsuits

Beginning in the mid-1930s, Black women in the South switched their legal strategies to sue municipal bus companies solely in tort, or for personal injury. Tort law was an area that oversaw many wrongs, including "negligence, civil assault, battery, and wrongful death."[46] These types of lawsuits were not at all new. Since the advent of railroads in the nineteenth century, Americans—including African Americans—had been suing railroads for personal injuries. Women were especially visible in such lawsuits.[47] Between 1900 and 1935, personal injury lawsuits made up 16 percent of the cases litigated in state supreme courts.[48] Furthermore, of the appellate personal injury suits brought between 1900 and 1920, 41 percent involved Black women.[49] This is an extraordinary figure. The disproportionate number of appellate lawsuits brought by Black women can likely be traced to the racial intolerance of the Jim Crow South. Since racism might have caused

Black women to lose in local courts, they appealed their cases to state supreme courts for review.

Tort lawsuits against bus lines suggest striking patterns across gender and race. When buses first appeared in the Jim Crow South, both Black and white women rode these vehicles, experienced bodily harm, sued, and often won. There are dozens of examples of white women who sued bus lines for injuries they sustained on buses in the 1920s, 1930s, and 1940s.[50] In addition, sometimes their husbands joined them in a lawsuit, alleging loss of companionship.[51] And at least fourteen Black women filed tort lawsuits for the bodily harm they experienced as bus riders in the 1930s and 1940s. In the case of Olivia and Everett Shankle, they sued together as a married couple.[52] But regardless of race, men were far less likely to file tort lawsuits as bus riders. White men sued for injuries when the cars they drove collided with buses, but there is little information to suggest that they sued for injury as bus passengers, and no evidence that Black men sued for injury as bus passengers.[53] In the first generation of the bus industry, it was more common for Black and white women to ride buses and experience bodily injury. Tort lawsuits against bus companies were almost always initiated by women in the Jim Crow South. Even though there were gendered patterns, it was still revolutionary that Black women used tort law to bring cases against white bus lines in the Jim Crow South.

For Black women, tort lawsuits presented many different considerations. Tort lawsuits were not the equivalent of civil rights laws. Tort law provided compensation in personal injury cases. Even though bus lines in the South practiced racial segregation, they had to treat all passengers equally. As a Louisiana statute stated, bus lines were expected to exercise a "duty of care on the operator of a motor bus to be the same as in the case of the operation of the electric street car or steam railroad." These Louisiana rules stipulated that bus drivers must exercise "the same degree of care which the law imposes on common carriers of passengers generally."[54] On the one hand, these decisions could be revelatory precisely because African Americans had such a fraught history with medicine and injury. Stretching back to the seventeenth century, slaveholders denied that people of African descent could feel pain or were even capable of bodily harm or injury.[55] But on the other hand, tort lawsuits did not address race relations or even matters of equity. They focused on assigning compensation for damages, but rarely did they grapple with the underlying causes of those damages, such as racial violence.[56]

For Black women contemplating a tort lawsuit, it was important to retain the services of a white lawyer. Even though the South was a racist and dangerous place for African Americans, a cohort of white lawyers specialized in personal injury cases and were willing to represent African Americans. These white lawyers could accrue high fees, especially if their clients received large rulings. While white attorneys held racially paternalistic views about their Black clients, they were often seasoned lawyers, savvy about the law, and well-versed in the racial etiquette of the Southern bar.[57] They always called on white witnesses to corroborate their Black client's testimony and often solicited the expertise of white physicians.

Personal injury lawsuits were a powerful tool to wield against bus discrimination, but Black women had to operate it with precision. They had to walk into the courthouse acting as though they trusted both the Southern white legal system and the bus industry. These racialized performances were key precisely because in personal injury lawsuits, juries decided nine out of ten cases. Black women plaintiffs enjoyed advantages over Black men because they were accorded the subtle privilege of womanhood, which meant that their bodies were more vulnerable to injury. When men brought a tort case to court, they could only point to injuries that affected their ability to work, whereas women could claim emotional injury and nervous shock.[58] Since these cases all revolved around bus travel, African American women could also score points with the judges and juries if they evoked gendered stereotypes and appeared ignorant about local geography and bus routes. It was not expected that African American women were savvy travelers, especially if they were bus passengers in unfamiliar locations. Black women's claims to geographic ignorance gave them crucial amounts of leverage in many of these cases.

But at the same time that Black women had more flexibility than Black men around the category of emotional injury and geographic literacy, their cases also differed from those of white women. Courts allowed white women to claim that injuries affected their quality of life, whereas Black women always had to maintain that injuries prevented them from working. White Southern courts expected that African American women labored in low-paying jobs as domestic servants, laundresses, untrained nurses, and cooks. Awarding Black women back pay for lost wages did not necessarily confer respect. The political economy of the Jim Crow South depended on Black women's low-paid labor to keep white households running and to preserve the existing racialized and gendered hierarchies of society. By granting Black women lost wages, white Southern courts normalized and calcified

Black women's service labor and ensured that Black plaintiffs would not be dependent on white society for welfare relief. There were also different perceptions about money. For many white Southerners, these amounts of money did not seem very large. But for Black Southerners trapped in an endless cycle of economic precarity, this money was life changing.[59]

There are a few reasons why Black women were especially successful with tort lawsuits in the South. Most white Southerners disliked large railroad corporations, and they transferred this hostility to the bus industry.[60] In the 1920s, 1930s, and 1940s—when bus travel presented a new form of transportation, typified by flimsy hardware and uneven services—many Southerners could relate to a story of a bus mishap. Hearing a complaint from a Black Southerner fit neatly within white citizens' familiarity with the hassle and general inconvenience of bus travel. In deciding to award damages to Black plaintiffs, white jurors could imagine that they might be in a similar position at some point in their life. This legal universality transcended the color line. Most importantly, white Southerners did not perceive personal injury lawsuits as threatening the racial order or having any impact whatsoever on the system of white supremacy.[61]

Despite the complex characteristics of these tort cases against the bus industry, there was a subtle revolution in these lawsuits. Even though they did not explicitly confront systems of racism or segregation, the fact remained that African Americans could enter the courtroom and expect to have their cases heard. They did not receive this type of respect when they entered a voting booth, a state house, or a governor's office. It was only in the courts where Black women could point to bodily injury, often at the hands of white men. Even though the NAACP was not aware that Black women waged tort lawsuits against the bus industry in this era, these cases helped bring awareness about abuses at the hands of bus drivers and create sympathy and sometimes respect for Black women plaintiffs among the Southern bar.

One of the first Black women to bring a tort lawsuit to a Southern court was Ollie Johnson, a forty-two-year-old laundress in Monroe, Louisiana.[62] In 1934, she boarded a city bus and paid the driver, Grover C. Kelly, a quarter for the five-cent fare. While Kelly was sorting through the coins to give her change, his foot pushed on the gas pedal and the bus moved forward. As she was walking down the center of the bus toward the section for Black passengers, the bus collided with an automobile driven by a Black man. This crash pushed Ollie Johnson to the ground, but on the way, her left shoulder jutted against the fare box. Her injuries were so severe that she could not get up off the floor of the bus. She was taken to the local sanitarium in Monroe. The physician who treated her suggested that she needed an operation on her shoulder. Since she could not afford to pay for it, she traveled to New Orleans to receive the surgery at the Charity Hospital. But the surgery was only a partial solution, and her physicians recommended an additional surgery that would cost more than $1,000 for her shoulder to heal properly.

Faced with daunting medical bills, Ollie Johnson hired a white lawyer named Norman Coon and sued the city of Monroe, Louisiana, on four counts.[63] In her petition, she stated that the white driver, Grover Kelly, had violated the city ordinance for failing to sound his horn, pushed his foot to the gas pedal even though a car had begun to turn, did not wait until she had reached her seat, and was negligent about traffic. In total, she sued the city of Monroe for $21,050. Her attorney called on the expertise of her physicians to narrate Johnson's bus-related injuries.[64] In his ruling, Judge James T. Shell sided with the bus company against Ollie Johnson and dismissed the lawsuit. He did not fault the driver for any negligence. Dissatisfied, Johnson appealed her case to the Second Circuit Court of Appeals in Louisiana, which reversed the ruling. Judge Robert M. Taliaferro, writing for the court, held that prior to her accident, Ollie Johnson was a "strong and robust woman" who had earned ten dollars a week as a laundress. He acknowledged that her injuries were so severe that she would be "partially disabled" for the rest of her life and that at this moment, she was "totally unable to work." He also noted that her medical bills were significant. Judge Taliaferro ruled that the city of Monroe owed Ollie Johnson $4,150 in damages.[65] By issuing this opinion, the court acknowledged Johnson's injuries and faulted the bus line—and implicitly the driver—for causing them. The damages of over $4,000 were significant, but the ruling also reinforced Louisiana's racial codes: The court wanted to ensure that the white doctor would be compensated for his services, and because he did not want Johnson to become a public charge, he placed the burden of her finances on the city of Monroe, Louisiana. With the ruling, Johnson received an acknowledgment from the legal system that her body was injured and that the condition was serious enough to warrant a fairly large sum of money.

In February 1938, a twenty-two-year-old Black woman and mother of two named Alma Porter experienced a similar type of outcome. At ten in the evening, Porter boarded a sparsely populated Missouri Pacific Bus in Newport, Arkansas. In one hand, she carried a suitcase, and in the other, she held her eighteen-month-old child. Porter was recently divorced and thus the sole support for both herself and her child. Porter's status as a divorced woman had the potential to undermine her claims to respectability, so her case was more delicate than that of other African American women. Thirty-five miles into the trip, the driver veered off the road, the bus collided into a mailbox, and the wheels flew off. The bus rolled over several times before it crashed. As the passengers flew in the air, Alma Porter hit her head, fractured her left leg between her knee and hip, and sustained many bruises and abrasions. Her injuries confined her to bed for three months in a full leg cast. In the aftermath of her injuries, one of her children died. It was not stated whether Porter's injuries on the bus factored into this death. Porter hired the white law firm of Richardson & Richardson and sued the bus company for the negligence of its driver, Clyde Fiveash. At trial, Porter testified about her injuries, discussing how her leg was in a cast for over a month, and she was confined to bed rest for three months, which prevented her ability to earn her weekly wages. Her occupation was not listed, but in the court proceedings, her lawyers emphasized that she earned five dollars a week, presumably in some service position. In response to her compelling testimony, a jury in Arkansas awarded her $2,500 in damages. But the bus company appealed the decision to the Supreme Court of Arkansas, arguing that these damages were excessive and that there was no negligence on the part of the driver. On appeal, the court held that the damages awarded to Alma Porter in the Randolph Circuit Court were not excessive. Writing for the court, Judge J. Seaborn Holt focused on the permanent physical injuries that she had suffered, the emotional toll of the incident, and her time in confinement. The other judges sustained the amount.[66] For Alma Porter and Ollie Johnson, it was critical that they had legitimate injuries and had previously held jobs before their accidents.

The previous year, Della Martin, a Black woman in Mississippi, had received another victory in her personal injury lawsuit. At thirty-seven years old, she was three months pregnant and lived with her family in Madison County, where her husband labored as a watchman in a lumberyard.[67] In August 1936, she arranged to visit her parents in Summerland with her three young children in tow, their ages stretching from eight to four to only eighteen months old. She and her children boarded a Tri-State bus and sat down in the back. The bus driver was new and unfamiliar with the route. At some point into the trip, Martin realized that the driver had taken a wrong turn. After a passenger corrected him and guided him onto the correct road, Martin called out that her stop was nearing, but the driver did not stop the bus. It is possible that since Della Martin was sitting in the very back, the driver might not have heard her. Since Martin's last visit to

Summerland, the state had constructed a new highway, and this landscape was unfamiliar to her. Confused, she and her children departed the bus at Knight's Filling Station, which was four miles from her parents' home. It was an extremely hot day in August, with the temperature reaching ninety-five degrees. With no money in hand, Martin arranged to leave part of her luggage at the filling station and set off to walk to her parents' house.[68] Her youngest child was not able to walk and had to be carried. Later into the walk, her four-year-old also needed assistance. When she finally arrived at her parents' home, she collapsed. Her personal physician diagnosed her with permanent heatstroke and determined that she would never be able to work in the heat. This was crucial. Even though Martin's current life stage was consumed with raising children, her case hinged on her ability to work in the future so that her family would never pose a public burden on the state of Mississippi.

Della Martin sued the Tri-State Transit Company for breach of contract. She hired two distinguished white lawyers in Madison, Mississippi: Dick C. McCool and J. Paul White.[69] At trial in the Circuit Court of Madison County, Martin testified that when she purchased this bus ticket, she had expected it to be a seamless trip to reach her final destination. Martin and her attorneys strategically emphasized a few key points. First, Martin highlighted the physical hardships of her bus trip. It was obvious that the heat on that summer day and being stranded far from her destination had contributed to her poor health outcomes. Perhaps through the coaching of her attorneys, she also drew on stereotypes about race and gender. She framed herself as lost and unfamiliar with the landscape and in need of the kindness of strangers to reach her destination safely.

The jury sided with Della Martin and awarded her a sum of $1,925 in damages. The Tri-State Transit Company appealed the decision, contending that Martin should have arranged for another type of transportation to avoid these types of injuries. The Supreme Court of Mississippi upheld the circuit court's decision. The bus company had failed in its duty to transport Della Martin and her children to their appropriate destination. Writing for the court, Judge Virgil A. Griffith emphasized that Martin's injuries from this exposure to the dangerous heat were severe, compounded by her condition as a pregnant woman. The opinion pointed to the testimony of her physician, noting that she would never be able to work in this type of heat, "as she had always theretofore been accustomed to do." This was key. Furthermore, the court agreed that the Tri-State Transit Company had exercised "negligence" in failing to transport her to her final destination. The

The bus industry in Mississippi and throughout the Jim Crow South was quite rural. Here, this Black woman landowner in Mississippi waits for a bus on a wooden bench deep in the piney woods. *Source*: Dorothea Lange, *Negro Landowner Waiting for the Bus. Mississippi*, LC-USF34-017805-E, Farm Security Administration Collection, Prints and Photographs, Washington, DC.

opinion emphasized that her condition of pregnancy, compounded by the blistering heat, made her vulnerable to this type of illness.[70] Most importantly, the court used her case to emphasize that Della Martin's impoverished condition and inability to secure her own alternative transportation was irrelevant. "The poor are entitled to avail of the facilities of public carriers upon the payment of the public rate," the court announced, "and are not required to have an additional sum to provide against the consequences of a breach of the contract of carriage."[71] In this groundbreaking opinion, the court used Martin's case to issue a broader ruling about the duties and obligations of bus carriers.

For Della Martin, this sum of money was significant. Mississippi embodied the worst of Jim Crow segregation and disenfranchisement, and yet the Supreme Court of Mississippi awarded her $1,925 and ruled that the bus line was obligated to convey her to her destination. This decision demonstrated respect of Della Martin as a person, taking into account her status as a pregnant woman, her labor as a mother, and her indigent condition. But at the same time that this decision expressed care and attention toward Martin, it did not address any of the structural systems of Jim Crow that implicitly created her conditions of poverty and discrimination. As the legal historian Dylan Penningroth notes, "Before the civil rights movement, winning a tort suit showed the world that Black people's lives had value, that whites might have to pay for what they did."[72]

Although it was not widely covered in the press, one newspaper did report on the case. Under the headline "Poor Have Rights That Cannot Be Denied," a newspaper article in the *Commercial Appeal*—a newspaper in Memphis, Tennessee—profiled the case. The article discussed the fact that in this case, the Supreme Court of Mississippi upheld the rights of an impoverished woman.[73] The Jackson, Mississippi, *Daily Clarion-Ledger* summarized the case under the headline "Rights of Traveler."[74] In bringing this tort suit to court, Della Martin expanded the rights of travelers and put the burden on the bus industry to uphold those rights.

Martin was fortunate that Justice Griffith wrote the opinion. A native of Lawrence County, Mississippi, he was born in 1875, two years before the stunning interracial experiment of Reconstruction ended. Coming of age in the era of Reconstruction's slow demise might have informed his attitude about race relations. Griffith attended law school at the University of Mississippi. After practicing law and serving as a chancery judge, he was elected to the Mississippi Supreme Court in 1929. In 1936, just two years before he ruled in the Della Martin bus case, Griffith was part of a very controversial decision, *Brown v. Mississippi*. In it, three poor African American men who labored as sharecroppers were accused of murdering a white planter. The men confessed to the alleged murder while undergoing brutal physical torture. A white mob hung one man from a tree to force his confession, while the other two men were bent over chairs and whipped with a leather strap studded with metal buckles. While enduring these brutal beatings, the three men confessed to the crime. Earl Brewer, the former governor of Mississippi, questioned whether these men had experienced due process. The case traveled to the Supreme Court of Mississippi. A truly bizarre legal team of Brewer and two white lawyers recruited by the NAACP tried the case. In their ruling, the justices maintained that the three men had received due process and should be convicted and receive the death penalty. But Virgil A. Griffith issued a sharp dissent, in which he critiqued the barbarous practices.[75] The case traveled to the United States Supreme Court, and the justices overturned the conviction, contending that law enforcement was not permitted to use force to extract a voluntary confession.[76]

Even though he presided over such high-profile cases, Justice Griffith also heard quieter ones, like the one waged by Della Martin. This was a pure stroke of luck for Martin. While Justice Griffith was indeed a white Southerner, he had developed a reputation for racial fairness, and perhaps even empathy for the plight of African Americans in his home state, and he displayed that sense of judicial equity in his dealings with Martin.

In the 1930s, Della Martin was not the only Black woman who found herself stranded in an unfamiliar location. In 1938, Linnie Eaddy, a Black woman in South Carolina, experienced a similar situation. Eaddy had been born and raised in Florence, South Carolina, but had married and migrated with her husband to New York City, where she labored as a cleaner at Mount Sinai Hospital. In March 1938, Linnie Eaddy returned to South Carolina to introduce her new baby to her extended family. On March 27, 1938, Eaddy, accompanied by her four-month-old infant, purchased a bus ticket to transport her from Marion, South Carolina, to Scranton, South Carolina, with a stop in Florence. She bought the ticket from the Greensboro-Fayetteville Bus Lines. The initial trip was uneventful, but when the bus wheeled into Florence, she had to disembark and wait for the next bus. When the bus finally arrived, she boarded with her infant and handed over her ticket and luggage to the driver. By this point it was getting dark, and she realized that she was unfamiliar with the area. After some time, when she thought she heard the driver announce "Scranton," she departed the bus with her baby and luggage. She had been let out at a gas station operated by white people, and after making an inquiry, Eaddy realized that she was in Effingham, not Scranton. It was pouring down rain, very cold, and darkness had descended. Linnie Eaddy was alone in a strange place with her four-month-old baby. Walking through the streets, she knocked on the door of a house, and a Black woman answered. After Eaddy explained the situation, the woman provided towels for Eaddy and her baby, and determined that they would need to catch a train to Scranton.

She knocked on the door of her neighbor, a white man, who gave Eaddy his lantern so that she could flag down the train. Because of the kindness of these two strangers—one white and one Black—Eaddy was able to board a train and travel to her brother's house. But because she and her baby had been exposed to the torrential rain and cold, they were both sick for several weeks after. Once they returned to New York City, they both needed medical care.[77]

Eaddy hired the white firm of McEachin & Townsend and sued the Greensboro-Fayetteville Bus Lines, alleging negligence in depositing her in the wrong place in the elements when her ticket specifically listed Scranton, not Effingham, as her final destination. Here Eaddy relied on a script similar to Della Martin's. The bus driver had stranded her in an unfamiliar location. But as a litigant, Eaddy had to navigate a more complicated personal history than Martin. Eaddy had chosen to migrate from South Carolina to New York City, which might have generated hostility in the Southern bar. As a result, Eaddy strategically tapped into gendered stereotypes about women's geographic illiteracy to explain the confusion about her destination. In her testimony, she emphasized the kindness of the two strangers she encountered: one Black woman and one white man who generously gave her a lantern so she could flag down the train. These details made her more sympathetic to the jury and demonstrated that she appreciated the hospitality of the Jim Crow South. When white Southerners heard these details, they waxed poetic about the kindness and hospitality, not the violence and brutality, of the Jim Crow South. In court, a jury awarded Eaddy $100 in actual damages and $400 in punitive damages. In response, the Greensboro-Fayetteville Bus Lines appealed the decision to the Supreme Court of South Carolina, arguing that the award of punitive damages was "improper and excessive." The Supreme Court of South Carolina affirmed the awarding of both actual and punitive damages, holding that "the driver of the bus carrier clearly owed a duty to the passenger, and he breached that duty when he permitted the passenger to exit the bus which was not her destination in the night and while it was raining." The court also ruled that "there was a carrier-passenger relationship, and the driver breached his duty."[78] This ruling, then, demonstrated that Linnie Eaddy was like any other passenger who deserved equal treatment by carriers. While not an enormous amount of money, it affirmed Eaddy's rights as a customer, even though she was now a resident of New York City, not South Carolina. Unlike Della Martin, Eaddy did not have major injuries, which helps to explain the smaller amount of money she received.

Not only did Black women sue for being deposited in the wrong location, but in very delicate ways, they contested bus drivers' use of force. In 1938, Olivia Shankle sued her bus driver in tort for assault, alleging that he had punched her in the face in DeRidder, Louisiana. Like many others, she signaled that she needed to depart the bus, but he ignored her. After a conflict, the bus driver punched her in the face. She received some compensation, but on appeal, the First Circuit Court of Appeals of Louisiana agreed that she should receive more money. Writing for the court, Judge Samuel A. LeBlanc noted that Sam Brickley's "attack" on Olivia Shankle was inappropriate. While Shankle's reactions may have been "irritating," he emphasized the power imbalance between a Black woman and the white Southern bus driver. He also highlighted Shankle's respectability, describing her as a woman of "good reputation," and lamented that this incident had caused her "considerable embarrassment, humiliation, and mental suffering."[79]

The decision of the First Circuit Court of Appeals in favor of Olivia Shankle epitomized the radical possibilities of tort law. Even though the court did not weigh in on the inequalities that existed in Shankle's life—such as disenfranchisement, her employment in a segregated school, and her lack of electoral representation—he did acknowledge her subjective experience as a Black woman and both the physical and emotional violence she sustained at the hands of the bus driver. Regardless of her race, it was wrong for a large bus driver to attack a woman. This case bore a striking resemblance to Laura Fischer's case in Indiana in 1927, over ten years earlier, when a white judge had also faulted a bus driver for attacking a Black woman. Laura Fischer was awarded $500 and the bus driver served time in jail. But Laura Fischer was able to hire a Black lawyer and make race explicit in her lawsuit, whereas Olivia Shankle had to delicately state her injuries without acknowledging the racist and misogynist undertones that undergirded this act. She had to file this lawsuit as a Black woman who willingly sat in the back of the bus yet felt a claim of injustice. She, like Fischer, received $500. But if Shankle had filed her suit on claims of racism or segregation, her lawsuit would have been dismissed immediately. Juxtaposing the cases of Laura Fischer and Olivia Shankle demonstrates that while it was possible for Black women to receive justice from the bus industry through the courts, region very much dictated the types of lawsuits that they waged.

One year after Shankle sued Tri-State Transit Company, another Black woman brought an injury lawsuit against a bus driver. In 1939, Jennie Bibbs Didlick, a teacher at the Booker T. Washington High School, was riding a Southeastern Greyhound bus in her home state of Kentucky on a trip from

Winchester to Lexington. When she boarded, she had taken a seat near the back, but when the white driver ordered her to sit in the rear, she refused. The driver grabbed her briefcase, jostled her arm, and shoved her off the bus. Didlick decided to sue the bus company. She hired a white lawyer who called on white witnesses to testify on her behalf. One white witness described how terrible it was for a white male bus driver to assault a Black woman passenger. Didlick knew this lawyer because he had previously employed her father. Her lawyer made two key points in the case. First, Kentucky was one of the states that had never amended its state constitution to mandate bus segregation, making the bus driver's actions illegal. And second, he emphasized the viewpoint of a white witness: The bus driver's rough handling had caused Jennie Bibbs Didlick bodily harm. The suit was successful. Although she sued for $2,500, she received only $200, which she split evenly with her lawyer.[80]

Even though Didlick's damages were small, her case demonstrated the ways that she was able to use the law to receive a bit of justice for her experience. For Didlick, it was precisely her relationship with white Southerners that was critical to the victory in her case. Her father, Ben Bibbs, had labored as a tobacco worker in a warehouse in Lexington, Kentucky, and later as a janitor.[81] At some point, he had worked for a white lawyer, and Didlick was able to draw on that personal connection to help her litigate the case. In addition, she was able to ask fellow white passengers on the bus to testify on her behalf. For Didlick, these two sets of connections with white Kentuckians were critical to her legal victory. While $200 was not very much, this case demonstrated the change that had taken place. Consider that nine years earlier another teacher, Lucille Brumfield, had sued for racial segregation in Kentucky and lost. For Jennie Bibbs Didlick, suing for personal injury—not segregation—translated to a more favorable legal outcome and a small amount of money in recognition of the trauma and racial violence that she had experienced.

In their lawsuits, Black women cited not only bus drivers' violence but also their negligence. In the late 1930s, Fannie Grant, a laundress, was riding on a municipal bus in Baton Rouge.[82] When it was her turn to depart, she signaled to the bus driver that she wanted to get off the bus. But the driver failed to bring the bus to a complete stop and the door closed on her dress, causing her to fall to the street. The bus company claimed that Grant was clumsy. When the case went to trial, both sides called Black and white witnesses, who offered conflicting reports on the events. Ultimately, a jury awarded her $1,554, citing loss of wages, expenses, and funds for "physical pain, mental anguish, and suffering." The trial judge, John Hugo Dore, reduced her award to $753.[83] But even though Judge Dore lowered her damages, he did not question her injuries.[84]

In addition to suing for personal injury, Black women filed lawsuits to recover lost luggage. In September 1936, Marie Peterson, a twenty-three-year-old teacher in Memphis, was visiting Birmingham, Alabama. She purchased a bus ticket on the Dixie Greyhound Lines to transport her back to Tennessee.[85] When she boarded the bus, she handed the driver her handbag and fur coat and took a seat in the back. When the bus wheeled into Carbondale, Alabama, the driver announced a ten-minute rest stop, which was not on the trip's itinerary. Peterson departed the bus and walked to a café. When she returned five minutes later, the bus had left the station. She was able to procure another ticket to Memphis, and the bus company recovered her bag, but not her coat. Dixie Greyhound refused to refund her. Angry at the loss, Peterson hired a Black attorney, Augustus Arvus Latting, and sued Dixie Greyhound for fifty dollars.[86] Attorney Latting argued that "bus companies, like railroad companies, are common carriers and are liable as insurers for baggage placed in their exclusive custody and control." Even though the stakes in this case could not have been lower—a sum of fifty dollars centered around a fur coat—both sides took this lawsuit seriously. Dixie Greyhound hired four white lawyers to defend the company, contending that the bus company was responsible only for driver negligence, not a loss of luggage. Latting argued that the company had an obligation to refund Peterson's personal items. In a Tennessee lower court, Judge George B. Coleman ruled in favor of Peterson and awarded her $32.50 in damages.[87] Dissatisfied, Greyhound appealed the decision to the Tennessee Court of Appeals. The court contended that because Marie Peterson had not checked her bag, the bus line was not necessarily liable for this lost item. But the court also ruled that because the driver had failed to announce that the bus was departing early from the rest stop, the company had become the insurer of the coat and was responsible for its return.[88] The Tennessee Court of Appeals ruled in favor of Marie Peterson and sustained the amount awarded in damages.[89]

For African Americans living across the country, Marie Peterson's lawsuit marked a tremendous victory, demonstrating that a Black woman passenger could sue for the loss of luggage in a Southern court with a Black attorney. An article in the *Chicago Defender* celebrated Peterson's successful verdict, noting that her case resonated with thousands of Black passengers who had similar experiences in segregated accommodations. The article termed it "refreshing" that Peterson's all-Black legal team had bravely challenged Dixie Greyhound's legal counsel before two white judges. Neither Marie Peterson nor her African American lawyer called on any white witnesses. Instead, Peterson offered her "uncorroborated testimony."[90] It is equally noteworthy that Dixie Greyhound spent hundreds of dollars in litigation costs over a fur coat, demonstrating that the bus industry worked at every moment to undermine and contradict its Black passengers.[91] But not all Black women were successful in challenging the bus industry in their lawsuits.

Invisible Injuries: Lawsuits That Failed

Beginning in the late 1930s, some Black women began to experience setbacks in their tort lawsuits. In 1939, Lou Owens, a Black woman in her sixties, boarded a bus in Shreveport, Louisiana, to travel to Mansfield, a nearby city.[92] During the course of the trip, the bus drove near a road grader. When the driver sharply pulled the bus onto the shoulder, Owens was thrown off her seat, hit her head, and lost consciousness. She attributed this injury to recklessness on the part of the driver, claiming that he was driving at a high speed despite the unevenness of the road and the presence of debris. She hired a white attorney, J. D. Barksdale, to defend her. Even though Owens may have suffered specific injuries, she had a weak case. She did not present testimony from any physicians who may have treated her injuries, and no Black or white witnesses were willing to corroborate her story. Plus, as a woman in her sixties, she was no longer working, making her injuries less compelling. These factors might have explained why she lost the case, both in the First Judicial District Court and then in the Court of Appeals of Louisiana for the Second Circuit. The court concluded that Owens did not prove negligence.[93]

In 1941, a Black woman named Rosa Valdry sued the Baton Rouge Bus Company for a sum of $4,000. In 1940, Valdry had boarded a Baton Rouge bus to visit the dentist for a postoperative procedure. The bus started to move forward as she was moving to a seat in the rear, causing a major "jerk." Valdry crashed against a seat, which had an iron rod sticking out of it, and hurt her back. Even though she called out that she was injured, the bus driver did not hear or respond. When she arrived at her job as a domestic worker, she was in crippling pain. The Baton Rouge Bus Company dispatched its company physician, Dr. T. Jeff McHugh, who treated Valdry on four separate occasions. He determined that her injuries were related to her recent dental surgery, not her incident on the bus. Despite the fact that Valdry's white employer and her brother and sister testified to her injuries, the First Circuit of the Court of Appeals in Louisiana sided with the bus company and elected not to award Valdry any damages.[94]

Rosa Valdry was not the only one to receive a setback in Baton Rouge, Louisiana. When Leathy Hughes boarded her bus, she deposited her fare and began to walk down the aisle. Suddenly, the driver lurched the bus forward, and she fell onto one of the seats where there was a metal bar, causing immediate back pain. When she eventually returned to her home, she limped to bed and was subsequently admitted to the Charity Hospital in New Orleans for her injuries. She sued the Baton Rouge Electric Company for $3,500, charging negligence on the part of the driver. The court sided with the bus company, and she also lost on appeal, though since Hughes was poor, the court ruled that she did not have to pay court fees.[95] The decision, however, was not unanimous. In his dissent, Judge Ott sided with Hughes, pointing out patterns of negligence that he discerned on the part of the bus driver.[96] These three defeats demonstrate that the courts could be discerning about injuries and that the bus industry and their legal teams worked hard to avoid paying costly fees. Even though these three women lost their cases, it was during this period that Black women litigants secured over $10,000 in damages from the bus industry.

$10,617.50: Making Sense of These Cases

Between 1931 and 1943, Black women filed fifteen strategic lawsuits against the bus industry in Southern courtrooms, winning twelve cases and losing three. In total, Black women received $10,617.50 in damages from the bus industry, although they had to pay their attorneys and court fees. Nonetheless, especially for poor women like Della Martin, Jessie Garner, and Alma Porter, damages of over $1,000 represented a tremendous amount of money. Conversely, Black women in the Jim Crow North received only $2,860 in damages for their lawsuits, demonstrating that torts offered an excellent legal avenue to hold the bus industry accountable.

In the broad canvas of race relations and civil rights, these cases were rather narrow in scope. They did not integrate the bus industry, and they did little to alter the behaviors of white bus drivers. In addition, the money that the white bus industry had to pay did not transform the political economy of the Jim Crow South. These were not reparations; they were damages. These cases demonstrate that while Black women were always pressing against systems of white supremacy and racial violence during the early civil rights movement, systemic change was nearly impossible to achieve in the absence of major court rulings, mass mobilization, and growing support among white power players, whether locally, nationally, or internationally.

While these cases did not jump-start the modern Black freedom struggle, they registered a significant impact on both the bus industry and the Jim Crow legal system. First and foremost, the bus industry paid attention to these tort lawsuits. *Bus Transportation* began publishing a legal column, which reported news about various court decisions. The trade journal covered the personal injury lawsuits filed by three Black women plaintiffs—Leathy Hughes, Olivia Shankle, and Rosa Valdry—but did not disclose the race of the litigants, demonstrating that it was the content of the case that mattered, not the racial classification.[97] Even though the bus industry did not desire the patronage of Black women passengers or exercise a tremendous amount of care in their transportation, these decisions forced the industry to pay attention to the details of the cases in order to avoid further lawsuits. Interestingly, rather than simply settling out of court, the industry chose to litigate these cases and, when dissatisfied with the decision, appeal them, which ended up costing thousands of dollars in lawyer fees.

These decisions also registered an impact on the Jim Crow legal system. Through her lawsuit, Olivia Shankle forced Judge Samuel LeBlanc to remark that the bus driver's violence was unacceptable. In no other context in the Jim Crow South would it have been permissible for a white man to denounce this type of violence against a Black woman. Cumulatively, these appellate cases ruled that buses must transport poor passengers to their final destinations, that buses were responsible for upholding racial segregation, and that buses must compensate passengers for lost luggage. This evidence attests to the far-reaching impact of Black women's lawsuits in the South, demonstrating that the bus industry was indeed paying attention to these lawsuits. The historian Dylan Penningroth argues that African Americans' "legal activity helped shape legal institutions, practices, and doctrines."[98] Through these lawsuits, Black women carved out a space in the Jim Crow South where they could seek justice in the deeply unjust bus industry. Black women in the South recognized that they would never receive a victory like Laura Fischer or Paulina Stevens had. Instead, they worked within the constrained, racially coded system of the Jim Crow South to force the buses and courts to reckon with their humanity as passengers and their expectations as paying customers. It was in the relatively neutral space of a courtroom—not the corporate headquarters of Greyhound or even the offices of the NAACP—that bus companies were compelled to pay attention to the law. Through their personal injury lawsuits, African American women not only forced bus companies to pay them damages but also invited white judges to grapple with the nature of injury, their vulnerable status in the Jim Crow South, and the fragility of their bodies.

When the United States entered World War II, the color line on buses reached a critical tipping point. In the Jim Crow South—marked by the rise of Black military bases, internal migrations, and a racially tense climate—buses became even more fraught. In Southern states, white bus drivers, soldiers, and military police escalated their attacks on Black women passengers. This violence became so entrenched and quotidian that Black women filed fewer lawsuits for personal injury. But in the North, Midwest, and Washington metropolitan region, African American women continued to wage lawsuits around segregation and civil rights. Drawing on the lessons they learned from the verdicts in the 1930s and 1940s, African Americans brought the issue of bus segregation to courts at the appellate and federal levels, and they won. And unlike the legal outcomes for Jessie Lee Garner, Sadie Patillo, and Ellen Harris, these victories were not hollow ones but in fact based on the injustice of segregation. These cases even convinced the US Supreme Court to rule on interstate bus segregation in the landmark case *Morgan v. Virginia*. Chapters 5 and 6 investigate African American women's chaotic, surprising, and ultimately history-making experiences on buses during World War II.

Part III The War on the Bus

We want a statement and justice if we are Americans. Anyone of us may be beat-up by these very same people who are supposed to protect us—namely, the police and bus drivers, who carry guns. In fact, right thru in here any Negro woman, other Negro army nurses may be attacked and pommeled unless the government we are trying to support gives us the protection a woman deserves as a birthright.

—Tuskegee Nurses to the Attorney General, Alabama, 1942

"Colored Woman Wins Civil Rights Verdict"

—*St. Joseph News-Press*, February 17, 1944, about Maggie Mack's case against Dixie Greyhound in Missouri

5 If We Are Americans

Black Women and Bus Violence in Deep South World War II

In September 1942, 2nd Lt. Norma L. Green, a twenty-eight-year-old trained nurse, was exhausted. Green had been working hard days and long nights at the Tuskegee Medical Hospital in Alabama, treating men who were training to be pilots. She was miles away from her home. Like thousands of Black soldiers, nurses, and war workers, this global conflict had pulled her from her home in Richmond, Virginia, and planted her on military bases in the Deep South. She was first stationed at Camp Livingston in Louisiana, then transferred to Tuskegee, Alabama. Both states were dangerous, notorious for their reputations of racial and sexual violence against Black women.[1] At Tuskegee, Black military personnel labored under the command of Col. Frederick von Kimble, who enforced strict policies of racial segregation in the base's dormitories and dining facilities, engendering feelings of low morale.[2] Adding to her mounting stress level, her supervisor had informed her that she was being deployed overseas to Liberia as part of the first Black medical unit to travel abroad.

Green had planned a shopping trip to the neighboring city of Montgomery. Since canteens on military bases did not carry Black hair products, it is possible that the army's requirements for straight hair motivated this excursion. Day after day, newspapers reported cases of white bus drivers harassing Black soldiers in uniform, which is perhaps why she elected to wear civilian clothes. Tucking a roll of cash into her purse, Green purchased a round-trip Greyhound bus ticket to Montgomery on Saturday morning. After she completed her shopping, she walked to the bus station in order to travel back to the hospital. She slipped into her seat and waited for the bus to pull out of the station. Norma Green was a light-skinned woman, and when she first boarded the bus, the driver thought she was white. But when he discovered that she was Black, he immediately demanded that she exit the bus. Green protested, explaining that she needed to return to Tuskegee for her afternoon shift and could not be late. The armed bus driver called the police and, within minutes, a white officer appeared. Tears welled in Norma Green's eyes as the white officer arrested her, shoving her into a police car with four other officers who waited there hungrily. In the car ride to the station, the five officers beat Norma Green mercilessly, leaving her with a black eye, a broken nose, and cracked ribs. Her cries of terror and fright became fainter and fainter and then silent, as she lost consciousness. The officers threw her into a jail cell in Montgomery, where they stole $100 from her purse, doused her body with a bottle of whiskey, and cradled her fingers around the empty flask. There was not a hint of subtlety in their actions. These white police officers were determined to evade responsibility by perpetuating a false narrative about Black women and criminality, framing her as a drunken delinquent rather than a military nurse working to fight Nazism and fascism.[3] A seemingly banal conflict over a bus seat in Montgomery, Alabama, had escalated into state violence against a Black woman lieutenant in the army.

When Norma Green regained consciousness, police officers charged her with disorderly conduct. After she informed them that she was, in fact, an army nurse, they released her at three o'clock the next morning. A group of nurses from Tuskegee drove to Montgomery and brought Green back to the hospital.[4] Her injuries were so severe that she spent a week recovering before she was deployed overseas. The white administration at Tuskegee issued strict orders to the staff, warning them not to disclose any information about Green's condition. It took twelve days for the Black press to report the story. The *Atlanta Daily World* first broke the news of Norma Green's assault, prompting Black activists and ordinary citizens living across the country to politicize her case and press the Department of Justice *and* the War Department to conduct formal investigations into the attack. Green's experiences with bus segregation and racial violence in Montgomery, Alabama, occurred thirteen years before Rosa Parks would famously refuse to give up her seat, leading to the Montgomery Bus Boycott. Norma Green's arrest and assault demonstrate how the wartime climate triangulated bus segregation as the federal government became a complicit actor in the South's racist transportation system.

World War II brought the deep state to the Deep South. By the 1940s, Alabama, Florida, Georgia, South Carolina, and Virginia had all granted bus drivers police powers, allowing them to carry guns and conduct citizen's arrests.[5] Even though the drivers were not formally deputized as officers of the peace, the Black press began to report on the escalating violence of bus drivers, who at times enforced racial segregation with bullets, pistols, belts, and blackjacks. During World War II, white bus drivers shot many Black male soldiers and harassed and assaulted thousands of African Americans, whether they were military personnel, industrial war workers, or ordinary passengers. Not only did bus drivers escalate their tactics as the war strained the South's transportation systems, but hundreds of thousands of white soldiers and white military officers streamed into the region. The military mobilized its own police unit, the military police (MP), who patrolled military bases, buses, and trains. MPs often, but not always, worked in tandem with bus drivers to enforce segregation in conflicts that arose over bus seats. In this tense wartime climate, white bus drivers, white civilian officers, and white MPs formed a dangerous triumvirate of powerful men to harass, surveil, and assault Black passengers. During World War II, buses in the Jim Crow South became proto-jails.

World War II marked a transformative era in the bus industry. During World War I, buses were in their infancy stages, and the government had largely relied on automobiles and trains for transportation. But by World War II, buses had become a vital instrument in the government's wartime strategy. Once the United States entered World War II, the government made transportation a federal priority. On December 18, President Franklin D. Roosevelt signed Executive Order 8989, which created the Office of Defense Transportation (ODT) to oversee the nation's rail, road, and water transportation industries. He appointed Joseph B. Eastman, a member of the Interstate Commerce Commission, to direct the ODT. As a government agency, the ODT coordinated transportation for the US military and industrial war production while also convincing civilians to ride trains and buses instead of driving individual cars. By 1941, thirty-three million passenger cars and trucks were on the road, and asking ordinary Americans to conserve the nation's rubber by riding public transportation instead of driving cars was a challenging position.[6] Eastman issued a public statement asking citizens in the United States to consider changing their travel plans. Specifically, he advised that American citizens should not participate in any "meetings, conventions, or group tours that were not closely related to the war effort." While he did not ban vacations altogether, he strongly urged citizens to consider riding trains and buses to reach their destinations.[7] And Eastman recognized that transportation was a crucial ingredient in the United States' success in the war. "We must have driver and mechanics for essential motor transport," Eastman stated, arguing that they were "as vital to the war effort as soldiers and sailors."[8] With this statement, then, the government urged all Americans—including Black women—to ride the bus as part of their patriotic participation in the war effort, thereby making the federal government even more of a complicit actor in bus segregation during this period.

The exigencies of wartime industrial production shut down most bus manufacturing. Interstate companies, such as Greyhound, ran older buses or purchased tractor trailers and converted them into "victory buses." These large vehicles could accommodate forty-five seated passengers and fifty standing passengers.[9] Not only were more Americans clamoring to ride a limited supply of buses, but gasoline rations meant that vehicles had to slow to a speed of thirty-five on the highway, which made trips take longer.[10]

Black women experienced heightened bus violence in cities and towns throughout the Deep South. As residents of the region, Black women passengers witnessed the everyday brutality that was meted out to soldiers, nurses, and military persons in the war. This racially charged environment created a culture of fear for all African Americans, and these feelings were heightened on buses—vehicles that had to travel at a slower pace to ration gasoline; that were overloaded with passengers; and that employed bus drivers who enforced the color line with blackjacks, guns, and brute force. Black women from all walks of life encountered this mounting bus violence, stretching from elite teachers and domestic servants to mothers and schoolgirls. Many were brand-new bus riders, as the war had prompted thousands of Black women to migrate from rural areas and move into cities and towns to labor as domestic servants, making bus commutes a daily necessity.

Black women passengers articulated many different responses to the unrelenting violence and abuse that erupted on buses during World War II. Some merely accepted that harassment and assault were an everyday part of bus travel in the Deep South. Others demanded answers, whether it was asking their white employers to contact bus lines or pressing federal agencies to investigate high-profile cases. A few Black women alerted the National Association for the Advancement of Colored People (NAACP) about the worsening climate or gave chilling accounts to Black newspapers.

Many Black women riders fought back. During the 1920s and 1930s, some Southern Black women had relied on a strategy of respectable Southern citizenship in their battles against bus violence and abuse, filing lawsuits for personal injury that traveled to the appellate level and resulted, at times, in life-changing amounts of money. In these lawsuits, most Black women had strategically constructed themselves as upstanding citizens who deliberately followed racial segregation laws and still sustained physical injuries at the hands of bus drivers and vehicles. But during World War II, the climate shifted. Bus drivers escalated their violence, the white military descended on the Deep South, and, as the nation fought a war against

Nazism and fascism, most Southern Black women did not receive *any* of the wartime benefits accorded to other marginalized groups.[11] Southern white women secured higher-paying jobs in wartime industries to advance their economic prospects, while thousands of Black male soldiers used military service as an instrument of citizenship. Even if Black women were directly tied to the state—as nurses, Women's Army Corp (WAC) members, or soldiers' wives—neither the federal government nor Southern state governments deemed Black women worthy of safety and protection.[12] Black women's exclusion from wartime labor opportunities and most military service inspired them to adopt a much more militant and combative demeanor on the bus. Black women and girls cursed at bus drivers, fought back against white passengers, and armed themselves with blackjacks, nail files, pistols, screwdrivers, and umbrellas as protection in bus conflicts. Black women absorbed the daily collective abuses of this racist Southern climate and wove it into their resistance on the bus, using their words and bodies to articulate pointed political critiques of bus driver violence, the wartime economy, and the profound degradation of their lives in this heightened moment of conflict.

While many historians have written about Black male soldiers' experiences with the bus industry during World War II, most have neglected to discuss Black women.[13] Few scholars have recognized that Black women *also* encountered similar types of violence and hostility. An investigation of racialized and gendered practices on buses during World War II demonstrates that drivers seized on the violent policing tactics they had perfected on Black women passengers and applied them to Black male soldiers and Black women war workers, nurses, civil servants, and soldiers' wives, sometimes to deadly ends. This chapter chronicles Black women's war on the bus in cities and towns throughout the Deep South, defined as North Carolina, South Carolina, Tennessee, Texas, Alabama, Georgia, Mississippi, and Florida. In these states, many Black women expressed their political opinions through their behavior on wartime buses. Through their actions—whether it was refusing to abide by racial segregation, cursing at drivers and passengers, or defending themselves against violence—Black women critiqued their exclusions from wartime industrial service; their relegation to domestic labor; and their overpolicing at the hands of bus drivers, military police, and police officers. By protesting their "place" on the bus, Black women vented their heightened frustrations with their servile position in the Southern economy and their second-class citizenship in the United States. These everyday practices of resistance formed a crucial instrument in Black women's survival in Deep South cities and towns during World War II.[14]

We *Can't* Do It: Racism and Sexism in the Wartime South

In 1943, newspapers in Alabama reported that the Bechtel-McCone-Parsons Corporation would open an aircraft modification center in Birmingham and employ twenty-two thousand workers. Notably, officials announced that thirteen thousand of those jobs would go to women. Gathering in a mass meeting at the Sixth Avenue Baptist Church, 1,300 Black women expressed their desire to labor at this factory and help build airplanes for the war. But these aspiring war workers quickly learned that all the jobs designated for women workers would go to white women. The company planned to institute a training program for a hundred Black workers, but it limited participation to men.[15] Even though this news was disappointing, it was not especially surprising. Factories throughout the Deep South did not envision Black women as part of the wartime industrial labor force.

During World War II, Black women witnessed how the categories of manhood, womanhood, Blackness, and whiteness mapped onto the political economy of the Deep South. As the region's economic landscape pivoted to wartime production, hundreds of thousands of men were drafted into the military while thousands of Black men and white women streamed into well-paying wartime industrial jobs. Not only were white women recruited into wartime labor positions, but as new workers, they were also afforded racialized patriarchal protections from violence. Opportunities and privileges abounded for white women in the South, while for Black women, doors of economic possibility slammed shut.[16] Very few Southern industries—including shipyards and defense plants—ever hired Black women workers. The historian Karen Tucker Anderson notes that wartime industries in the South were perpetually understaffed precisely because they preferred labor shortages to hiring Black women. Anderson concludes that World War II did not significantly disrupt the South's labor practices.[17] When Black women felt a glimmer of hope that they could obtain a wartime job, they fought relentlessly because these jobs would be life changing. Even the most menial jobs in wartime industries paid more than domestic service.[18] But few Black women ever successfully reached these industrial positions, and most prospective job seekers in the South were turned away. When a Black woman in Memphis, Tennessee, wrote to the mayor inquiring about war labor opportunities, he replied that there were no positions beyond domestic labor.[19]

There were even reports that industrial managers who refused to hire Black women in factories offered them jobs to work as maids for their wives, a deeply insulting but not uncommon phenomenon.[20] It was only in the North and West where Black women workers achieved a modicum of wartime labor opportunities.

There were several reasons why Black women were excluded from wartime industries. Southern industrial plants preferred to hire Black men. In Southern factories, Black men had already been laboring as janitors and cleaners, so it was logical for these factories to promote Black men to technical and advanced positions rather than hire Black women workers.[21] Factories also reasoned that white women would refuse to work alongside Black women. Some employers and politicians even intimated that Black women had venereal diseases and could infect white workers.[22] Even though Black women could report cases of racism to the Fair Employment Practices Committee (FEPC), this government office was understaffed, had a meager budget, and was ineffective in combating discrimination in the South.[23] And the Women's Bureau never hired a Black woman to investigate labor discrimination during the war.[24] Black women in the Deep South had every reason to be skeptical about their prospects for economic advancement or first-class citizenship, and these feelings of cynicism only worsened as the war progressed.

As Southern white women poured into higher-paying industrial jobs in the Deep South, they left lower-paying jobs in domestic service, altering the region's economic landscape. This labor vacuum prompted 50 percent of Black women working in rural areas to migrate during the war. Some Black women relocated to Northern states, but many moved to the urban South, where they became domestic servants for white families, trading one exploitative employer for another.[25] In most cases, these new domestic servants had to ride city buses to travel to white neighborhoods. Even though Black women were confined to the back of the bus, they had a front-row seat to the vicious, if quotidian, violence that was now part of everyday life in the Deep South. Black women's departure from rural areas was so significant that farmers in the Carolinas, Georgia, and Alabama recruited Barbadian workers to perform agricultural labor.[26] While most Black women in the Deep South continued to work as domestic servants during the war, a small number served in the military as nurses or WACs, laboring in segregated bases and hospitals. Military canteens on these bases carried white women's hair products but nothing for Black women. To conform to military regulation, Black women in the military had to travel by bus to neighboring cities to access the hair products that they would need, which created even more opportunities for Black women to experience abuse and assault.

For all Black women living in the Deep South, World War II marked a moment of startling visceral contradictions. Every day—in white newspapers, magazines, and wartime reels—Black women were greeted with images of white women performing industrial labor in the war effort. As Black women gazed at these smiling women who were valued for their important contributions, they knew that their race and sex excluded them from these high-paying jobs. White women experienced an elevation in their labor, while Black women faced a degradation. Even Black newspapers perpetuated these contradictions. Articles in the *Birmingham Daily World* celebrated Black women's achievements during World War II but highlighted women who left the South and received wartime jobs in industry or the government. All of Black women's civil rights victories during World War II—whether it was becoming bus drivers and streetcar conductors or waging successful lawsuits against racial segregation—occurred outside the Deep South.[27] Articles in the Black press touted the Double V campaign, in which African Americans supported the war effort abroad but simultaneously pressed for civil rights on the home front.[28] It was only outside the Deep South where Black women were able to point to concrete change in terms of the Double V campaign. Black and white press coverage offered daily reminders that some women were making wartime breakthroughs, but never Black women in the Deep South.

The Southern bus industry hired white women in a range of positions throughout the war.[29] Municipal bus companies tapped white women to work as drivers and announcers, stationed at the front of the bus.[30] There is no evidence that the Southern bus industry ever extended this same type of promotion to Black women. The most senior position a Black woman ever held in the Southern bus industry was as a manager. In Jackson, Tennessee, Naomi Clingman served as the manager for Greyhound's segregated waiting room, where she sold the *Chicago Defender*. This was an incredible act of defiance, and it is likely Greyhound's Southern executives were unaware that Clingman was selling a newspaper that offered weekly reports on the brutality of Greyhound and other bus lines during the war.[31]

As new residents of Southern cities and towns, Black women navigated the municipal bus system in a moment of heightened traffic congestion, chaos, and—most importantly—policing. The historian J. Mills Thornton contends that in the Deep South, key differences distinguished the rural areas from the cities and towns. Segregation was neither a "universal" nor a "uniform" system. It was enforced differently throughout the South depending on the demographics. In rural areas, white supremacy was the dominant racial system, while in towns, it was racial segregation. In rural places, African Americans were economically tied to white landowners, who maintained "social discipline" over Black agricultural workers, making power diffuse. But in cities and towns, this control was transferred to the police and, by extension, bus drivers, who surveilled Black women's everyday activities and enforced racial segregation with brute force.[32] As Black women moved from rural areas into Southern cities and towns, they encountered policing power and state power with more frequency. Since buses were now part of Black women's daily commutes, this power was clearly manifest in the interactions between white drivers and Black passengers.[33] And in the World War II period, buses in the Deep South had become potent symbols of white supremacy. The historian Robin D. G. Kelley argues that buses in the Jim Crow South—equipped with the signs and signifiers of white supremacy—represented "daily visual and aural reminders of the semicolonial status black people occupied in the Jim Crow South." Kelley notes that public transportation, "unlike most forms of public space, was an extension of the marketplace." Daily trips could be expensive, a significant consideration for working-class women. Kelley argues that Black passengers "experienced public transportation as a form of economic exploitation."[34] During World War II, Ella Baker served as the NAACP's director of branches, traveling throughout the South to recruit Black citizens into local NAACP chapters. Understanding that buses were dangerous and seething with tensions, she rode the train whenever possible.[35]

Not only were Black women exposed to more policing on buses in Southern cities and towns, but they also gained a bird's-eye view into the military as a site of brutal exploitation for African Americans. Beginning in the early 1940s, the government opened segregated training camps, military bases, and hospitals in the Deep South, making them literal tinderboxes of racial violence over the next four years. Eight of these important bases included Fort Benning near Columbus, Georgia; Camp Shelby in Hattiesburg, Mississippi; Fort Bragg in Fayetteville, North Carolina; Camp Hood near Killeen, Texas; Fort Jackson near Colombia, South Carolina; Camp Claiborne near Alexandria, Louisiana; Camp Blanding near Starke, Florida; and Fort Knox near Louisville, Kentucky.[36] Any Black women who lived near these bases or visited them would witness the horrible abuse of Black male soldiers who were stationed there—or experienced it themselves.

"The Race Question Is Getting Worse": The War on the Bus Begins

In April 1942, Myrtle Smith, a maid in Anniston, Alabama, noticed that her daily commute on the city bus was becoming a ride of terror. The bus driver frequently cursed at passengers, issued threats, and forced Black soldiers to stand rather than sit in the white section. In an act of desperation, she wrote a letter describing her experiences to the *Pittsburgh Courier.* Smith noted that the situation was becoming more "acute" and feared that it would soon be "impossible" for working-class Black Alabamians to ride buses because of the threatening and violent behavior of the bus driver.[37] Terrified for the safety of her life, she asked the editor to withhold her name. *Pittsburgh Courier* editor Robert L. Vann did not publish Smith's letter, but he did send it to the national office of the NAACP, alerting officials of something they already knew: that the situation on buses for Black civilians and soldiers was worsening, daily. In the coming year, African Americans throughout the Deep South would experience a surge in brutality, and nowhere was that stronger than in Alabama.

There were many reasons why Alabama developed a notorious reputation for violence. The state housed four Black training camps—at Fort McClellan, Brookley Army Air Field, Maxwell Field, and Tuskegee—bringing Black soldiers, nurses, and WACS from diverse parts of the United States into these segregated military bases. The state's wartime economic shifts prompted 25 percent of Alabama's Black residents to migrate from rural areas into the three big cities: Birmingham, Mobile, and Montgomery. Alabama was more urbanized than most Southern states, and all three cities had their own municipal bus lines, which created many opportunities for white male bus drivers to harass African Americans.[38] Between 1939 and 1943, Frank M. Dixon, a Democrat, served as governor. While every governor of Alabama ardently supported racial segregation, Dixon was noteworthy for his extreme positions.[39] In July 1942, Governor Dixon forbade state agencies from accepting wartime contracts that contained the nondiscrimination language of Executive Order 8802 because he feared that it would be enforced through the FEPC.[40] "The present emergency," Governor Dixon argued, "should not be used as a pretext to bring about the abolition of color lines in the South." Of course, wartime industries in no way threatened to dismantle the existing racial order. But Governor Dixon's profound hostility toward the empty language of nondiscrimination signaled the state's unrelenting racist climate, which was palpable on the state's buses.[41]

As World War II descended on Alabama, bus drivers attacked Black women riders with their uniforms and accessories. In June 1942, Hannah Coefield, a nineteen-year-old pregnant woman, was riding the bus home from a long day of work at a shirt factory in Montgomery, Alabama. When a white man boarded and asked for her seat, she refused to move. Enraged, the white bus driver grabbed his belt and beat Coefield while a white passenger pinned her to the ground. The driver then called the police, who arrested her, charging her with both disorderly conduct and inciting a riot. Newspaper articles remarked that the city's rapid population growth had created overcrowded conditions on the buses, and drivers were quick to use brute force. Even though it was obvious that this bus driver had brutally assaulted a Black pregnant woman, he was not charged.[42] Later that year, Mildred McAdory, an activist with the leftist Southern Negro Youth Congress, was traveling on a bus in Alabama, raising money for a tin can drive. A fellow rider grabbed the bus's "Colored" sign and placed it on a different compartment, presumably to create more space for Black passengers. When the bus driver interrogated McAdory about the incident, she refused to disclose who had moved the sign, and he invoked his powers as an officer of the peace to arrest her. Police officers boarded the bus, grabbed her, and beat her with a blackjack. The next morning, she was fined ten dollars.[43] These two examples demonstrate how bus drivers reflexively used belts and blackjacks as weapons against Black women passengers.

In addition to bus conflicts that were well chronicled in the Black press, incidents erupted that were only documented in the records of municipal bus companies. On city buses in Birmingham, tensions flared between Black passengers and white drivers. Only one year into the war, the city's population expanded by 13 percent, straining the Birmingham Electric Company, the city's local bus service. When the war erupted, many drivers were drafted, bringing in a cohort of new and inexperienced men. Additionally, the Birmingham Electric Company hired white women to stand in the front of the bus. Equipped with microphones, these women announced stops, eased the process of passenger boarding and exiting, and provided updates. A newspaper article praised these women for offering a "little old-fashioned southern courtesy."[44]

Black women passengers in Birmingham politicized the city's wartime climate on city buses. According to these transportation files, Black women often sat in the white section, requested to move seats, reported bus driver abuse to managers, and pushed aside white passengers who insulted them.[45] This tenor of resistance likely indicates that white bus drivers and passengers harassed Black women riders but also that Black women fought back, emboldened by the wartime climate, the unique demographic shifts in Birmingham, and possibly their new status as bus riders. This evidence demonstrates that Black women from all stations in life began to experience more abuse on buses throughout Alabama in the first year of the war. The company began to track these incidents, attributing them to a marked rise in passengers as well as charged resistance from "younger Negroes."[46] It is likely that many of these Black women riders were domestic servants, perhaps recent migrants to Birmingham who were unfamiliar with the coercive policing practices that existed on buses. Theophilus Eugene "Bull" Connor served as Birmingham's commissioner of public safety. The son of a train dispatcher, he would become the most notorious police chief in the country during the Black freedom struggle, famously deploying hoses and police dogs on civil rights activists. As the city's public safety commissioner, Connor monitored the mounting violence on buses and ordered that bus companies install boards to physically separate Black and white passengers.[47] Conflicts on the Birmingham Electric Company's buses surged, prompting the local chapter of the NAACP to meet with the bus line to ameliorate conditions for Black riders.[48]

Not only were buses dangerous sites for Black women civilians in the state, but they were also vicious for Black military personnel, including soldiers and nurses. In August 1942, white bus drivers shot *two* men in Alabama: Pvt. Henry Williams in Mobile and J. B. Butcher in Birmingham. Private Williams, a twenty-nine-year-old soldier, was stationed at Brookley Army Air Field in Mobile. He boarded a city bus and asked the driver, Grover E. Chandler, to help him with his luggage. This request annoyed Chandler, prompting him to punch Williams in the stomach. Chandler then grabbed his pistol and shot Williams three times in the head and neck, killing him instantly.[49] Even though police officers arrested Chandler, he was never charged with Williams's murder. Fifteen months later, Chandler enlisted at Camp Shelby, while Henry Williams's family searched for answers.[50] In the aftermath of Williams's murder, his sister, Mary S. Robinson, politicized his case. She wired Secretary of War Henry L. Stimson, "asking for an immediate and thorough investigation into the death" of her brother. Her husband, Grant Robinson, traveled to Mobile to investigate the facts of the case but was unable to learn anything more.[51] Only a few days after Private Williams's murder, a white bus driver shot J. B. Butcher, a Black civilian in Birmingham. When twenty-two-year-old Butcher boarded the bus, he dropped a dime in the fare box and demanded change. Enraged, the bus driver snapped at him. Butcher reached for his knife, but the driver whipped out his pistol, shooting Butcher in the lower abdomen three times. Butcher was admitted to Hillman Hospital in critical condition with a 50 percent chance of survival.[52]

After these twin shootings in August 1942, African Americans, and even some white Americans, knew that the racial climate in Alabama was worsening by the day. An editorial in the *Montgomery Advertiser*, the city's white newspaper, lamented this recent violence, soberly remarking that these Black men were both unarmed and shot without reason. Not only did the editorial critique the wanton abuses of power that white bus drivers had recently displayed, but it also faulted Governor Dixon for contributing to this surge of racist violence in the state.[53] A few weeks later, white bus drivers and police officers attacked and arrested Norma Green in Montgomery, Alabama.

Norma Green's bus assault in September 1942 marked a watershed moment, demonstrating unequivocally that state violence in Alabama had now claimed a *woman* as its victim. When Green did not show up for her evening shift on Saturday evening, rumors began to circulate. Fear rippled through the halls. Terrified that she might be dead, a group of Tuskegee nurses piled into a car, drove to the jail, and brought their colleague back to the hospital. Norma Green was now a patient, wounded from a battle on a Montgomery bus. White authorities at Tuskegee gave her a stern lecture, forbidding her from speaking to anyone about the incident. As soon as she was healed, they informed her, she would be deployed to Liberia to provide medical assistance to the Black troops. White authorities at Tuskegee needed Norma Green—her bruised body a potent symbol of bus driver and police violence—to leave the hospital so that nurses and soldiers would stop asking questions.

Emotions at Tuskegee were visceral as every nurse realized she could be next. Balancing fear with facts, Tuskegee nurses crafted a pointed letter to Attorney General Francis Biddle, explaining that a disagreement about segregated bus seats had escalated into state violence against a Black woman. "If we are Americans," the nurses wrote, "we want a statement and justice." Educating the attorney general about what it was like to be Black women in the rogue state of Alabama, they wrote that Green's assault could have happened to any of them, committed by the "same people who are supposed to protect us—namely, the police and bus drivers who carry guns." The Tuskegee nurses rhetorically linked police officers and bus drivers, naming both as perpetrators of violence against African American women. At any moment, Black women "may be attacked and pummeled" "unless the government we are trying to support gives us the protection a woman deserves at birthright."[54] Thirty-eight Tuskegee nurses signed this typed letter, their black and blue signatures matching Norma Green's bruises.

One Tuskegee nurse, Almeria Plaskett Roberts, wrote a separate letter to her parents in Bucks County, Pennsylvania, urging them to contact Attorney General Biddle to investigate. She lamented that the whole incident was being covered up and issued a clarion call for the truth. "The race question is getting worse than ever down here," Roberts told her parents, "and something must be done about it."[55] Living in Pennsylvania, her parents could exercise more influence than she could in Alabama, even as a nurse in the army.[56]

While nurses at Tuskegee contacted the Department of Justice, Mabel Keaton Staupers, the executive secretary of the National Association of Colored Graduate Nurses, wrote a letter to Secretary of War Henry Stimson, urging him to "use his power to guarantee protection to Negro nurses who are forced to serve in segregated units." The federal government had encouraged Black women to serve in the Deep South, where they did not have any rights. Staupers warned that the combined impacts of Green's assault and government inaction made it "increasingly difficult" to recruit Black women to serve as nurses in the war effort.[57] Other Black women's groups—including the National Council of Negro Women and the Women's Auxiliary of the Brotherhood of Sleeping Car Porters—also called on the government to punish Norma Green's perpetrators.[58]

Black men also rallied to Norma Green's defense. Black residents of Tuskegee wrote a letter to President Franklin D. Roosevelt in which they denounced the brutal attack on Norma Green. Linking Green's "lurid incident of maltreatment" with the ongoing abuse of Black passengers on buses, the men noted that those Alabama residents had purchased automobiles to avoid bus violence.[59] This pressure—from Tuskegee nurses, Black women's organizations, and ordinary citizens—eventually worked, and the Department of Justice investigated Norma Green's assault, although no one was ever charged. But regardless of any investigation, the damage had been done. Bus violence against African Americans in Alabama was out of control. Within just two months, white bus drivers and police officers had attacked one Black civilian and two members of the military, and one soldier was dead. In January 1943, William H. Hastie, a Harvard-trained Black attorney, resigned as Negro adviser in the War Department. In his public statement, Hastie characterized every white person in Tuskegee, Alabama, as deputized to carry a gun.

In the first year of the war, African Americans in Alabama witnessed the brutality of bus drivers and police officers as the federal government averted its eyes. Men were dying on the battlefields, but they were also being murdered on buses in the Deep South. The attack on Norma Green demonstrated that her womanhood could not protect her from this state-based violence. As the war dragged on, African Americans across the country learned the devastating consequences of bus violence in the Deep South.

"She Fears for Her Life": State Violence Spreads

As World War II stretched across the European and Pacific theaters, thousands of Black women streamed into the Deep South. Some dressed in uniforms as they enlisted in the new WAC program or joined the growing ranks of lieutenants in the army's nurse program. But most women who visited the Deep South were more indirectly connected to the state: They were the daughters, sisters, and especially wives of Black men training in military bases throughout the Deep South. For the past twenty years, it had been migrant women traveling to the South as visitors; now, it was military wives.

Only one year into the war, it was clear that violence was mounting on bus lines in the Deep South, and this affected soldiers, WACS, nurses, and the spouses of men serving in the military. It is never productive to rank the oppressions between Black men and women in this era. All African Americans experienced this crushing racism and violence, but Black women in the Deep South bore the additional burdens of sexism and anti-citizenship. Authorities in the Deep South—including military officers, soldiers, military police, and bus drivers—treated Black women with suspicion. In Savannah, Georgia, and Memphis, Tennessee, military bases required Black women to carry health cards verifying that they were free of venereal disease.[60] Health cards were not about protecting Black soldiers from disease; they were a proxy for policing Black women's bodies. (There is no evidence that white women had to carry such cards.) Just as industrialists and Southern politicians justified Black women's exclusion from wartime labor by suggesting that they were infected with venereal diseases, military bases operated from the same racist logic.

One Black woman who soon absorbed this reality was Audrey Riley. In the late 1930s, Riley had been a noted singer at New York City's Cotton Club. But when the war erupted, she married her husband, Theodore, and gave birth to their first child. Theodore Riley was drafted into the war and stationed at Camp McCain in Grenada, Mississippi. Audrey and her child moved from Philadelphia, Pennsylvania, to rural Mississippi so that the family could be close. In June 1943, she and her husband purchased tickets to travel on a Tri-State Bus. Audrey boarded the bus first, and her light skin allowed her to pass as white. But when Theodore attempted to board, the driver snapped that "no n****** ride this bus," insisting that the couple leave. Audrey protested, and the driver hissed that she was a "n***** bitch," and she called him a "cracker." Grabbing his blackjack, the driver started to beat Audrey Riley. Theodore tried to protect his wife, but the driver began to assault him. A military police officer then intervened. He grabbed Theodore, scooped up Audrey, and carried her into the provost marshal's office, where the couple was arrested and thrown in jail. At the trial the next morning, Audrey Riley was not permitted to speak and fined $350. When the couple left the jail the next morning, an armed mob of white men gathered outside, ready to lynch the couple. A military police officer interceded again and took the couple back to Camp McCain. Once there, a minister advised Audrey Riley to notify the NAACP immediately, which she did.[61]

After reading Audrey Riley's letter, the NAACP contacted William Hastie's replacement, Truman K. Gibson, but there was nothing that Gibson could do.[62] No institution in World War II—including the military, the federal government, the local police, or the bus companies—could protect Black women. Audrey and Theodore Riley were injured, shaken, and fearful for their safety in Mississippi. Because he was a soldier, the military carried some responsibility for Theodore Riley's life, and he was transferred to Fort Meade in Maryland to recover from his injuries.[63] But neither the state of Mississippi nor the federal government bore any burden for Audrey Riley's physical and psychological injuries, nor did these governments even acknowledge them. She fled to her mother's house in Baltimore.[64] Women like Audrey Riley paid a heavy price during the war. As they boarded buses bound for military bases, they were keenly aware that they lacked state protection.

Phrania Henderson Barnes was another military wife with no state support. A resident of Cleveland, she and her husband married young. She gave birth to their daughter, and her husband was soon drafted into the army.[65] In 1944, she and her one-year-old daughter boarded a bus bound for Fort McClellan in Anniston, Alabama, so that her husband could have a family visit before he traveled overseas. She and her baby took a seat in the back. As more passengers boarded, the driver barked at her to "get up, N*****," so that a white woman could sit down. Since she had a baby on her lap, she refused to do so, and the white woman told the driver that she did not mind standing. The driver called the police, and officers arrested Phrania Barnes and deposited her and her baby at the police station. Officers considered finding a United Service Organization worker to supervise the baby, but they ultimately released Barnes. When she returned to her home in Cleveland, she immediately contacted the *Cleveland Call and Post* to narrate her story. The paper ran a feature on the front page. The headline declared, "Jail Soldier's Wife, Baby After Refusal to Take Back Seat on Southern Muny Bus" and featured her photograph.[66] This article educated African Americans—both of Cleveland and across the nation—about the cruelty of the Southern bus system, in which the wife of a soldier and her baby were treated as criminals, not patriotic citizens.[67] While Black women supported their husbands in the military, the state bore no responsibility for their safety.

And these abuses that Black women experienced existed alongside the everyday brutality and shootings meted out to Black soldiers. Between 1942 and 1946, white male bus drivers shot dozens of Black soldiers, in addition to murdering Henry Williams in 1942, Edward Green in 1944, and Booker T. Spicely in 1944. After each murder, leaders at the NAACP pressed the War Department and the Department of Justice to investigate. But these bureaucratic processes were ineffective, giving the veneer of government diligence beneath a foundation of abject indifference.

Each shooting was different, but every discharged bullet demonstrated that the combination of Southern white bus drivers' weapons and hostility toward Black soldiers proved a dangerous mixture. In March 1943, Loomis Farmer, a white bus driver, shot Cpl. Reuben Pleasant at Maxwell Field in Montgomery, Alabama. Pleasant, a resident of Maryland, had been on furlough. After he clashed with Farmer over a seating arrangement, Farmer shot him in the right leg.[68] The NAACP politicized the case, but Attorney General Francis Biddle concluded that there was no "federal jurisdiction" in the assault on Reuben Pleasant.[69] In March 1944, Edward Green, a Black soldier from New York City, was stationed at Camp Livingston in Louisiana and boarded a bus. After an altercation over seating arrangements, the bus driver, Odell Lachney, shot and killed him.[70] Immediately after the shooting, a crowd gathered around the bus, and a Black woman in the crowd shouted at the driver, demanding answers. Even though police officers arrived, they only symbolically arrested Lachney. A newspaper article lamented that "local cops did not arrest Lachney in the real sense of the word," noting that he was "escorted" to the police station in "hero style."[71]

While NAACP leaders exercised their due diligence to alert federal bureaus and work to bring some justice for Edward Green and his family, feelings of cynicism and helplessness about violence in the Deep South clouded the office. Because witnesses saw Lachney murder Edward Green, the police arrested him, and he was charged. But at the trial, a jury met for ninety minutes, and he was exonerated.[72]

Two months later, civil rights activists finally achieved some momentum in the long-standing struggle against segregated transportation. In June 1944, Representative Francis J. Myers—a Democrat from Pennsylvania—and Assistant Secretary of War John J. McCloy convened a gathering of Black and white power brokers to craft a solution to the mounting problem of racist transportation violence in the Deep South.[73] As leaders negotiated the terms of a deal, bus violence persisted.

On Saturday, July 8, 1944, Black soldier Booker T. Spicely boarded a Duke Power Company Bus. Spicely clashed with the bus driver, Herman Lee Council, who shot him twice. The police arrived and transported Spicely to Duke Hospital, where he died soon afterward. Virginia Foster Durr, a local white woman who was outspoken on civil rights, held an organized protest outside the hospital.[74] After Spicely was pronounced dead, police officers arrested Herman Council. He was given a $2,500 bail and was released before his case was heard by a grand jury.[75] Spicely's murder sent shock waves through the Black community because it occurred in Durham, North Carolina, an upper South state with a reputation for racial moderation. The governor of North Carolina, J. Melville Broughton, announced that the state would appoint one of its "ablest prosecutors" to try Council for second degree murder.[76] This response typified North Carolina's seemingly milder attitude on race relations. Raleigh's *News and Observer* published an editorial declaring, "The Law Is Supreme." This newspaper was edited by the noted segregationist Josephus Daniels, who was nearing the end of his life. While Council's bond was "low," the paper was optimistic that the North Carolina courts would treat the case with all due attention. The editorial noted that this case would determine whether justice was colorblind in the state and optimistically concluded that "North Carolina is proud of its record in such matters and that record will be preserved in the Durham case."[77] But in September 1944, a Durham superior court jury acquitted Council.[78]

In the aftermath of the Booker T. Spicely murder, the *Baltimore Afro-American* published a political cartoon titled "Disarm Dixie Bus Drivers or Give Soldiers a Gun Too."

Disarm Dixie Bus Drivers or Give Soldiers a Gun Too

Source: *Baltimore Afro-American*, July 22, 1944. Courtesy of the AFRO American Newspapers Archives/Afro Charities.

This political cartoon captured the complexities of racialized and gendered violence on buses, depicting the ways that it affected both men and women. The image featured a white bus driver who looked and acted like a police officer as he stood above the prone body of a Black male soldier. Right next to the driver was a Black woman cradling a small baby. This woman was likely a soldier's wife, riding the bus to visit her husband on a military base, and also served as a visual representation of real victims. Recently, stories about Audrey Riley and Phrania Barnes had raced through the Black press.[79]

On July 8, 1944, the same day that Herman Lee Council murdered Booker T. Spicely on a bus, the War Department issued Memorandum 97, which integrated buses on military bases. Specifically, this order forbade "the practices of Jim Crow in army post exchanges, theaters, and transportation facilities." Leaders at the NAACP celebrated that the War

Department had finally intervened to address deadly violence on Southern buses.[80] This order was a revelation for Black members of the military, an institution composed almost entirely of men. While it represented a crucial victory in the fight against bus segregation, the order also underscored Black women's inaccessible path toward full citizenship in this era. In the Deep South, thousands of Black men and hundreds of Black women on military bases could use this order as a recognition that the federal government intended to protect them. In the Jim Crow North, Black women in industrial factories could use their wartime labor as a ladder to citizenship rights. Black women in the Deep South—including soldiers' wives, maids, cooks, mothers, and elderly women—were accorded no such protection on buses.

While African Americans celebrated this order, white Southerners expressed concern about the dangers of integration. Alabama Governor Chauncey Sparks denounced this memorandum, maintaining that it "aggravates rather than helps." Governor Sparks insisted that it fractured "an essential principle of race relations in the South." Furthermore, Bull Connor contended that segregation was one of Alabama's "sacred institutions," and dismantling it would create "terror, bloodshed, and calamity for both races."[81]

Only a few months after the order was handed down, two Black WACs ran into trouble on a bus in Alabama. Pvt. Roberta McKenzie was a native of Lee, Arkansas, and Pvt. Gladys Blackmon was from Oklahoma. Both women were stationed at Camp Sibert in Etowah County, Alabama.[82] On Saturday, December 23, two days before the holiday, Blackmon and McKenzie boarded a bus for the neighboring city of Gadsden, Alabama, to buy presents. The bus was relatively empty, and both women slipped inconspicuously into seats near the back. When the bus pulled into Alabama City, more passengers boarded, and the driver demanded that Private McKenzie move to the back. She complied, but after a while she rejoined Private Blackmon. When a white woman passenger boarded the bus, she demanded that the two WACS move to the very back of the bus, and they refused. The white woman exited the bus and returned with two police officers.

The white officers marched onto the bus and grabbed Blackmon and McKenzie, twisting their arms. Their force was so strong that they knocked Gladys Blackmon's hat and purse to the ground. Hurling epithets at the women, the officers shoved them into a patrol car and raced to the police station. After putting them in a cell, they banged Gladys Blackmon's head against the door several times and punched both women in their breasts.

The military police arrived, loaded Blackmon and McKenzie into a carryall truck, and transported them back to Camp Sibert.[83] When the War Department learned about the incident, they collected the testimonies of Blackmon and McKenzie. They also contacted the NAACP and asked them to investigate.[84] When the news reached Thurgood Marshall's desk, he termed the case "dynamite."[85] But nothing materialized. Gladys Blackmon and Roberta McKenzie, like thousands of Black women, served the war effort and yet the government refused to protect them from physical and sexual violence at the hands of white bus drivers and police officers. The War Department memorandum was only a piece of paper. Black women in the Deep South continued to face the disturbing reality that their race and sex chained them to the cellar of Southern society—a place where they were vulnerable to wartime violence with no benefits from wartime opportunities. And they began to fight back.

Organized Resistance

As bus violence spread, Black women throughout the Deep South recognized that organized resistance was necessary. Black communities and individual women continued to work through established channels to protest mounting bus violence.[86] Women met with bus lines and officeholders, filed lawsuits, and even formed a grassroots organization to protest transportation violence. Even though Black women occupied a marginal position in the Jim Crow South, they marshaled their resources to address bus violence.

Once World War II erupted, Black girls noticed a surge in violence on buses traveling throughout the Jim Crow South. Riding a bus now put Black girl riders in the proximity of numerous armed white men, including bus drivers, soldiers, and MPs. Black girls experienced the same visceral reactions to the war as did their mothers, aunts, sisters, and grandmothers. Around them, they watched as their fathers and brothers were sent off to war, and their mothers and sisters were denied wartime jobs. Those circumstances also shaped Black girls' political and social subjectivities. Black girls in the Jim Crow South had to navigate what the historian LaKisha Simmons calls a "double bind." On the one hand, they had to experience the unrelenting constraints, trauma, and violence in the Jim Crow South; on the other hand, they had to comply with the expectations of the Black community and conform to their idea of what a "Black girl" should be.[87]

For Black girls, this "double bind" became an unrelenting knot by World War II.

In 1943, Julia and Emily Harris, teenage sisters in Augusta, Georgia, were the latest victims of violence. Boarding the city bus, the sisters paid their fare but discovered that they had given twice the amount and asked the driver for change. The bus driver struck Julia Harris on the head and drew a gun on her because she would not "shut up." Emily Harris managed to climb out the window, but the bus driver called the police and demanded that they be arrested and charged with disorderly conduct. Fortunately, the girls' father, Norman Harris, arrived at the scene and intervened. Rather than seeing his daughters arrested and charged, he insisted that they be taken to the hospital, where doctors stitched Julia's head wounds. As a tailor with his own shop, Norman Harris was a prominent member of Augusta's Black middle class, which kept his daughters from being arrested and treated as girls, not women. Historians note that in many instances, Black girls were not accorded the privilege of girlhood, and this could affect the sentences and criminal punishments meted out to them.[88] Two months later, another Black girl faced a bus incident. Doris Lyons, a sixteen-year-old high school student in Durham, North Carolina, boarded a city bus. The driver asked her to move to the back, and she replied that all the seats were taken. Officer Wade Gates, a plainclothes detective, was also on the bus. He echoed the bus driver's message, but Lyons refused to budge. Angered, Officer Gates grabbed Lyons, assaulted her, and forcibly ejected her from the bus, kicking her schoolbooks to the ground. Detective Gates's symbolic "kicking" of Lyons's schoolbooks was deeply insulting to her aspirations to graduate from high school. After Lyons was arrested, her mother came to the police station to secure her release and contacted attorney Caswell "C. J." Gates, who had previously represented Ellen Harris in her bus lawsuit (see chapter 4).[89]

Black girls continued to be unsafe on buses throughout the South. In March 1944, Dorothy Foster and Mildred McGowan—aged ten and twelve—boarded a Duke Power Company Bus in Spartanburg, South Carolina. Both girls were from poor families. Dorothy Foster's father worked as a sharecropper, while Mildred McGowan's widowed mother supported the family as a domestic servant.[90] The girls boarded the bus to attend a church service. Walking toward the back of the bus, Dorothy Foster stumbled over the foot of a white woman, who slapped her. Foster retaliated, and the bus driver bounded to the back of the bus clutching his blackjack, and proceeded to hit both girls on the head and face so hard that they both required stiches. In police court, Dorothy Foster was fined $15.75 and charged with disorderly conduct. The local Black community in Spartanburg rallied to the girls' defense and filed a damage suit against Duke Power Company.[91] Black communities in Georgia and South Carolina knew that if this case went uncontested, bus violence against Black girls could set a dangerous precedent. These communities banded together to hire lawyers to defend Black girls and bring charges against abusive bus drivers in the face of unrelenting violence.

Black women also filed at least four injury lawsuits against bus companies in the Deep South, and three won three cases.[92] In Columbus, Georgia, in October 1943, Mabel Smith ran to catch her bus, but she missed it and expressed frustration. The white driver, enraged by her irritated reaction, stopped the bus, ran half a block after Smith, and beat her skull with a blackjack. Police officers arrested the driver, R. H. Martin, and held him with bail. In front of a grand jury, Mabel Smith appeared in court, her head covered in bandages. Smith wisely enlisted the testimony of her physician, Dr. Thomas H. Brewer, who narrated her wounds and accompanying illness.[93] Martin's arrest and trial represented a rare instance when white bus drivers were held accountable for their assaults on Black passengers. These victories were exceptions, as most working-class Black women and girls did not have the resources to hire lawyers and sue in court. Instead, they used their actions on chaotic city buses to articulate their anger over everyday bus violence and their broader exclusions from the war effort.

"This Great Democracy": Black Women's War on the Bus

As the war dragged on, Black women's conflicts on buses surged. Their transportation struggles were deeply connected to the state but also stubbornly detached from them. With so many training bases in the Deep South, city and interstate buses overflowed as soldiers, war workers, and civilians competed to board. Out of every resident of the Deep South, Black women were the least tethered to the war effort, as they were largely banned from wartime labor industries and the military. But the war's economic transformations pulled them away from rural farms and brought them to cities and towns in the Deep South, where they became domestic servants and bus riders.[94] The war did not bring Southern Black women into battlefields or factories; rather, it trapped them on crowded buses and confined them to stifling kitchens in white houses. In this subtle way, Black women's labor was part of the larger wartime state project. But domestic service did not confer citizenship rights on par with military service or industrial labor. And Southern Black women were keenly aware of these exclusions.

Black women used their daily bus commutes to articulate critiques of wartime racism and sexism, drawing attention to the crushing violence of the Jim Crow South. Practicing resistance on a spectrum that stretched from the very subtle to the deeply overt, Black women and girls cursed at drivers, denounced discrimination, carried weapons, intimidated white passengers, and protested segregated seating arrangements. There were complex stakes in these daily transportation battles. On the one hand, Black women bore a heavy price for this behavior, facing arrest, charges of disorderly conduct, steep fines, and the real threats of physical and sexual violence. On the other hand, it was through their resistance that they could most effectively communicate that the Southern system of bus segregation with untenable. They lobbied their white employers to register complaints with bus companies. And they recruited members of the Black and white military to use their power to intervene against bus segregation, sometimes with terrifying consequences. By the end of the war, the federal government was aware that it was a complacent actor in some of the worst violations of human rights, perpetrated not in Asia or Europe but in the Southern part of the nation. Even though Black women fought a long and hard war on the bus, neither ordinary civilians nor prominent wartime women such as Norma Green, Audrey Riley, Gladys Blackmon, or Roberta McKenzie—all of whom were heavily covered in the Black press and whose stories reached the desks of the War Department and the Department of Justice—ever received compensation for their racist treatment on the bus. The federal government turned a blind eye toward the human rights abuses that festered in the Deep South, a region steeped in centuries of violence. During World War II, this racist violence could no longer be hidden or concealed. It was visible to all.

As bus passengers, Black women frequently cursed at white riders, sharply critiquing the culture of wartime discrimination in the Deep South. In August 1944 in Mobile, Alabama, police officers arrested Black women bus passengers for swearing at two white women and a soldier, calling them "white trash."[95] Although the circumstances of this incident are unknown, it is possible that Black women's reference to "white trash" hinged on the fact that white women benefited from lucrative wartime jobs in wartime production in Mobile as well as the racist violence perpetrated against African Americans at Brookley Army Air Field.

In July 1944, a Black woman boarded a Valley Coach Bus traveling from Augusta to Aiken, South Carolina. As the white bus driver would later complain, she spent the duration of the trip "talking loudly about racial discrimination." Even though the driver tried hard to silence her, she carried on for the entire ride. Not only was this Black woman informing the bus driver about her own personal distaste for racial discrimination, but she was educating her fellow passengers. In Aiken, she was turned over to local police. This would be the same police force that would attack Isaac Woodard two years later, brutally gouging out his eyeballs and contributing to a global outcry about bus violence.[96]

In August 1944 in Greensboro, North Carolina, a Black woman rang the bell for her stop. "I'll cut your god-damn head off," she threatened the driver as she departed the bus.[97] In all these examples, Black women exhibited a well-developed political consciousness, which richly critiqued the racist political economy of the South and the US military. But anytime that a Black woman dared to speak back, she bore the profound danger that the Southern racial order would retaliate—violently.

In September 1944 in Winston-Salem, North Carolina, an African American woman named Mary Fleming boarded the bus. She cursed the white passengers, and the driver ordered her to be quiet. When she got off the bus, the driver started to follow her, but then she pulled out a gun. She was later arrested and charged with disorderly conduct and public drunkenness.[98]

By the middle of the war, Black women began to board the bus armed, whether with actual weapons or everyday objects they could deploy as protection. Stretching back to the beginning of the bus industry in the 1920s, bus lines equipped drivers with all kinds of weapons, including billy clubs, guns, and pipes. Now, in the charged climate of World War II, Black women prepared to fight back against the bus drivers who policed them as passengers. In August 1944 in Chattanooga, Tennessee, a Black woman boarded a bus and took a seat near the front. When a white male passenger grabbed her by the shoulders and attempted to move her to another seat, she snatched her nail file and cut him in the face. In Charleston, South Carolina, on Christmas, two white naval officers asked a Black man to move to the back of the bus. A Black woman appeared with a knife and cut both officers. In August 1944, a Black woman boarded a bus in Jacksonville, Florida, with two men. She was shouting obscenities and carrying a gun, threatening to shoot all the passengers. In July 1944, a white sailor hurled epithets at a Black woman, and she stabbed him in the neck with a knife. But Black women could pay a heavy price for these actions. In April 1944, a Black woman shoved a white boy aside on a bus, claiming that she was just as good as he was. The next day, the boy's parents drove alongside the bus with a shotgun.[99] This visible threat against a Black woman passenger illustrated the dangerous climate of violence in the Jim Crow South.

World War II created new circumstances for Black and white women to interact with each other. Migration and urbanization meant that many Black women were now laboring as maids for white women. Recognizing that white women could wield power and authority with bus lines, many domestics implored their white employers to contact bus companies when there was a problem with transportation. In Birmingham in July 1944, one employer called to complain that her cook's bus had broken down and all the passengers had to depart. When a new bus arrived, the cook was not permitted to board.[100] Not only did Black and white women interact through the prism of employer-servant relations, but they also encountered each other on buses. As labor shortages swept the Southern bus industry, municipal companies in the South tapped women to work as drivers. Bus driving represented another area where white women advanced while Black women were held back. No Southern bus system ever hired African American men or women to labor as bus drivers. The promotion of white women to bus drivers created even more opportunities for tense, if understudied, confrontations between Black and white women.[101]

But it was most common for Black and white women to encounter each other as fellow bus passengers. On a daily basis, Black women witnessed how white women were accorded war work and praised for their patriotism, while Black male soldiers and Black women passengers were abused on buses. Even though the evidence is not present, the subtext of these encounters suggests that Black women channeled their resentment and anger about exclusions from the war industry into their interactions with white women passengers. For example, in Knoxville, Tennessee, in December 1945, near Oak Ridge, a group of Black women were traveling on a bus with white women. When they were boarding the bus, one of the Black women pushed a white woman. The next day, these tensions escalated into a full-scale fight on the bus between Black and white women passengers, including verbal attacks, clothes tugging, and knives. Between eight and ten Black women participated in this fight.[102] It is very likely that these white women labored at Oak Ridge, a site of the Manhattan Project, which was working on the atomic bomb. White women, not Black women, received these labor opportunities, leading Black women to vent their frustrations with these racial and sexual barriers on tense wartime buses. The historian Sarah Haley notes that "arrests for public quarreling was a technique to control Black working women's independence, public image, and community life," and that observation is an apt description for what was happening on buses.[103] In a July 1944 incident, white women complained that Black women would not let them move on the bus. And in Greensboro, North Carolina, a Black woman named Elsie Mae Wall boarded a bus and sat near a young white woman, who was a war worker. The bus driver forced Wall to move to the back. When she exited the bus, she passed the white woman and threatened to "beat her up." The next day, the parents of the white women arrived at the bus office. The woman's father told the bus driver that if he did not "maintain order on the bus," he would ask his daughters to quit their defense jobs because he would not "tolerate such insolence."[104] This example not only captures the racial tensions of World War II buses but also highlights the double privileges that white women experienced as the beneficiaries of wartime jobs and the recipients of racialized patriarchal protection.

In the Deep South, Black male soldiers wrestled with a complicated paradox on buses: they had to reconcile their military status and their masculinity when they witnessed injustice, especially when it was meted out to Black women. Most white male bus drivers resented Black male soldiers, which caused them to double down on their violent behavior. But on occasion, Black soldiers could try to use their uniform to intervene when they witnessed injustice. This situation reached a breaking point in October 1944 in an episode that demonstrated that the white South valued Jim Crow more than military service or civic patriotism. In Warrensville, South Carolina, an elderly Black woman—wearing glasses and accompanied by a small boy—boarded a Valley Coach bus. She was seated next to a white man, who was drunk. Since this man's position in the back of the bus violated the Jim Crow laws, she asked the bus driver to reseat the man, presumably because she feared for her safety. When the driver refused to reseat the man, she asked for a refund of her bus ticket. The driver told her to get off the bus. Curling his fingers into a fist, the bus driver struck the woman on the head, knocking her to the floor of the bus. Shaken and injured, the Black woman staggered off the bus. The bus driver would have attacked her more, but several white soldiers on the bus grabbed him to prevent him from further assaulting the Black woman.[105] Eleven Black male soldiers were also aboard the bus and seated in the back. They yelled out in protest, and the driver angrily grabbed the bus's money box and exited. He then called the police, who came and arrested the Black soldiers.

The next morning, all eleven soldiers were charged with disorderly conduct and sentenced to a fine of twenty-five dollars or thirty days on a chain gang. Only three of the soldiers were able to pay the bail money, which meant that eight were put on another bus, this one headed for Aiken, South Carolina, where they would serve out their punishment.[106] One of those soldiers was Aubrey E. Robinson Jr., a student at Cornell University and a future judge in Washington, DC. In a letter published in the *New Republic* in 1944 titled "Negroes in the Army," Robinson described the indignity of this experience. Writing to an audience of readers across the nation, he described the feeling of being "forced to take off my military uniform and put on the filthy black and white striped clothes of a convict and have an iron riveted to my right ankle." He noted that "the entire series of events was like one long nightmare" and that his time on the chain gang was one that "I shall never forget and one that I did not believe could happen in 'This Great Democracy.'" A native of New Jersey, Robinson called racism in the South a "cancer in our own nation."[107] One of the workers on the chain gang had just served overseas for twenty-eight months, been wounded on the battlefield, and received a Purple Heart.[108]

The violent practices of bus segregation in the Jim Crow South extinguished the flame of American democracy. In the confined space of a bus, Black women and men bore witness to the everyday brutalities meted out to one another. World War II brought Black soldiers face-to-face with the commonplace indignities that Black women had endured for years. And it revealed to Black women the humiliating worlds that Black soldiers inhabited as they trained to defend the nation within the iron cage of racism and indignity. Black men paid a heavy price for defending Black women on the bus—in this case, serving on a chain gang in the Deep South. This sacrifice was matched when Black women protested the bus drivers who continued to murder Black soldiers.[109]

Two months after the war ended, a bus driver raped a Black woman on a bus in rural Georgia. The details of this case demonstrated unequivocally that buses would never be safe for Black women. On a sunny morning in November 1945, Charlotte Wright—a fifty-three-year-old Black mother of nine, grandmother of one, and cotton sharecropper—boarded a Southern Stages bus in Brown's Crossing, Georgia, bound for Milledgeville to sell her family's cotton crop.[110] This was not Charlotte Wright's first bus trip. As soon as Southern Stages had started running their buses in the early 1930s, she had been a regular rider.[111] On that morning, she was alone; the only other person on the bus was the driver, W. C. Davis. A few minutes into the ride, Davis steered the bus off the highway into a secluded section surrounded by pine trees. "Auntie, you give me bad luck this morning," he said, and told her that she had to do something for him. He asked if she was married, and she said that she was. He then grabbed her and prepared to rape her. She protested but was powerless against his force and might. She objected and objected, but he proceeded to violate her body, again and again. When he had finished, he asked her if she would tell anyone. She said no. "He told me if I did," Charlotte Wright recalled, "he would kill me." When the bus driver finally finished, he resumed his bus route. Wright eventually summoned the strength to pull the cord at her stop and quickly departed. Dazed, Charlotte Wright wandered through town. She sold her cotton and sent off a money order. She then found a close childhood friend and confided in her. This friend then told her brother, Reuben Pitts. Devastated at the news that a white bus driver had raped the sister of a close childhood friend, Pitts traveled to Milledgeville, Georgia, where he reported the rape to the police.[112]

The case reached the desk of Solicitor General Carter S. Baldwin, who later testified that "while he had plenty of evidence to show," it was his "opinion that being a colored woman and a white man and no corroborating circumstances, I doubted whether I could do anything, but waste time and money of the County."[113] In other words, Baldwin did not believe that Charlotte Wright could receive justice in Jim Crow Georgia.

Davis kept his job and his bus route. One month later, he raped a white woman named Azilee Whittle, a twenty-one-year-old white mother of two and wife of a soldier.[114] Whittle had been visiting her wounded husband in the military hospital. When it was over, she threatened to report him, but he snapped, "They won't do nothing to me but call me to the office and talk to me about it." Davis was speaking a partial truth; he had just raped Charlotte Wright and was still employed. But Whittle called the police and was asked to travel to Milledgeville, where she met with Carter S. Baldwin, the solicitor general. Baldwin told her that they had a case and issued a warrant for the arrest of W. C. Davis.[115] After it was confirmed that this white bus driver had likely raped two women, Baldwin contacted Charlotte Wright and requested that she come to the jail at Milledgeville. Baldwin asked ten white men in the community, including W. C. Davis and his attorney, Marion Ennis, to line up. Baldwin did not have a bus driver uniform for Davis, so he asked him to wear a soldier's uniform. When Wright scanned the sea of men, she spotted Davis instantly. In August 1946, the case went to trial. While the case centered on W. C. Davis's rape of Azilee Whittle, Charlotte Wright testified at the trial, and her testimony was admitted as evidence without objection. In his testimony, Davis claimed that he never would have even wanted to sleep with Charlotte Wright, let alone rape her, but also testified that Azilee Whittle had seduced him. Davis's testimony perfectly captured the racialized and sexualized positionalities of Black and white women in the Jim Crow South. Both were vulnerable to patriarchal rape.[116] But all Davis had to do was to state that he reviled Charlotte Wright, and he would be believed. After all, the entire system of Jim Crow rested on the idea that Black women were dangerous, could not control their sexuality, and therefore could not be victims of rape. To counter Davis's testimony, Whittle called witnesses from her family and her church to affirm her respectability. The jury found Davis guilty of rape, and Judge George S. Carpenter sentenced him to the penitentiary for one to six years. Davis appealed the case, and it traveled to the Supreme Court of Georgia, which affirmed the ruling of the lower court.[117] W. C. Davis served time in prison—not for the rape of Charlotte Davis but for the rape of Azilee Whittle. Although this case demonstrated that buses were sites of patriarchy and could be dangerous for both Black and white women, it is not surprising that Davis was only punished for raping a white woman. Neither the bus industry nor the Jim Crow legal system was especially concerned about Black women's safety.

Losing the Southern War on the Bus

As World War II ended in the Deep South, Black women could point to very few victories in their battles against bus segregation and everyday patterns of violence. A few Black women successfully sued for injuries, but these women were outliers. Even though Black women were tied to the state in the Deep South—as nurses, war workers, and soldiers' wives—the government refused to protect them. In the Deep South during World War II, Black women experienced the least amount of citizenship rights of any group. While it was true that thousands of Black male soldiers endured everyday harassment and brutality on buses and training bases, some of them even being shot and killed by white bus drivers, they also shipped off overseas to do battle, using military service as an avenue for citizenship rights. In addition, the War Department had finally come to understand that transportation posed a problem for Black male soldiers, and it integrated buses on military bases. Some Black men, along with white women in the Deep South, were able to elevate their labor prospects through high-paying jobs in war industries.

In the Deep South, Black women were largely shut out of wartime citizenship, whether through the military or through war industries. Instead, they had to ride buses seething with tension in order to labor as domestic servants. By the middle of the war, as bus drivers and police officers harassed Black women from all walks of life—including nurses, WACS, mothers, schoolgirls, teachers, and domestic servants—Black women brought the war on the bus. They politicized the war by cursing, defending themselves, attacking white passengers, and picking fights. Black women's politicized resistance demonstrates how they articulated their precise exclusions from wartime citizenship rights and wove them into the substance of their everyday actions on their daily bus computes. The story of Black women's experiences on buses in the Deep South during World War II reveals more continuity than change. The only constant in Black women's lives was the unrelenting reality of violence, rape, and sexual assault on the bus.

But this was not the story in the rest of the nation, which demonstrates the profound difference that region made. In the North, the Midwest, and the Washington metropolitan region, which included the Southern state of Virginia, Black women were able to more fully connect the war with a quest for citizenship rights. In these regions, Black women fought hard for industrial labor jobs, and a few hundred thousand successfully obtained them. The bus industry was so desperate for drivers that it hired Black women to steer the bus. And, most importantly, Black women's legal battles against bus segregation finally reached new heights as they brought precedent-setting cases to higher courts. Their actions did not greatly differ from those of their counterparts in the Deep South. These women also politicized the wartime climate, cursed drivers, and resisted their abuse, all while facing physical violence and sexual assault. But because of their location outside the Deep South and their relationship to the war, they were able to make the act of sitting wherever they pleased a right of wartime citizenship and, in turn, help to create a new political narrative for the national imagination of democracy.

6 I Know My Rights

Black Women's Rides for Citizenship Outside the Deep South During World War II

On Saturday, April 4, 1942, at eight o'clock in the morning, Maggie Mack, a twenty-three-year-old airplane worker, boarded a Dixie Greyhound Bus in Hayti, Missouri. Mack was accompanied by her disabled sister, and they were bound for Springfield, Missouri, a city two hundred miles away. When the bus wheeled into Steele, Missouri, more passengers boarded, and the bus driver ordered the sisters to move to the back seat. Mack protested, stating that there were other empty seats, and it would be painful for her disabled sister to move. The driver snapped that they were in the South. After she refused a second time, he called a police officer, who boarded the bus with a large revolver in his holster. Hurling a racial epithet at Mack, the officer slapped her across the face, grabbed her by the arm, and violently shoved her into the back seat. Mack was horrified that the bus driver "stood by, abetted, assisted and encouraged" the police officer to assault her. Bruised and frightened, she hired three white attorneys and filed a lawsuit against Dixie Greyhound, faulting both the bus driver and the police officer.[1]

Mack v. Dixie Greyhound traveled to the Eastern Division of the Judicial District of Missouri, and Mack and her attorneys requested that a jury hear the case. In the pre-court proceedings, as lawyers were selecting jurors, they noticed that two potential jurors were Black men, and Dixie Greyhound's attorney asked these men whether they were part of the National Association for the Advancement of Colored People (NAACP) or the March on Washington movement. After hearing responses to the affirmative, these Black men were not seated.[2] Nonetheless, at the conclusion of the trial the all-white jury returned with a victory for Maggie Mack, awarding her $1,500 in damages.[3] Not only did Mack's case mark the first time a federal district court ruled in favor of a Black woman over a bus assault for bodily harm, but the Associated Press covered the case, generating coverage in the *New York Times* and local newspapers across the country. As World War II raged around the world, newspaper readers were greeted with bold headlines, declaring, "Negro Wins Bus Suit," "Colored Woman Wins Civil Rights Verdict," and "Negress Wins Judgement."[4]

World War II raised the stakes of bus segregation, enabling women like Maggie Mack to seize on their wartime labor as leverage in their fight for citizenship rights. World War II had recently upended Mack's life. The daughter of Mississippi sharecroppers, she had migrated to Missouri, where she became a teacher.[5] When Mack learned that there were high-paying jobs in war industries, she moved to Milwaukee, Wisconsin, where she assembled airplanes. As millions of people like Maggie Mack relocated for wartime jobs and military service, they witnessed new racial orders, prompting many Black and white people to publicly question racial segregation, especially on buses. These internal migrations, coupled with the political dimensions of the conflict, pushed Black women to take bolder stands against bus segregation. Despite their legal victories in the 1920s and 1930s, it was during World War II when Black women's lawsuits against bus segregation and racial violence gained more visibility, traveled to higher courts, and began to influence policy and public opinion. By the end of the war, Black women like Maggie Mack brought the issue of bus segregation to the forefront of the nation's conscience.

At the beginning of World War II, while anti-Black racism held strong as the overarching system in the Jim Crow North, faint cracks appeared in the foundation. It was in Northern and Midwestern states where Black women's fight for wartime jobs resulted in employment, whether in factories or federal offices. The employment of thousands of Black women war workers strained buses and brought the matter of bus segregation into sharp relief. Black women drew on their earlier practices of litigiousness, suing bus companies for segregation and racial violence, but it was during World War II when their cases traveled to federal and state supreme courts and, ultimately, the Supreme Court. Black women litigants evoked the discourse of war citizenship to politicize their cases and fashioned their narratives into bold newspaper headlines and compelling testimonies in federal and appellate courtrooms. By 1943, municipal bus companies were so desperate for workers that they hired Black women as bus drivers, a sharp and symbolic reversal in the industry. In Cleveland, Detroit, and New York City, Black women slipped on the police-inspired uniforms of the white male drivers who had harassed them. As industrial workers, government clerks, soldiers' wives, and bus drivers, a broad swath of Black women across the Jim Crow North could connect their wartime labor and everyday sacrifices to the state. By fighting for the right to ride, select their own seat, and even drive the bus, Black women pushed their bus battles for full citizenship rights onto the national narrative of wartime hardship and struggle, helping to lay the groundwork for the nation's postwar racial reckoning. By the end of the war in 1945, those cracks in the foundation were beyond repair.[6]

Transporting Brown American Womanpower

In April 1943, editors at *Opportunity*, the organ of the National Urban League, devoted an entire issue to African American women and World War II, celebrating "Brown American Womanpower." This volume brimmed with articles highlighting Black women's employment in different aspects of the war, including military service, nursing, and industrial and clerical labor. In a key article, "Negro Women Are American Workers, Too," writer George E. DeMar chronicled the unique struggles that Black women faced in their industrial jobs, stretching from racial prejudice in hiring practices to the barriers toward entry in intensive training programs. For Black women, time was critical, since war workers labored around the clock to produce military equipment, including airplanes, bombs, and cartridges. But bus segregation and racial violence could and did undermine Black women's perceived character as industrial laborers and government clerks.[7]

When the United States entered World War II, many Black women were already working outside the home. The majority of Black women labored in personal service and agricultural work, but some held more lucrative positions as clerks, beauty culturalists, seamstresses, dressmakers, teachers, or trained nurses.[8] On the eve of the war, 40 percent of Black women held paid labor positions, as compared to only 25 percent of white women.[9] But during the war, over five million white women were able to secure industrial jobs, as compared to only six hundred thousand Black women. Significantly, among this cohort of Black wartime workers, four hundred thousand had previously labored as domestic servants. Even though only 18 percent of African American women worked in wartime jobs, they entered industries where they had previously been excluded, including aircraft plants, electrical companies, foundries, shipyards, and steel mills.[10] Despite these small numbers and the persistence of racial discrimination, these wartime jobs were transformative, enabling Black women to earn higher wages, perform work usually done by white men, and potentially join a labor union.

But Black women had to *fight* for these wartime labor positions. Most factories in the Deep South refused to hire Black women war workers. It was only in the North, the Midwest, and the Washington metropolitan region where Black women were able to secure industrial positions. In 1942, nearly a year into the war, the *Afro-American* reported that sixty-five factories in eighteen states employed Black women war workers. While Black women labored in a variety of industries, they were especially prominent in aircraft manufacturing. By the end of the war, Black women were constructing airplanes in fifteen different plants across the West Coast, the East Coast, and the Midwest.[11] They were also well represented in the navy yards of Washington, DC, and Norfolk, Virginia. By 1943, over two thousand Black women were employed at the Washington Navy Yard.[12] These types of opportunities were nearly elusive for Black women in the Deep South.

Yet racial discrimination was rampant, and many industries stubbornly refused to hire Black women as industrial workers. In 1941, the US Bureau of Employment Security conducted investigations, discovering that 51 percent of the defense job openings were not available to Black workers. States with especially high rates of discrimination included Michigan, Ohio, and Indiana.[13] In 1942, thirty thousand women in Detroit were employed in wartime labor positions, and only one hundred were Black women.[14] Out of 280 automobile factories that employed women, only 74 of them were willing to hire Black women. The National Metal Trades compiled its own research, concluding that out of 62 plants that hired women, only 29 would consider Black women workers.[15] Some Black women were able to submit appeals to the Fair Employment Practices Commission (FEPC) and testify in hearings, but that government agency was underfunded throughout the war, which made it difficult to investigate cases of labor discrimination.[16]

Between 1940 and 1950, almost 1.5 million African Americans moved out of the South and streamed into the North, the Midwest, and the West.[17] Many left farms in the rural South to labor in domestic service or war work. But agricultural sectors in the white South resisted this migration because they were losing a cheap source of their labor. For example, in June 1944, a group of five hundred Black workers in Florida learned of job opportunities at the Campbell's Soup Factory in New Jersey. In Florida, if African Americans purchased bus tickets under suspicion that they were leaving the state, police officers were permitted to board the buses and detain these potential Black travelers. Those arrested could be held for up to seventy-two hours.[18] Despite these police limitations, many aspiring Black workers left the South and migrated North in search of wartime opportunities. At the Edgewood Arsenal at Aberdeen Proving Ground, Maryland, hundreds of Black women produced gas masks. Some of these workers already lived in Maryland, but others had moved to the region from diverse states, including Alabama, Georgia, New York, Pennsylvania, and Virginia.[19] None of these women lived in Aberdeen and had to travel to the arsenal by private car or bus.[20]

If Black women were able to secure positions in wartime factories, buses were essential for their daily commutes. While most Black women lived in cities, factories were located on the outskirts of urban areas, forcing these women to travel significant distances for paid labor.[21] A bus conflict could make Black women workers tardy for their jobs, further fueling stereotypes about African American women being lazy or incompetent. At the Picatinny Arsenal in Dover, New Jersey, Hortense Johnson labored as a munition's inspector but lived in New York City.[22] In an article titled "What My Job Means to Me," she detailed her job at the Picatinny Arsenal but also described her daily bus commute. Each day she traveled forty-five miles to and from work, the trip sometimes involving ice, wind, and sharp turns. She wrote that her long and stressful day ended only when her bus transported her safely to her home.[23] Even though industrial workers like Hortense Johnson had to endure long bus rides and on-the-job racism, they seized on these opportunities because their wartime labor linked them to the state and demonstrated their aspirations for full citizenship rights in the United States.

Since housing for Black war workers was limited and expensive, some cities constructed dormitories, which meant that Black women were necessarily reliant on buses for transportation. At this time, bus shortages were threatening the already precarious positions that Black women occupied as war workers, so they marched on the front lines against transportation shortages. In 1943, Sarah Campbell Johnson—a war worker in Norfolk, Virginia—lived in Roberts Park, a housing complex for local defense workers. Johnson and her fellow workers labored around the clock in local plants in three shifts, and they needed consistent bus service to perform this wartime labor. Johnson contacted the Virginia Electric and Power Company, demanding that they furnish more buses for workers. As a war worker, she had more leverage to demand bus service than if she were merely an ordinary civilian. And now that buses were part of the state wartime project, the Virginia Electric and Power Company had more of a duty to respond to Johnson.[24]

Not only did Black women struggle with the lack of bus service, but as war workers, they also faced abuse at the hands of drivers and fellow passengers. In April 1944, very late in the evening in Bayonne, New Jersey, Jennie McCoy and Ethel Perry ended their shifts at the American Radiator

Company plant. They boarded a crowded bus with two white sailors, who had been drinking. The sailors objected to riding in the same bus with Black women war workers. In a turn most surprising, a police officer arrested the sailors. The next morning in police court, the sailors were each fined ten dollars and heavily censured for their "undemocratic attitude."[25] This scenario would have played out very differently in the Jim Crow South. It is undeniable that Black women's status as war workers granted them a small but crucial amount of leverage in their fight against bus inequalities. These Black women war workers successfully demonstrated that the right to ride a bus to their industrial jobs was a fundamental, and even patriotic, act of citizenship in this period.

"Doing Their Bit for Democracy": Government War Work

Not only did African American women work hard to obtain industrial jobs, but thousands also secured coveted positions as clerks, stenographers, and typists in wartime federal agencies. By 1944, two hundred thousand African Americans labored in government positions.[26] Even though civil service jobs were posted across the country, it was in the nation's capital where Black women achieved the most significant labor gains because the city already had a tradition of hiring Black workers. But these jobs were part of the Civil Service Commission's War Service Regulations, which meant that they were temporary and did not offer permanent status.[27] Nonetheless, as government agencies expanded to oversee the vast wartime apparatus, positions opened in the Navy Department, the Labor Department, the Census Bureau, and other offices, and Black women eagerly applied for these positions. Government labor—literally and symbolically—connected Black women with the state, enabling them to draw on this service to make claims to citizenship in ways they had not experienced since the Civil War and Reconstruction.[28]

During World War II, Black women from the North, South, and Midwest all streamed into the Washington metropolitan region, seizing on these coveted opportunities for government work and higher-paying jobs in domestic service.[29] In late December 1941, only two weeks after Pearl Harbor, an article in the *Birmingham Daily World* celebrated that Theresa L. Nash, a local high school graduate in the city, had just taken the civil service exam and received a job in the War Department. As a Black woman in Alabama, Nash knew that her prospects for government work would be nonexistent, which prompted her to relocate to the nation's capital.[30] Similarly, a newspaper article in the *Cleveland Call and Post* in September 1942 carried the headline, "Want a Job? Uncle Sam Is Hard Up for Stenographers," inviting Black women in Cleveland to move to Washington, DC.[31] Many pieces in the Black press reminded readers that government work was just as significant as industrial positions.[32]

Black women's government labor made bus segregation a charged battleground in the Washington metropolitan region. Maryland, Virginia, and Washington, DC, all had different laws, which were unevenly enforced. Racial segregation was legal in Maryland but not on buses, which meant that the color line was randomly applied on transportation. Most Black workers lived in Washington, DC, a city that also practiced racial segregation but not formally on transportation. During World War II, space constraints forced government offices to relocate across the Potomac River to Virginia, a state where racial segregation was legal on buses, and featured armed drivers who were deputized to conduct citizen's arrests. None of these three states had a civil rights law. When Northern Black women arrived in Washington, DC, to pursue government war work, the *presence* of racial segregation and the *absence* of civil rights protections raised alarms, prompting them to publicly articulate their critiques. A Black woman from Chicago who moved to Washington, DC, was shocked at the city's segregation, noting that bus drivers were "insulting" to passengers.[33]

Thousands of Black women government workers rode buses in their daily commutes, and each day, race relations worsened. One of the subtle ways that the government privileged white women workers over Black ones was through the assignment of shifts. In July 1942, it was reported that the War Department allowed white women to work daytime shifts, while Black women had to work at night. Not only did these shifts make Black women more vulnerable to racism and sexual violence, but they also made the logistics of segregated transportation more difficult to maneuver.[34] A year later, the *Cleveland Call and Post* discussed the cohort of Black women workers in the Census Department in the Department of Labor. The building was so busy that workers were employed in three sets of shifts around the clock. Transportation was chaotic, as women workers had to "push" onto buses to avoid being tardy for work.[35] Just as these wartime industrial worker opportunities were fragile for Black women, so, too, were the opportunities for Black women clerical workers. Any charge of lateness could seriously jeopardize a Black woman's prospects for advancement and undermine her claims to full citizenship rights.

Soon, the complicated logistics of bus segregation in the Washington metropolitan region became too burdensome. Buses in Washington, DC, did not require segregated seating, but they did in neighboring Virginia. This meant that women traveling on these buses had to literally move to the back when the vehicles rolled across the Potomac River into Virginia. In January 1943, two Black clerks at the Navy Annex in Arlington became the first women caught in this logistical chaos of transportation. On Thursday, January 7, 1943, just after midnight, Mildred I. Turpin and Caroline K. Johnson boarded the Arlington and Fairfax bus bound for Washington, DC, selecting seats near the front. The driver ordered the women to move to the back, and they refused. Police officers arrived and reinforced the driver's message. Turpin told the officers that "government employees can sit anywhere in the bus," to which he replied, "You are in Virginia and not in Washington." Neither Turpin nor Johnson would relent, and the officers arrested the clerks. In court, each woman pleaded "not guilty" and was fined five dollars. The judge later approached the women, informed them that they did not have to pay the fine, and dismissed the case.[36] The Black press quickly circulated the story of Turpin's and Johnson's arrest, highlighting the contradictions of Black women who were laboring for a patriotic cause but were still subject to inequality and humiliation.[37] An editorial in the *Baltimore Afro-American* stated, "It is bad enough under any circumstances when American citizens are subjected to such humiliations; but after innocent young women have slaved all day, doing their bit for democracy, it is even worse."[38]

One year later, Lola Walters, a government clerk in Washington, ran into trouble in her home state of Pennsylvania.[39] On Sunday evening, she boarded a Greyhound bus to return to DC for her job on Monday morning. When Walters entered the nearly empty bus, the white driver insisted that she take a seat in the back. Since Pennsylvania had a civil rights law, Walters refused to do so. After receiving verbal threats, she exited the bus and called the police, who informed her that this matter was not in their "jurisdiction." Because she was detained and unable to ride this bus, Walters did not report for work on Monday morning, which fueled broader stereotypes that linked Black women workers with laziness and tardiness. For Lola Walters, this case of bus segregation threatened to destroy her standing as a government worker and broader claims to first-class citizenship during World War II.[40] Walters immediately notified the NAACP's national office, which contacted the Interstate Commerce Commission (ICC).

The ICC investigated the Pennsylvania Greyhound Lines and interviewed the driver, who reported, on the record, that Lola Walters was intoxicated and disruptive.[41] In this case, it was the white bus driver's word against hers. Walters, as well as the civil rights community, was grateful that this case reached the ICC for an investigation, but the commission ultimately honored the account of the white bus driver over that of the Black woman war worker.

These stories from industrial workers and government clerks offer a new narrative about Black women in World War II. Not only did African American women have to fight tirelessly to secure wartime labor positions, but the circumstances of crowded buses, compounded by interpersonal racism, only deepened Black women's efforts to link wartime labor with citizenship rights during World War II. Even though women such as Lola Walters, Mildred Turpin, and Caroline Johnson all experienced violent and disturbing conflicts on the bus, war service emboldened them to claim bus service as a right of full citizenship. And by the middle of the war, Black women began to demand higher-paying jobs in the bus industry.

Driving the Bus: "What Our Women 'Can' Do"

During World War II, Black women cracked the most indestructible ceiling in the bus industry: They became drivers. Since its inception, the bus industry had practiced a rigid hierarchy of racialized and gendered hiring practices, restricting Black women to service positions while enthusiastically hiring white women to many white-collar and skilled jobs, stretching from ticket agents and printers to conductorettes and tour guides. Once the nation entered World War II, the bus industry enthusiastically looked to white women workers to fill the roles previously held by men: drivers and mechanics. For the bus industry, white women drivers became their visual representation of Rosie the Riveter. A series of articles in *Bus Transportation* epitomized the industry's celebratory, and vaguely feminist, discourse about hiring white women drivers, featuring headlines declaring, "Women Can't Drive?," "So They Took Women . . . and Like 'Em," and "Remanning with Women." These pieces waxed poetic about white women driving municipal buses across upstate New York, San Diego, and Oakland. Bus lines also hired white women as mechanics to repair buses, calling them "electricionettes."[42] By 1943, the Women's Bureau reported that 12,415 women across the country were working in the bus industry, demonstrating that white women were making significant gains in wartime transportation jobs.[43] Most bus companies were thrilled to recruit white women to drive their buses and serve as the public face of their companies.[44] While it was mostly municipal bus lines that hired women as bus drivers, on rare occasions massive interstate lines, such as Greyhound, tapped women for these longer rides.[45] The industry never explicitly stated why they preferred to hire women for municipal over interstate driving positions, but it is likely that they reasoned that longer trips required stamina, strength, and endurance that white women did not have.

Unsurprisingly, the bus industry was less enthusiastic to hire Black women workers. By the middle of the war, there were eight thousand vacant transportation jobs, which threatened industrial production.[46] In January 1943, the Office of Defense Transportation announced that 269 city buses sat idle in Detroit because there were no drivers. As the arsenal of democracy, Michigan was awash with industrial plants and high-paying jobs for white women. In fact, one of the workers who inspired the Rosie the Riveter campaign worked at Michigan's Willow Run bomber plant. Within a few days of this announcement, Detroit's Department of Street Railways (DSR) announced the employment of Lois Wright, making her the first Black woman bus driver in the nation. A twenty-seven-year-old migrant from Georgia, Wright was a widow who was raising two young sons. This job with the DSR was a lifeline. A newspaper article in the *Detroit Evening Times* carefully introduced Wright to the city's residents. Detroit was reeling with racial tensions, marked by the massive migration of Black and white Southerners into the city for high-paying wartime jobs.[47] Strategically avoiding any discussion of Wright's race, the article praised her talents as a driver, her bravery as a widowed mother, and even her physique, noting her height and weight. Warning passengers not to be concerned about a "terrible woman driver," this article applauded Wright's ability to "shift a mean gear" and "control a massive bus steering wheel with the skill of a veteran."[48] This story was freighted with meaning. By highlighting both her body and her competence as a driver, the article cast Lois Wright as a Detroit wartime citizen bus driver. Wright had the fitness and skills to become the first Black woman bus driver in the nation.[49]

In contrast, a newspaper article in the Black-owned *New York Amsterdam News* explicitly discussed Lois Wright's race: "Mrs. Wright is a perfect example of what our women can and will do," the article proudly stated, "if given the opportunity to participate fully in the war effort."[50] This piece in the *New York Amsterdam News* boldly stated what the *Detroit Evening News* omitted: Thousands of Black women were eager to participate in the war effort as workers and were equally excited to perform this labor as patriotic citizens. Featuring a photograph of Lois Wright wearing her police-inspired uniform, she flashed a bright smile as she gripped the bars at the front of the bus, delighting in the authority and responsibility of her position. Even though race relations continued to worsen in Detroit, culminating in a deadly race riot in June 1943, Lois Wright was not the city's only Black woman bus driver. By the end of the war, 20 percent of Detroit's bus drivers and streetcar conductors were African American.[51]

Detroit's pioneering example encouraged other municipal companies to hire Black women drivers. In September 1943, the Triboro Coach Corporation in Queens, New York, announced that they were recruiting African American women to work as drivers, inspectors, and porters. The company expressed a preference for women whose husbands were serving in the military.[52] And in April 1944, the Cleveland Transit Authority hired Edna Letheridge Hawke to become the city's first Black woman bus driver. "The reason I took the job," Hawke told the *Cleveland Call and Post*, "was to prove to skeptical people that colored girls could do as well as any others in the job."[53] Even though Hawke broke through employment barriers, African American women found Ohio to be slow in hiring bus drivers of color. Black Ohioans pressed the Akron Transportation Company to hire Black women drivers, but they were unsuccessful.[54] Even as Greyhound faced labor shortages, Black women had mixed results in securing employment with the company. Greyhound advertised jobs for workers in the baggage room at the company's grand headquarters in Cleveland, but when two Black women inquired about the jobs, they were told that the positions were no longer available.[55]

During World War II, the transportation industry also hired Black women to operate streetcars. One of San Francisco's first Black streetcar conductors was the future writer and poet Maya Angelou. During World War II, she saw white women conductors skillfully steering the city's iconic streetcars up and down San Francisco's hills. After months of waiting, she finally qualified to become a conductor. As she later noted in an interview, "It cost me the earth, but I got the job."[56] The fact that Maya Angelou fought so hard for her job as a streetcar conductor demonstrated that these were not only high-paying positions but also symbolic ones, allowing Black women to command positions of authority that had previously been the domain of white men. The collective pressure that women like Lois Wright, Edna Letheridge Hawke, and Maya Angelou put on the transportation industry demonstrates their heightened claims for wartime citizenship. When buses

FIRST WOMAN BUS DRIVER TAKES OVER

In this image, Lois Wright clutches the bars of the Detroit city bus as she revels in becoming the first Black woman bus driver in the nation. It was revolutionary for Wright to slip on the police-inspired uniform of bus drivers who had harassed thousands of Black women passengers and steer a bus in wartime Detroit. *Source*: Used with permission of *New York Amsterdam News* from "First Woman Bus Driver Takes Over," *New York Amsterdam News*, January 30, 1943, 1. Permission conveyed through Copyright Clearance Center, Inc.

first debuted on American roads in the late 1910s and early 1920s, the industry deliberately hired white men to labor as drivers and police Black women passengers to enforce Jim Crow. The highest position a Black woman could aspire to in the white bus industry was as a cleaner. But during World War II, the gears had shifted so much that Black women were now steering buses in the Jim Crow North.

Despite the acute need for bus drivers, every city in the South refused to hire African Americans. Even in Washington, DC, a city where segregation was becoming more precarious every day, the Capital Transit Company remained steadfast in its opposition, explaining that many Southern war workers would be deeply opposed to Black drivers. The Capital Transit Company limited its 523 Black laborers to trackmen, cleaners, and janitors. African Americans in Washington, DC, took their complaints to the FEPC but were unable to reverse these patterns of employment discrimination.[57] In 1942, Greyhound bus terminals in Norfolk, Virginia, began to hire Black girls to work in their waiting rooms, but this is the only evidence that African Americans made gains in the interstate bus industry.[58] Of course, the bus company in the South that was truly receptive to Black women workers was the Safe Bus Company, where Black women had always worked. It is unclear whether Safe hired Black women to drive its buses during World War II. But at a symposium after World War II, H. C. Woodland, the chair of the board of the Safe Bus Company stated, "Many areas in transit work are now open to women workers."[59]

The employment of Black women drivers on municipal bus lines in Cleveland, Detroit, and New York City demonstrated the profound differences between the Jim Crow North and the Jim Crow South by World War II. This employment helped to confer a measure of citizenship for Black women drivers, but this new authority mapped onto municipal, not interstate, buses. Between 1941 and 1945, Black women throughout the Jim Crow North linked their labor to the state, allowing them to make more progress in the quest for full citizenship rights they had been pursuing since the period of emancipation and Reconstruction. As industrial workers, government clerks, and city bus drivers, Black women performed the identity of war citizens, enlisting in jobs that helped the nation defeat the Axis powers. Unlike most white women who were *recruited* as workers, most Black women had to *fight* for their positions, whether it was assembling an airplane, fastening a cartridge, typing government documents, or transporting workers on a bus. Black women achieved significant victories in the bus industry in the Jim Crow North during World War II—whether it was riding as workers or driving.

Yet the Washington metropolitan region remained a hotspot of contests over bus segregation. The different laws in Maryland, the District of Columbia, and Virginia, coupled with the wartime climate in the nation's capital, created a charged context for Black women war workers and soldiers' wives to contest the legality of bus segregation. During World War II, five Black women war citizens brought these issues to the Supreme Court of Virginia and ultimately the US Supreme Court, thereby fastening the connections between bus segregation and the modern Black freedom struggle.

Bringing Bus Segregation to the Supreme Court of Virginia

In wartime Virginia, across a period of only fourteen months, five Black women were arrested on buses for defying segregation. All five contested their charges, and the Supreme Court of Virginia heard all their appeals. Sarah Davis won her case, Hortense Randolph's case was dismissed on a technicality, and Barbara Lewis was granted another trial. Ethel New and Irene Morgan lost their cases, but the US Supreme Court agreed to hear Morgan's case and ruled in her favor. These five cases marked a critical tipping point in contests over bus segregation. All five of these Black women were war citizens. Sarah Davis and Ethel New were married to soldiers, Hortense Randolph labored as a government clerk, and Barbara Lewis and Irene Morgan were industrial workers. These wartime connections furnished compelling contextual evidence in their legal cases and media coverage, alerting both the courts and the nation that the tide on bus segregation was receding. Even though these cases occurred in Virginia, a Southern state, issues of both geography and mentality loomed large. Virginia was a stalwart practitioner of Jim Crow segregation, but it was also located next to the nation's capital. White residents of Virginia—including newspaper editors, local citizens, and state supreme court justices—realized that the brittle system of bus segregation was breaking, and this ideological evolution resulted in successful legal revolution for Black women war citizens. Virginia was a strategic Southern state for bringing bus segregation cases to higher courts. Virginia's location next to the nation's capital created uneven enforcement of segregation laws, and this fluidity was only heightened because the federal government had constructed annexes in Arlington, Virginia. Untangling the threads between federal and state authority was complicated. There were also a few sympathetic white Virginians who tried to improve conditions for African Americans, largely within a discourse of paternalism.[60] These factors worked favorably toward Black women and bus segregation. But on the other hand, Virginia was still a Southern state with clear segregation laws and bus drivers who were deputized as officers of the peace, putting it in company with Alabama, Georgia, Florida, and South Carolina. And white Virginians, like all Southerners, always articulated defenses of states' rights in the face of federal intervention. These contests began on a city bus in Norfolk, Virginia, in June 1943 at eight o'clock in the evening when Sarah Morris Davis boarded, her patience for bus segregation eroding by the minute.

Sarah Morris Davis was one of thousands of Black women whose life had been upended by World War II. A beloved elementary school teacher in her late thirties, she was a pillar of Norfolk's Black middle class and was active in social and religious causes.[61] When the war erupted, soldiers streamed into Norfolk for training, and she fell in love with Vernon Davis. A native of Portsmouth, Virginia, he had moved to New York City in the 1930s, where he joined the National Guard and then became a staff sergeant. Vernon and Sarah got married in April 1943, and their wedding was featured in the *Norfolk Journal and Guide*.[62] In June 1943, just two months after her wedding, Sarah Davis boarded a Virginia Electric Power Company bus. There was only one available seat—between two white men on a bench near the front of the bus—and she selected it. The bus driver ordered her to vacate this seat and select another one. When she asked him which one, he replied, "I don't care where you sit, as long as you get up and get on in the back of the bus."[63] At the time, there were several white passengers seated in the rear of the bus, but the driver did not force them to move. The driver repeated his request, barking at Davis to move, but she refused. According to court testimony, Davis told the driver, "Well I am going to sit here." After he explained the segregation law to her, she replied, "I know what I am doing; I can read." When he repeated his request a final time, Davis told the driver, "I know my rights."[64] This tense exchange suggested that Sarah Davis's tolerance for bus segregation had disappeared. Telling the driver that she "knew her rights" suggested that she was knowledgeable about Virginia's segregation statute, while her remark that she "could read" is evidence that she had been politicized by the war.

The driver steered the bus to the police station, where he procured a warrant for Sarah Davis's arrest. In police court, Sarah Davis was fined five dollars for violating Virginia's segregation statute.[65] She hired Walter Davis, a Black attorney. One month after her arrest, Sarah Davis appeared in circuit court, where she contested her violation of Virginia's segregation statute on two claims. First, she and her attorney contended that the street

TABLE 6.1 Black women's bus lawsuits during World War II

Year	*First name*	*Last name*	*Occupation*	*State*	*Incident*	*Outcome*	*Amount*	*Attorney*	*Attorney's race*	*Judge*	*Court*
1944	Maggie	Mack	War worker	Missouri	Segregation	**Victory**	$1,500	Claude Cooper	White	Richard Duncan	Eastern Division of the Judicial District of Missouri
1944	Sarah	Davis	Soldier's wife	Virginia	Segregation	**Victory**		Walter Davis	Black	John W. Eggleston	Supreme Court of Virginia
1944	Hortense	Randolph	War worker	Virginia	Segregation	Technicality	$2,500	James H. Raby	Black	Edward Hudgins	Supreme Court of Virginia
1945	Barbara	Lewis	War worker	Virginia	Segregation	Retrial		William S. Diguid	Black	Campbell	Supreme Court of Virginia
1946	Irene	Morgan	War worker	Virginia	Segregation	**Victory**		Thurgood Marshall	Black	Harold Burton	United States Supreme Court
1947	Ethel	New	Soldier's wife	Virginia	Segregation	Defeat	$10,000	Oliver W. Hill	Black	J. Spratley	Supreme Court of Virginia

Sources: *Daviś*, 202 Ga. 13; *Lewis*, 184 Va. 69; *Mack v. Dixie Greyhound* (1944); *Morgan*, 184 Va. 24; *New*, 186 Va. 726; *Randolph*, 183 Va. 420.

where Sarah Davis was arrested was a "public street" and not part of the state highway system, which meant that state laws could not apply. Virginia's segregation statutes only mandated racial segregation on highways, not city streets. And Davis and her attorney argued that the "arbitrary, unjust, and unreasonable police power" that the bus driver had exhibited violated the Fourteenth Amendment of the Constitution. The judge rejected these arguments and affirmed the police court's ruling, sustaining Sarah Davis's five-dollar fine and the charges for violating segregation. He also dismissed the motion for a new trial.[66]

While Davis pondered her next legal steps, another Black woman was arrested. In July 1943, Hortense L. Randolph, a nineteen-year-old clerk in the Navy Department in Arlington, was working late.[67] She missed the bus that she usually rode to her home in Alexandria, Virginia, so she walked to the Pentagon building, where she boarded an A, B, & W bus. When she entered, the bus was crowded with people. Since white passengers occupied nearly all of the seats in the rear, Hortense Randolph and another Black woman selected seats near the front. The bus driver ordered them to move back, and they complied. But Randolph's companion was annoyed. She told the driver that her son and brother were both solders. Alighting the bus, she called the driver "a damn dog." Hortense Randolph echoed her sentiments, charging that "all white people want is to dog Colored people around." The driver ordered her to be quiet, but Randolph continued to taunt him, snapping that he "ought to be over there with Hitler and his gang" and calling him a "white son of a bitch." Randolph's language was more strident than Sarah Davis's, and police officers arrested her for disorderly conduct. At the trial the next morning, Randolph was acquitted but had to pay fifteen dollars. Randolph hired a Black attorney in Alexandria, James H. Raby, to represent her. She sued the A, B, & W Bus Company for $2,500 on the grounds of malicious prosecution. When the case went to trial, the lower court ruled in favor of the bus company.[68] Within the span of only two months in the summer of 1943, two Black women in Virginia drew on the wartime climate to challenge bus segregation.

Sarah Davis's case gained national attention in November 1943 when the Supreme Court of Virginia agreed to hear her appeal. Newspapers in Arizona, California, Pennsylvania, Mississippi, Michigan, South Carolina, New York, Tennessee, and Washington, DC, all picked up the story, informing Black and white readers across the country that there was a "Jim Crow Case before [the] high court" in Virginia and that the state supreme court would "study Jim Crow law."[69] Since national newspapers covered the story, the local press in Virginia understood that the Davis case had major implications. The front-page headline of the *Richmond News Leader* proclaimed, "Court Opens Way to Ruling on 'Jim Crow.'"[70] An editorial in the *Richmond Times-Dispatch* went a step further, boldly calling for the end of racial segregation on buses and streetcars. Written by Virginius Dabney, a racial moderate, the editorial argued that bus segregation had the opposite of its intended effects. Rather than separating the races, bus segregation resulted in "closer interracial contact." Dabney argued that segregation was installed on streetcars in the early twentieth century, when African Americans were only one generation removed from slavery. But now, with wealth and education, Black Americans were better equipped to interact with white Americans. World War II had strained the buses in Norfolk, Portsmouth, and Newport News, making the system of segregation untenable and impossible to enforce. He observed that segregation on trains and "cross-country bus lines" had been "abandoned to a considerable degree, both in Virginia and other Southern states," and predicted that it was "on the way out."[71] Although the editorial incited a great deal of controversy, and even acrimony, it signaled that World War II had upended the racial order in Virginia. While no newspaper in the Deep South would dare oppose racial segregation on buses, this Virginia editorial signaled the difference that region made. After the editorial was published, the Richmond Civic Council convened a conference at the Richmond Beneficial Hall to outline a program for ending racial segregation on the state's buses, trolleys, and trains.[72]

As the United States entered the third year of war, Black women continued to bring the issue of bus segregation to high courts. In February, aircraft worker Maggie Mack marched to the federal courthouse in Missouri. An all-white jury sided with Mack and awarded her $1,500 in damages.[73] Her compensation was not the largest sum that a Black woman had ever received for injury, but her lawsuit in a federal court charged that the driver and officer had enforced segregation with violence. Mack's legal victory against Dixie Greyhound signaled a shifting tide as courts now looked more favorably toward Black women plaintiffs, especially since they were tied to the state.

One month after Maggie Mack's victory, Sarah Davis and her attorney traveled to Richmond, Virginia, and argued the case in front of the Supreme Court of Virginia.[74] While Davis and her attorney awaited the decision, Hortense Randolph learned that the Supreme Court of Virginia agreed to hear her case.[75] The Black and white press followed this news with trained attention, noting that these cases were mounting in the Virginia Supreme

Court and that their pending decisions could have major implications for the doctrine of racial segregation.[76]

In the summer of 1944, as Black and white citizens in Virginia eagerly scanned their newspapers each morning, three more Black women were arrested for defying segregation on Virginia buses across the state. In June, Ethel New was arrested in Lynchburg; in July, Irene Morgan was arrested in Middlesex County; and in August, Barbara Lewis was arrested in Lexington. These three arrests in three months not only demonstrated the chaos of bus travel in wartime Virginia but also showcased Black women's increased politicization.

In June 1944, Ethel New, a soldier's wife, was arrested in Lynchburg, Virginia, after visiting her husband. A resident of Kentucky, she was married to a soldier who was stationed at Camp Pickett.[77] At the time of her visit, she was three months pregnant. In Blackstone, she purchased a bus ticket to return home to Kentucky. When she first boarded the bus, it was packed, forcing her to stand for the first leg of the trip. When passengers disembarked from the vehicle, she selected a seat near the front of the bus, but the driver ordered her to move back. She refused, prompting the bus driver to call two white police officers, who tried to persuade her to move seats, but she refused.

As tensions on the bus escalated, both the bus driver and Ethel New addressed the wartime climate. She told the bus driver that she had been visiting her husband at Camp Pickett and that "he was a soldier wearing the uniform of the United States, a representative of our country, and she had as much right to ride there as anybody else." The bus driver matched her politicized stance, ordering her to "be a good soldier, as good a soldier as your husband, and come on and get in the back seat." The officers then grabbed Ethel New by her arms and legs and pulled her off the bus. Her tears became screams. Bruised and injured, she had to wait another two hours before she could catch a bus to Kentucky, where she visited her doctor. He informed her that her injuries were severe, and she would likely miscarry her pregnancy. A few days later, her fetus died.

Four days after Ethel New suffered her miscarriage, the Virginia Supreme Court released its decision in the Sarah Davis, ruling in her favor and overturning her conviction. The court held that both Black and white passengers must comply with racial segregation. Writing for the court, Supreme Court Justice John W. Eggleston held that drivers were charged with the responsibility of enforcing the "fairness" of segregation and that it applied to both races.[78] This was a controversial opinion and prompted a robust dissent from two other justices. Justice Henry W. Holt held that the matter of racial segregation was "settled law," and he faulted Davis for sitting in the white seat. But he acknowledged that bus drivers often behaved poorly, noting that not all were "knights of the round table." Justice Holt's remark hinted that bus drivers had a poor reputation—and rightly so. But he also critiqued Davis's case, noting that it was not about money but rather "an assault on the segregation statutes themselves." Despite these dissents, the Supreme Court of Virginia ruled in favor of Sarah Davis and faulted the bus driver for failing to enforce racial segregation.[79] Davis's case generated widespread press coverage in both Black and white newspapers.[80]

It is likely that news about Sarah Davis's victorious lawsuit encouraged other Black women to appeal their cases. Only three weeks after the Supreme Court of Virginia handed down its decision in the Davis case, Irene Morgan was arrested in Middlesex County and chose to contest her conviction.[81] Leaders at the NAACP were delighted when Irene Morgan entered their offices.[82] Like Sarah Davis, she had been arrested for defying the statute, not on a charge of disorderly conduct. And only five weeks after Irene Morgan's arrest and conviction in Virginia, Barbara Lewis became the third Black woman that summer to be arrested in a case that would reach higher courts. In August 1944, Lewis, a sixteen-year-old war worker from New York City, was traveling by bus to visit her extended family in Blackstone, Virginia. A few miles outside Washington, DC, the driver ordered her to sit in the very back. Lewis refused, telling the driver that these white passengers "ain't a damn bit better than I am." After a long and protracted battle, the driver lost his patience and began to assault Lewis, physically and sexually. He kicked her in the knee, punched her in the breasts, and reached for an iron pipe.[83] Lewis snatched the pipe and struck the driver on his neck. He grabbed the pipe out of her hands and tried to smash her head, but a Black male passenger grabbed it. Lewis then called the driver a "dumb son of a bitch," and he drove the bus to a police station and officers arrested her. In court the next day, she was charged with disorderly conduct and fined fifty dollars.[84] Lewis returned to New York, where she visited the NAACP's national office.

Barbara Lewis's story mirrored that of so many anonymous Black women in the Deep South. As a sixteen-year-old girl, she, like so many others, expressed frustration that she was forced to adhere to the indignity of Jim Crow. She vented her frustrations by cursing, snapping at the driver, and making snide comments at fellow passengers. But unlike the thousands of Black women and girls who defied racial segregation in the Deep South,

Barbara Lewis was a war worker from New York City, she had access to the national office of the NAACP, and she would soon have the attention and sympathy of people around the world.

Barbara Lewis appealed her conviction to the Circuit Court of Nelson County. During the trial, her lawyer, William S. Diguid, noted that African Americans were not permitted to serve on a jury in that county.[85] The clerk from Nelson County testified that in his twenty-four years as a clerk, not a single African American had ever sat in a jury box despite the fact that there were over 350 Black people who would be qualified to serve at that time. Based on that inequity, he motioned for the jury to be dismissed, but the motion was denied.[86] A jury heard from both sides before charging Barbara Lewis with two crimes: disorderly conduct and criminal assault. The jury sentenced her to six months in jail and a $200 fine. Abram P. Staples, the Virginia attorney general, had instructed the jury to give her a maximum sentence because "she was a New York girl" who came to Virginia to disrupt established racial practices.[87]

The Lewis case demonstrated that the stakes of bus segregation in Virginia had now escalated. She was only sixteen years old, but the state treated her like a grown woman, sentencing her to six months in jail and a heavy fine. Out of the plaintiffs—Sarah Davis, Hortense Randolph, Ethel New, and Irene Morgan—it was Barbara Lewis whose case became a compelling narrative that resonated the most with the politicized Black community. Shortly after her trial concluded in October 1944, pieces about her case appeared in the *Baltimore Afro-American*, the *New York Amsterdam News*, and the *New Journal and Guide*, alerting readers that she was suffering financially and intended to appeal the case. The *New York Amsterdam News* allowed Lewis to write her own article and narrate her version of the events. "Fights 'Virginia' Justice" featured a photograph of Lewis, in which she is wearing her war worker uniform and grinning broadly. To any reader, Lewis's bright personality and youth were instantly palpable.

Not only did Barbara Lewis's case reach Black readers across the country, but it resonated with Black soldiers in the United States, who had suffered similar types of abuses, both on buses and military bases. A group stationed in the Pacific raised money among soldiers, sending the *New York Amsterdam News* $133 for the NAACP's Barbara Lewis Defense Fund. "It's needless to say how we feel about such demonstrations of fascism," the soldiers wrote, vowing that "when we return, we will do all in our power to help abolish it as we are helping her."[88] A group of Black sailors who were stationed in Hastings, Nebraska, also wired money because Lewis's story hit close to home. Two months earlier, Hastings was the site of a three-day riot between Black and white sailors.[89] After reading about Lewis's story, these sailors pooled their money and sent forty-five dollars for the Barbara Lewis Defense Fund.[90] The Lynchburg chapter of the NAACP also joined Lewis's legal defense, holding a mass meeting at the Court Street Baptist Church.[91] Since Lewis was only sixteen years old, the Black press—and the Black community more broadly—deliberately treated her as a girl, a privilege that the white justice system certainly ignored.

As the United States entered its final year of the war, Black women's legal cases against segregation and racial violence on buses in Virginia had reached a critical turning point. It was now routine, not extraordinary, for the Virginia courts to weigh in on the legality of racial segregation. Black soldiers and citizens viewed Black women's battles against segregated seating arrangements, racist bus drivers, and everyday abuse as passengers as a crucial dimension of the Double V for victory in the war effort. As the fighting raged on in the European and Pacific theaters, Hortense Randolph awaited a decision in her case from the Supreme Court of Virginia, Barbara Lewis and Irene Morgan worked on their appeals, and Ethel New prepared her lawsuit.

In January 1945, Hortense Randolph learned that the Supreme Court of Virginia declined to overturn her conviction on a legal technicality. The court held that Randolph had failed to "make the transcript of evidence as part of the record." The court ruled that in order for evidence to be part of the record, it had to be certified by the trial judge.[92] While this ruling did not result in a victory for Hortense Randolph, the case was nonetheless significant because it had traveled to the Supreme Court of Virginia.

As Randolph received the disappointing news, other Black women waited on their appeals. In January, Barbara Lewis and her attorney learned that the Supreme Court of Virginia had granted a writ of error in her case. In an article announcing the news, the *Richmond News Leader* noted that Lewis's case marked the third time that the Supreme Court of Virginia would weigh in on bus segregation.[93] Two months later, Irene Morgan and her legal team were informed that the Supreme Court of Virginia had also agreed to hear her case.[94]

In the spring of 1945, industrial workers Barbara Lewis and Irene Morgan and their lawyers traveled to Richmond, Virginia. Lewis's attorney, William S. Diguid, contested Barbara Lewis's charge of disorderly conduct on a bus since the word "bus" was not part of Virginia's segregation statute, while Morgan's team of lawyers argued that Virginia's racial segregation statutes posed an undue burden on interstate buses.[95] A few months later, Ethel New and her attorneys pleaded her case in a law and equity court. New sued the Atlantic Greyhound Company for $10,000 in damages. In court, New and her physicians offered compelling testimony that her exposure to racial segregation and attendant rough treatment on the bus damaged her body to the point of pregnancy miscarriage.[96] But the jury ruled that her pregnancy miscarriage was unrelated to bus segregation.

In June 1945, the Supreme Court of Virginia handed down two decisions: a partial victory for Barbara Lewis and a defeat for Irene Morgan. In *Lewis v. Commonwealth*, the Supreme Court of Virginia reversed Barbara Lewis's conviction for disorderly conduct and ordered a new trial. The court held that when Virginia enacted its segregation statutes between 1899 and 1900, the statutes stated that passengers could be held for disorderly conduct while riding on a "car, caboose, or any part of a train carrying passengers or employees of any railroad or street railway." The court held that the precise absence of the word "bus" in Virginia's Michie's Code meant that Barbara Lewis could not be convicted of disorderly conduct on a bus and ordered a new trial. The court also held that Lewis did not have a "fair" trial because the court had charged her with both disorderly conduct and assault. But in a dissent, Justice Holt ruled that the jury had found her guilty of disorderly conduct. He wrote that while "disorderly conduct on a bus" was not explicitly written as a misdemeanor in Virginia's segregation statute, it was "plain that Barbara Lewis did make an assault on the bus driver." Justices Hudgins and Gregory concurred in Justice Holt's dissent. Even though Barbara Lewis's case was not unanimous, it was significant that the Supreme Court of Virginia ruled that she was entitled to a new trial.[97] In the aftermath of this case, the Virginia legislature revised its segregation statutes, stating that disorderly conduct could not occur on a bus.[98]

A few days after *Lewis v. Commonwealth* was handed down, Irene Morgan learned that the Supreme Court of Virginia issued its most definitive ruling that upheld racial segregation in Virginia. In a unanimous decision, the court held that Virginia's racial segregation statute "create[d] no such burden" on interstate commerce and that it was "not obnoxious to the Constitution." In this decision, Justice Herbert G. Gregory implied that this matter had reached a critical tipping point. For example, Justice Gregory wrote that "certain members of Congress have attempted to induce Congress to invade the so-called segregation field but so far without success." He then went on to list the three times when Representative Arthur Mitchell from Illinois had introduced legislation to outlaw racial segregation on interstate carriers, including restrooms and waiting areas. In his opinion, Justice Gregory baited the federal government. Acknowledging that this legislation had been introduced but was never successful, he critiqued this strategy, terming it "eloquent silence."[99] And next, it was clear that Virginia, as a Southern state, would likely not accede to this type of federal enforcement, especially in 1945. Additionally, to add some extra ammunition to this legal argument, Justice Hudgins cited *Davis v. Commonwealth*, demonstrating that the Supreme Court of Virginia believed in the fair enforcement of racial segregation for both white and Black Virginians, adding, "Until Congress pre-empts this legislative field by proper enactment, the States continue to have the right to segregate the white and colored races on public carriers." He concluded, "The statute challenged is a reasonable police regulation and applies to both intrastate and interstate passengers. It is not obnoxious to the commerce clause of the constitution."[100] The other six justices agreed with his opinion.

Newspapers across the country circulated news about Irene Morgan's legal defeat.[101] Many African Americans had been confident that Morgan had a solid legal case. In an act of desperation with little chance of success, her attorneys appealed the case to the US Supreme Court. One month later, in July 1945, Barbara Lewis and her attorneys traveled to Lynchburg, where her case was heard in the Nelson County Circuit Court. Even though the outcome of this case is unknown, it is significant that Lewis was able to have a retrial.[102]

In a stunning moment, on December 5, 1945, almost exactly ten years before the Montgomery Bus Boycott began, the US Supreme Court agreed to hear the Irene Morgan case. In March 1946, Morgan traveled to Washington, DC, where Thurgood Marshall, Spotswood Robinson, and William Hastie all argued the case. For William Hastie, this marked a momentous occasion. As an African American adviser to the War Department, Hastie had witnessed the federal government avert its eyes from the violence and brutality that was meted out to Black soldiers, war workers, and nurses. After all, Hastie had resigned his position four months after Norma Green's assault on a bus in Montgomery, Alabama. To be able to argue the case of another Black woman, Irene Morgan, who served the war effort as an aviation worker yet still experienced bus driver violence marked a fitting conclusion to Hastie's career during World War II. Morgan's legal team argued that "segregation on interstate facilities violated a Constitutional rule that states cannot enact laws that interfere with the flow of interstate commerce." They contended that Virginia's racial segregation statute posed an undue burden on commerce and that the varied segregation laws in different states created a confusing system for interstate passengers.[103]

In June 1946, the Supreme Court handed down its decision, favoring Irene Morgan in an 8–1 decision. The court ruled that Virginia's segregation statute posed a burden on interstate bus passengers because they might have to change seats repeatedly. These segregation statutes were not consistent across the country. Eleven states required segregation on buses, while eighteen did not. It was essential for interstate transportation to practice uniformity in order to "promote and protect national travel."[104] Indeed, this decision not only secured a victory for Irene Morgan—and the hundreds of women who had been arrested on interstate buses before her—but also signaled the increasing power of the bus industry in the United States.

Black newspapers across the country celebrated the *Morgan* decision. From Laura Fischer in Indiana in 1927 to Irene Morgan in Virginia in 1944, Black women had been at the forefront of legal campaigns against bus segregation for nearly twenty years. The fact that Irene Morgan was a war worker demonstrated that participation in World War II did matter, enabling her to claim a victory against segregation as part of the wartime battle for expanded Black civil rights. In the immediate aftermath of the *Morgan* decision, Greyhound, the company most responsible for interstate bus segregation, notified its carriers that they would have to comply with the Supreme Court ruling. However, it would soon become clear that the *Morgan* decision was just another empty ruling, symbolic rather than substantive. For one thing, Southern states refused to enforce the ruling. And in the same year that the Supreme Court handed down the *Morgan* decision, military veteran Isaac Woodard was brutally attacked on a bus in Aiken, South Carolina, the same town where Black soldiers were put on a chain gang in 1944 after protesting treatment of a Black woman passenger. In the attack, a police officer named Leonard Shull gouged out both of Woodard's eyeballs. Even though Black women and men had experienced racist violence and even death throughout the war, it was the Woodard assault that galvanized the nation and illuminated the crisis of bus violence. The *Morgan* decision, while significant, signaled that even the legal overturning of racial segregation could not change the culture of the Jim Crow South.

One person who paid close attention to Irene Morgan's case was Ethel New. Only a few days after the Morgan decision was handed down, New and her attorneys appealed her case to a higher court. At the jury trial, the jurors concluded that the bus company had complied with its policy of intrastate segregation and dismissed the charges of abuse.[105] Even though this was a defeat, New was determined to use Irene Morgan's recent victory as leverage for her case. In October 1946, New learned that her case would be heard by the Supreme Court of Virginia, and in September 1947, the court issued its ruling, which affirmed the judgment of the trial court.[106] This was a significant decision because it showed that the court refused to adhere to the Supreme Court's recent ruling in *Morgan v. Virginia.* As the historian Melissa Milewski has argued, the New case marked a watershed moment. In her lawsuit, Ethel New sued a bus company for personal injury. In doing so, she followed in the footsteps of so many Black women in the Jim Crow South, who entered segregated courtrooms and filed lawsuits for the ways that travel on a bus had injured their body.

And yet New's lawsuit was rejected. Her stunning defeat in court can be traced to two key factors. First, in her case, she had faulted not the bus itself or the bus driver per se but rather the system of racial segregation. Unlike the dozens of Black women who had sued bus companies in the Jim Crow South, New did not follow the proper racial script. She explicitly critiqued the system of racial segregation in the South, which was a compelling factor in her legal defeat.[107] But another reason why New may have been unsuccessful was perhaps that the Supreme Court of Virginia sensed that the country was about to change. After hearing all these cases—Sarah Davis, Barbara Lewis, Hortense Randolph, and Irene Morgan—the court defensively clung to the language of states' rights and racial segregation, signaling future legal battles that would rage in the South in the 1950s and 1960s.

Riding for Citizenship

During the World War II period, Black women achieved not only labor victories but also legal ones. It was in the North, the Midwest, and the Washington metropolitan region where Black women were able to connect the war effort with a quest for full citizenship rights in the United States, and buses were a vital part of this process. It was in these regions of the country that Black women illuminated the ties between their labor and the state. Whether they were factory workers, government clerks, or bus drivers, Black women's contributions to the wartime project were a factor in the nation's Allied victory. White women used the propaganda of Rosie the Riveter to demonstrate the patriotism of industrial labor. But Black women marshaled their wartime service and attendant civil rights cases to demonstrate that being able to sit in the front of the bus was a right of American citizenship and democracy. By bravely contesting the doctrine of racial segregation, Maggie Mack, Sarah Davis, Hortense Randolph, Irene Morgan, Barbara Lewis, and Ethel New all brought their cases into higher courts.

Even though these Black women are part of the historical record, they have largely been erased from historical memory. Recovering their narrative demonstrates that the fight to desegregate public transportation was explicitly a Black woman's struggle. Black women were the most marginalized and oppressed bus passengers, and yet they shaped the law and the industry the most. This movement began in the 1920s and 1930s, as Southern women migrated to Northern and Midwestern regions and called on their state civil rights statutes to protest racial segregation. As migrant citizens, Black women were able to use the courts and curry sympathy from some white judges and lawyers, but their cases were limited in scope and had little bearing on state or federal law. But now, as wartime citizens in these same places, Black women's labor was more directly tied to the state. Through their labor, their visibility, and their lawsuits, Black women nudged the nation to understand that equality on transportation was a right of American democracy.

Epilogue

You Don't Have to Ride Jim Crow

> I am especially delighted that my daughter has won the case and to know that I've lived to see an important result of her early training.
>
> —"Attorneys Hail Morgan Decision," *Baltimore Afro-American*, June 15, 1946, 11

> On her way to a doctor's appointment, she refused to give up her seat on a segregated Greyhound bus and appealed her subsequent arrest all the way to the U.S. Supreme Court. The Court's 1946 ruling banning segregation on interstate transportation was an early victory in the struggle for civil rights. It signaled the beginning of the end for Jim Crow. Over all the decades since, Irene Morgan has never asked for accolades, but today we honor her. We acknowledge our debt to her quiet and brave fight for freedom. And we acknowledge the fact that she was there before just about anybody else.
>
> —President Bill Clinton awarding the Citizens Medal to Irene Morgan, January 8, 2001

When World War II ended, a new generation of Black women passengers boarded city and interstate buses. Many of the struggles were the same: Buses continued to be sites of profound inequality, overcrowded with brusque drivers who policed passengers to maintain order. Regardless of region, Black women riders almost always outnumbered Black male passengers. And the fears of abuse and sexual assault hung in the air.

But the regional context of bus segregation shifted. In the Jim Crow North, racism and inequalities on public transportation became more structural and nuanced. In the 1940s and 1950s, as African Americans migrated into industrial and postindustrial cities, such as Chicago, Cleveland, Detroit, Indianapolis, New York, and Pittsburgh, white Americans fled to the suburbs and purchased cars. City and municipal bus lines now attracted an even greater proportion of Black urban riders.[1] During World War II, Black workers had gained a fragile foothold in the transportation industry. Now, in the postwar era, African Americans labored as bus drivers, mechanics, and ticket salespeople. Black activists used transportation jobs to pressure urban leaders to expand employment opportunities for Black workers.[2] As more and more African Americans slipped on bus uniforms and labored for municipal transportation companies in the Jim Crow North, the racial dynamics of bus riding became less pronounced. Black women continued to experience racism, sexism, and sexual assault on buses, but the lawsuits from the first generation, coupled with postwar movements to address urban inequalities, resulted in a markedly different bus experience.[3]

For Black women bus passengers in the Jim Crow South, this second generation revealed more continuity than change. Racial segregation remained the overarching racial order on city and interstate buses. The Southern bus industry continued to insist that white men labor as drivers. As white Southerners purchased cars, African Americans continued to ride segregated buses. The proportion of Black riders on municipal buses surged, while the number of seats in the Black section remained largely unchanged. This ratio was untenable, signaling that the chaos of Southern bus travel in World War II would persist in the postwar era.

In 1946, two matters of Southern bus segregation traveled to the forefront of national conversations. In February, Isaac Woodard, a twenty-six-year-old soldier from New York, was discharged from Camp Gordon in Georgia. During the war, he had served in the 429th Port Battalion and fought in the Pacific Theater. Excited to return home, Woodard boarded a Greyhound bus. When his bus wheeled into Aiken, South Carolina, Woodard protested the segregated seating arrangement with the white bus driver, who ejected him from the vehicle and handed him over to a white police officer, Leonard Shull. The officer beat Woodard mercilessly and gouged out both of his eyeballs. Woodard survived the attack, but the loss of his eyesight became a compelling symbol of bus violence in the Jim Crow South. It took some time for the national press to first report the story, but it soon became a lightning rod in conversations about race relations.[4] Across the Jim Crow North, thousands of concerned citizens wrote letters of support and crammed into urban arenas to raise awareness about Woodard's violent attack.[5] Despite so many outpourings for justice, Isaac Woodard never received any. An all-white jury in South Carolina deliberated for thirty minutes before acquitting Officer Shull of all charges except his admission that he had attacked Woodard. By December 1946, Woodard's assault inspired President Harry S. Truman to call for a national civil rights bill.

In June 1946, the US Supreme Court ruled in *Morgan v. Virginia* that interstate bus segregation was unconstitutional.[6] The legal coverage for the case underscored the importance of a woman as the plaintiff. In an article in the *Baltimore Afro-American*, Irene Morgan's father remarked, "I am especially delighted that my daughter has won the case and to know that I've lived to see an important result of her early training."[7] In the short term, it appeared that Greyhound and other interstate lines would comply with the Supreme Court ruling.[8] But within a month, Black bus riders reported that companies were ignoring the decision.[9] Southern states pressured bus companies to enforce racial segregation on interstate carriers, and neither the Interstate Commerce Commission (ICC) nor the Justice Department exerted any pressure on bus companies or individual states to enforce *Morgan v. Virginia*.[10]

In the aftermath of the Woodard assault and the *Morgan* decision, citizens in the Jim Crow North watched the spectacle of bus violence and segregation in the Jim Crow South. Activists in the interracial and nonviolent Congress of Racial Equality (CORE) organized a Ride of Reconciliation to test the enforcement of the *Morgan* decision on buses traveling throughout the South. CORE activists recruited sixteen Black and white volunteers and limited the participation to men. This decision was both ahistorical and short-sighted, marking a stunning rebuke to the hundreds of Black women who had been on the front lines against discrimination, particularly the forty-three plaintiffs from the first generation.[11] The presence of women passengers, CORE leaders argued, had the potential to "exacerbate an already volatile situation." Women would be included in the second ride.[12] Black women on the planning committee disagreed with this strategy.[13] Gendered blind spots in the male civil rights community persevered into the second generation.

The Ride of Reconciliation began in Washington, DC, where participants boarded buses bound for the South. Men sat in integrated pairs, testing whether bus drivers traveling across state lines would enforce the *Morgan* decision. In total, police officers arrested twelve men in six different episodes.[14] The fact that the Ride of Reconciliation started in Washington underscored the stark differences that now divided the North and the South. In the previous generation, Black women like Laura Fischer, Callie Stevens, and Paulina Stevens had experienced discrimination on interstate buses in the Jim Crow North, but a generation later, the focus was squarely on the South. The Ride of Reconciliation ended in defeat. CORE leaders concluded that the *Morgan* decision was not enforced in southern states, and waves of disappointment swept across Black activist communities. Segregation on interstate transportation remained intact.

But Black women continued to protest. In 1952, Sarah Keys, a WAC, boarded a Safeway Trailways bus from Fort Dix in New Jersey to her family's home in North Carolina. During the ride, the driver ordered her to switch seats, and she refused. She was arrested, and she contested the charges. After a long and protracted legal battle, her case went before the ICC, which ruled in November 1955 that segregated seating on all buses and trains had to end and ordered the removal of signs demarcating "white" and "colored" in interstate transportation terminals.[15] This ICC ruling not only affirmed the *Morgan* decision but underscored the persistence of Black women's lawsuits against segregated transportation. It was Sarah Keys's defiance, not the Ride of Reconciliation, that nudged this movement forward.

While national civil rights organizations strategized sweeping campaigns for Black freedom in the 1950s, women in the Deep South continued to fight for dignity on local buses. After World War II, Black businessmen opened their own bus company in Baton Rouge, Louisiana, running these vehicles as an alternative to the violence and humiliation of city buses.[16] But in 1949, the Baton Rouge City Council outlawed the city's Black buses.[17] By the early 1950s, conditions on Baton Rouge buses had become overcrowded and chaotic. In March 1953, the Baton Rouge City Council enacted Ordinance 222, which stated that passengers could select bus seats on a first come, first serve basis. The city's white bus drivers went on strike, refusing to drive these types of integrated buses. These white drivers were soon joined by their wives, who marched in support of their husbands. After a few days, city officials overturned Ordinance 222. African Americans in Baton Rouge, the majority of whom were women, responded by staging a boycott of city buses. With no riders, the bus system collapsed, and Black activists reached an agreement with the city, which would make more seats available for Black passengers while still preserving segregation. Even though the boycott lasted only four days and did not result in widespread integration, it was a pivotal moment for Black community activism and would serve as a model for future actions. But in the Jim Crow South in 1953, white bus drivers continued to play a central role in enforcing bus segregation, wielding significant political power.

The protests in Baton Rouge were rooted in a rich culture of Black women's activism that stretched across decades.[18] In the 1930s and 1940s, Fannie Grant, Leathy Hughes, and Rosa Valdry had sued Baton Rouge buses for bodily injury, and now the next generation staged a boycott. Patience for bus segregation across the Deep South was unraveling. Eleven months after the Baton Rouge bus boycott ended, the US Supreme Court overturned school segregation in *Brown v. Board of Education.* Black women everywhere, especially in Alabama, wondered whether this ruling would make any difference.

In 1954, Joanne Gibson Robinson, a professor at Alabama State College and head of the Women's Political Council, wrote a threatening letter to William A. Gayle, the mayor of Montgomery, Alabama, asking him if the recent Supreme Court ruling applied to buses. If he did not integrate city buses, she told him, Black women in Montgomery would stage a boycott.[19] In the next year, as momentum for a boycott spread, two Black women—Claudette Colvin and Mary Louise Smith—were arrested on buses for defying segregation. Each woman's arrest presented the opportunity to launch a boycott, but activists feared that neither woman had the respectability to serve as the public face of the struggle. But when Rosa Parks was arrested in December 1955, leaders knew that she had the alchemy of activism and pedigree to represent the boycott.

Rosa Parks was a seasoned bus rider, serving as a bridge between the first and second generations. "Protest," she recalled, "was in my blood." As a child in Alabama, she had watched her mother, Leona McCauley, stand up to white bus drivers and experience all degrees of mistreatment.[20] During World War II, Parks had worked as a seamstress at Maxwell Field in Montgomery, Alabama, witnessing firsthand the escalating violence on buses. Undoubtedly she would have heard about the arrest of 2nd Lt. Norma Green in 1942 over an incident about bus seating and the devastating details of her assault. And Parks was a beneficiary of the War Department's memorandum, enabling her to travel on integrated buses at Maxwell Field.[21] As the NAACP's investigator into the brutal gang rape of Recy Taylor in Abbeville, Alabama, in 1944, she knew that Black women were not safe, on or off the bus.

Rosa Parks and thousands of Black women in Montgomery, Alabama, made the boycott a woman's war. Even though Black men, including the Reverend Martin Luther King Jr., Fred Gray, E. D. Nixon, and others dominated media attention as the iconic leaders, it was Black women who had been the city's bus riders and were now the movement's walkers. The historical narrative of the Montgomery Bus Boycott has now dispelled the mythology of Rosa Parks as a tired accidental activist and recentered the importance of Black women in the story.[22] For 381 days, thousands of working-class Black women marched with their feet against the city buses in Montgomery. Photographs of Black women walking as they flashed beaming smiles appeared in national publications such as *Life* magazine and newspapers across the country. One woman, Mother Pollard, was a walker in her seventies. She famously declared, "My feets is tired, but my soul is rested."[23] These images and words resonated with the first generation of Black women who had ridden buses in the 1920s, 1930s, and 1940s. These passengers had written letters, spoken to newspaper reporters, notarized their testimony in affidavits, and filed lawsuits. And now, in this second generation, Black women drew on these traditions of protest to stage boycotts. Escalating their previous claim that their dollars and cents entitled them to ride in dignity, they now channeled these threats into collective action, staying off the buses entirely and depriving municipal buses of their hard-earned money. Of course, the boycott relied on a mixture of on-the-ground resistance and legal strategy. Shortly after the boycott began, Aurelia Browder, Susie McDonald, Claudette Colvin, and Mary Louise Smith all agreed to become plaintiffs in a civil action lawsuit challenging the legality of bus segregation. The case, known as *Browder v. Gayle*, was heard in the district court, which affirmed that segregation, even beyond education, violated the due process and equal protection clause of the Fourteenth Amendment. On December 17, 1956, the US Supreme Court upheld this decision.[24] Three days later, on December 20, a federal marshal handed the decision to Mayor Gayle, a fitting conclusion to a two-year struggle between Black women and the mayor's office over the matter of federal enforcement. On December 21, 1956, for the first time in history, Black women could select any seat on a Montgomery bus.

It is possible that 783 miles away in Akron, Ohio, Norma Green McNeil was watching this boycott, reflecting on her own experience. After she healed from her brutal attack over bus segregation in Montgomery, Alabama, in 1942, she shipped overseas to Liberia and nursed soldiers. Before the war ended, she met her husband, Noah McNeil, a native of Mississippi. After the war, he attended dental school through the GI Bill and the couple settled in Akron, Ohio, where she worked as a nurse at the city hospital.[25] It is not surprising that Norma Green McNeil opted to move to Ohio, a state with a civil rights statute. Norma Green McNeil never received any reparations for her attack. It might have provided some consolation to know that she was surrounded by women determined to take action, stretching from the nurses who wrote a pointed letter to Attorney General Francis Biddle to activists in the Women's Political Council who waited impatiently for a galvanizing bus arrest. It is only by telling this longer story that the dots can be connected between Norma Green's assault in 1942 and Rosa Parks's arrest in 1955. The Department of Justice investigated Green's attack but took no action. Fourteen years later, the Supreme Court issued a ruling and forced the local bus system in Alabama to uphold it.

This matter of federal enforcement was the reason why *Morgan v. Virginia* was only a paper law. By the end of 1960, the Black freedom struggle had entered a new era. Heartened by victories in Montgomery, Alabama, and Little Rock, Arkansas, and by the widespread success of the sit-in movement across the South, activists were finally ready to revisit the struggle to integrate interstate buses. By 1960, the *Morgan* decision, their key text, was fourteen years old. Subsequent rulings, such as the *Keys* case and *Boynton v. Virginia* (1960), formed the supporting evidence. Between May and December 1961, 431 civil rights workers—Black and white, women and men—boarded buses that traveled down to the South to test the enforcement of the *Morgan* decision. Only 25 percent of the riders were women, another failure to recognize that Black women had founded bus protest in the United States. Women riders were expected to wear dresses and high heels.[26] During the Freedom Rides, Americans learned what Black women riders already knew: Buses and contests over bus integration were violent. White Southerners punched Freedom Riders with bats, pipes, and bicycle chains while they bombed buses and set off tear gas. Many of the places that the Freedom Riders visited were cities that had witnessed Black women's bus protests in the first generation, whether it was a letter or a lawsuit. By the end of 1961, the federal government pressured the ICC to enforce the law and outlaw segregation in interstate travel. Irene Morgan's bus arrest in 1944 had finally reached its long and circuitous conclusion.

Even though Irene Morgan's case inspired the Freedom Rides and the lyrics in Bayard Rustin's song—"Get on the bus, sit anywhere, because Irene Morgan won her case"—her legacy remained as depoliticized as that of Rosa Parks. On that Greyhound bus in Virginia in July 1944, she had refused to move seats, snatched the arrest warrant out of the officer's hands, and kicked the sheriff. Morgan's resistance on the bus and lawsuit against segregation were routine behaviors for Black women passengers. But the failure to understand that Black women bus passengers were, in fact, political activists meant that male leaders in the Ride of Reconciliation, the Montgomery Bus Boycott, and even the Freedom Rides downplayed the role of women and cast Irene Morgan and Rosa Parks as quiet, timid, and tired. When President Bill Clinton awarded Irene Morgan Kirkaldy the Presidential Citizens Medal in 2001, he praised her for the "quiet and brave fight for freedom."

None of the details in Irene Morgan's encounter on that Virginia bus would indicate that she was quiet. And President Clinton immortalized her, wishing to "acknowledge the fact that she was there before just about anybody else."[27]

But Irene Morgan was not the first. *Policing Passengers* has revealed the hidden history of the first generation of Black women who took the bus industry to court, starting with Laura Fischer's victory in 1927 in Indiana and ending with Irene Morgan's success in the Supreme Court in 1946. Through their lawsuits, Black women passengers demonstrated that they could utilize state civil rights statutes to sue against segregation. They forced white judges in both Northern and Southern courts to hold that it was inappropriate for white bus drivers to assault Black women passengers, highlighting the physical, sexual, and racial power imbalances. Their cases also prompted courts to hold that buses had to transport impoverished passengers to their destinations, that buses were responsible for lost luggage, and that racial segregation was a system that had to be enforced fairly. Black women's activism taught the NAACP how to litigate these cases, and after years of experimenting, the US Supreme Court handed down the *Morgan* decision, stating that segregation on interstate commerce posed an undue burden. The narrative arc of this first generation of bus riders is a remarkable testament to the richness of the early civil rights movement and the litigiousness of working-class Black women in both the North and the South.

Yet there is a risk in romanticizing this resistance. Highlighting these legal victories obscures the physical and sexual violence and emotional abuse that Black women experienced in the early days of the bus industry. Black women arrested on buses became connected to the carceral state, spending time in jail cells, workhouses, and chain gangs. Several Black women lost pregnancies because of the abuse they sustained on a bus. A white bus driver raped Charlotte Wright, a grandmother in rural Georgia. Many white male passengers, often intoxicated, abused and assaulted vulnerable passengers. Sitting in the back of the bus exposed Black women to rain, snow, wind, and carbon monoxide, forcing them to seek medical care when they alighted. And hundreds bore the physical and emotional scars of these terrifying encounters with bus drivers and police officers. When drivers and officers arrested Black women for their refusal to abide by racial segregation, each arrest mattered. It gave Black women a criminal record and contributed to the prevailing cultural narrative that they were inherently deviant and disorderly.

Racism and missed bus connections also had real economic costs. For Black women migrants living on the edges of poverty, this was about more than inconvenience. Black women had to pay extra money to hold the bodies of deceased relatives, missed important hearings about property, and even lost the chance to say goodbye to relatives before they passed. Buses misplaced Black women's suitcases, handbags, coats, and money. Buses and rest stops were some of the most potent symbols that reinforced the Jim Crow color line. The bus industry sold to Sarah and violated Violet. On buses, Black women observed firsthand how the industry elevated white women passengers as it denigrated Black passengers. These racialized disparities stretched from bus driver treatment to the spatial configurations of buses to who was afforded dignity and privacy in sex-segregated restrooms. These inequalities were magnified during World War II, when white women became a valued part of the wartime state, while Black women, especially in the South, only experienced a surge of state-based violence as the government partnered with the bus industry.

The thirty-eight nurses at Tuskegee knew this well. In 1942, sobered by the news of Norma Green's assault, they wrote a letter to Attorney General Francis Biddle. "If we are Americans," they told Biddle, "we want a statement of justice. Anyone of us may be beat-up by these very same people who are supposed to protect us—namely, the police and bus drivers, who carry guns," they explained to the attorney general. "Any Negro woman," they stated, "may be attacked and pommeled unless the government we are trying to support gives us the protection a woman deserves as a birthright."[28] *Policing Passengers* has told the story of Black women passengers who experienced policing at the hands of bus drivers and police officers. Hundreds of Black women in this first generation contested their violent treatment on buses because it undermined their fervent belief in the promise of American democracy. Their fight lit a path for the postwar Black freedom struggle and continues to burn today, even as the flame of American democracy flickers.

Acknowledgments

Since I was a young child, I have always traveled on public transportation. When I was three, I remember riding the city bus in Baltimore with my father, traveling between our house, his office, and my day-care center. He always allowed me to press the yellow strip for our stop. When I started graduate school, I moved to Washington, DC, and rode the metro for seven years. As a lover of modern architecture, I reveled in the subway's stunning concrete stations, with their dramatic coffered ceilings. In my first job at Drexel University in Philadelphia, I took the city's rickety subway for two years, always appreciating the 1970s faux wood interior and orange plastic seats. I also taught Matthew Countryman's *Up South* and learned about the importance of transportation labor to the Northern Black freedom struggle. I was such a fan of public transportation that when I moved to Michigan, I arrived without a car. For two years I took, and adored, the Ann Arbor bus, despite the frigid temperatures. I was such an outlier in a state with a rich automotive history that I became iconic; rumors circulated about the "professor who does not have a car." Riding public transportation in Ann Arbor, Baltimore, Philadelphia, and Washington, DC, introduced me to the unique culture of each bus and subway line, the transit workers, and the daily commuters. These experiences piqued my curiosity about the role of transportation in shaping the everyday experiences of Black women before the 1950s. I have since discovered the incredible history of Black women's resistance in the face of the violent bus industry. It is my hope that any Black woman can ride in dignity, freedom, and safety.

I am honored to teach at Eastern Michigan University (EMU), a regional public university committed to educating all students. EMU has offered me incredible research support. I received a one-semester sabbatical and a one-semester Faculty Research Fellowship, and I used those semester releases to conduct research. I was also awarded a Summer Research Award, which allowed me to devote an entire summer to writing. I also want to acknowledge the Provost's Office and the Department of History & Philosophy, which funded small research trips. I was awarded a James H. Brickley Endowment Award, which provided a significant amount of money to start visiting legal archives in the South. As I was approaching the very end of writing, I learned about the devastating case of Charlotte Wright. With only a tiny bit of Brickley money left, I purchased a plane ticket to Atlanta so I could visit the Georgia State Archives in Morrow, unsure whether I would find anything. When I arrived that morning, I was greeted with a heavy box. When I opened it, I found Wright's entire case file. I will always tell this story because it underscores how EMU's research support allowed me to take research trips based on intuition and unearth archival gold. I want to thank Steve Pernecky in the graduate school, who oversaw these research awards and was always encouraging. Thank you to Rachelle Marshall, Carissa Blount, and Fran Calhoun for expertly processing my research trips and book image permissions.

This book project traveled in new and exciting ways when Marty Shichtman invited me to apply for a Kirk and Sharon Profit Social Justice Fellowship through EMU's Center for Jewish Studies. This fellowship supported my travel to archives in Ohio and Washington, DC, and allowed me to investigate the Jewish Americans who spoke out against bus segregation in the 1920s, 1930s, and 1940s. I want to thank Kirk Profit for funding this fellowship and asking insightful questions. Adding this layer to my research allowed me to explore the inner world of lawyer Milton Konvitz, whose legal career at the NAACP was very important for the Black women in this book, as well as the Jewish outpouring of support for the brutal assault of Isaac Woodard. I would also like to thank Katie Cangany and the Jewish Historical Society of Michigan, who hosted me to discuss this research and invited me to publish an article in *Michigan Jewish History*. This fellowship allowed me to play a larger role in Jewish studies at EMU, and it has been a delight to get to know Decky Alexander, Jeff Bernstein, and Bob Erlewine.

My academic job continues to grow. Since I started this book, I have chaired History, chaired the President's Commission on Women, and become the interim head of the Women's and Gender Studies Department. Embarking on a temporary career in administrative roles has been energizing and illuminating. As EMU's motto states, "If you want something done, ask a busy woman." It has been a joy to witness this tradition of feminist leadership in action, and I want to express my admiration for Kathryn Wilhoff, Kate Mehuron, Erin Kido, Debbie Ingram, Brooke Boyst, Alexis Braun Marks, Barbara Patrick, April Calkovsky, Nina Contis, Harriet Lindsay, all the members of the Women's Commission, my two deans—Dana Heller and Carol Bishop Mills—and my former department head and now associate dean, Peter Higgins. And I would not be successful in any of these roles without the support of another former department head and now associate dean (see a pattern?), Jim Egge. From the moment I started at EMU, Jim has been my cheerleader. It has been a delight to imagine, and then accomplish, so many ambitious projects with him, and I deeply appreciate his boundless energy, enthusiasm, and kindness. Thanks for gifting me *The Warmth of Other Suns*.

Writing a book can be a lonely process, but it has been wonderful to have the support of fellow writers in History, including Ashley Johnson Bavery, Joseph Engwenyu, Jesse Kauffman, John McCurdy, Richard Nation, and Steven Ramold. Ashley and Richard gave me incredible feedback on my lawsuit chapters, John pushed me to sharpen the introduction, and Steven read my World War II chapters. Toward the very end, Brendan Fay in Art History generously wrote me a long and detailed email about the Dorothea Lange photograph in chapter 4, and I am endlessly grateful. Joseph Engwenyu carefully read chapter 1 and offered excellent context for the *Highway Log*'s Swaziland cartoon. It is a testament to the intellectual breadth of EMU that I can turn to the expertise of United States historians, African historians, and art historians, and I am very grateful. My graduate student Hannah Doty put the bus companies and bus lines mentioned in the book into a spreadsheet and helped me keep track of the lawsuits. It has been a privilege to teach or know the following EMU students: Marie Sarnacki, Nada Al-Hanooti, Kari Havenaar, Alyssa Williams, Gaby Griffin, and Anisha Bhattarai. You are the future. The Honorable Daniel Opperman, EMU alum, has been supportive of this book from its inception. I am forever grateful for his kindness and generosity, whether it is through financing our History Book Party or creating a fund to support the publication of our book images. The History Section at EMU owes its strength to the tireless advocacy and financial generosity of Judge Opperman.

Michigan is a fantastic place to teach Black women's history because of the powerhouse scholars. I am very grateful to the kindness and support of Kidada Williams, LaKisha Simmons, Ava Purkiss, Jennifer Dominique Jones, Robyn Spencer-Antoine, Stephen Berrey, and LaShawn Harris. During the time I researched and wrote this book, I was privileged to participate in two seminars at Michigan, "Narrating Black Girlhood" and "Black Feminist Method," both of which were revelatory. "Black Feminist Method" transformed portions of my introduction, and I spent the entire three days in awe of the brilliance of the seminar participants, including Ava, Jennifer, LaShawn, Robyn, Mix Mann, Rianna Johnson-Levy, and Carina Ray. Thank you to the University of Michigan Humanities Collaboratory for funding this incredible work.

Writing a national book is a daunting challenge. I would like to thank the archivists at the Chicago History Museum; the Library of Congress, the Moorland-Spingarn Research Center, and the National Archives in Washington, DC; the Western Reserve Historical Society in Cleveland; the Alabama State Archives in Birmingham; the Walter P. Reuther Library in Detroit; and the Library of Virginia in Richmond. The Interlibrary Loan staff in Halle Library at EMU has been wonderful and facilitated my access to hard-to-find newspapers and periodicals. I would also like to thank the staff in the Special Collections Research Center and the Buhr Shelving Facility at the libraries of the University of Michigan, Ann Arbor, which allowed me to gather images from *Bus Transportation*.

Adding a legal history dimension to this project utterly transformed this book. In 2019, my sister started law school and gave me access to her legal database. That password was a game changer, enabling me to locate some of the first tort cases. And then, in October 2023, I traveled to the law library of the Supreme Court of Virginia and met Gail Warren. Gail was incredibly generous. Not only did she locate the appellate briefs and trial transcripts for all of the Virginia Supreme Court cases, but she put me in contact with every state supreme court law librarian. Because of these connections, I was able to track down materials for twelve cases in the Jim Crow South. I would like to thank Thomas P. Davis and James B. Fish at the law library of the Supreme Court of North Carolina; State Librarian of Mississippi Stephen Parks; Bryan Hastings of the Parish Clerk of Court in Baton Rouge, Louisiana; Janet Meyer, law librarian of the Supreme Court of South Carolina; and Stephen Spence, archivist at the National Archives in Kansas City, Missouri.

I am grateful for the Michigan friendships of Ashley Johnson Bavery, Nora Krinitsky, Kim Barrett, John McCurdy, Kit French, Alexis Braun Marks, and Jim Sanouris. In the last year, Jim became my walking partner and is always up for "processing." It remains a joy that Ashley is my friend and colleague. John is my confidant and my role model as a historian. My college friends, Molly Gower and Lindsay Theile, continue to bring great joy to my life. I am so happy we all call the Midwest home.

My group text of Greg Argeros and Melissa Jones is one of my daily delights. Greg and Melissa are simply my favorite people. They are always on my side, and their support is my daily beacon of sanity in a seriously crazy world. Since I have been in administration, Greg and Melissa always brighten my office. These two people make me laugh every single day, a true gift.

I am honored to be publishing a second book with the University of North Carolina Press. From the beginning, Brandon Proia expressed enthusiasm for this project and asked terrific questions about Greyhound. I was a little bit panicked when he left UNCP but utterly delighted when Dawn Durante joined the press. I had admired her career from afar, and it was a dream that I got to work with her. From our first Zoom meeting, Dawn has been 100 percent supportive. I am so grateful for her advocacy, her instincts as an editor, and her deep knowledge of publishing. I am equally honored to be a part of Justice, Power, and Politics. I want to thank Heather Ann Thompson and Rhonda Y. Williams for recommending my book for inclusion in this distinguished series. Everyone at UNCP has been wonderful, and I am always inspired by the social justice mission of this press. I want to thank my two anonymous readers, whose rich insights and brilliant suggestions improved this book immeasurably.

Jim OD, a brilliant writer, sent me beautiful songs written in the 1940s, 1950s, 1960s, and 1970s, and then thoughtfully analyzed them with me. Those epically long conversations inspired my ideas and sharpened my prose. Knowing you feels natural, like sunshine feeding daisies. CBW, SRT.

I met CD on my first research trip to the Western Reserve Historical Society, and it was my favorite discovery. Seeing him on every research trip to Cleveland has been the most unexpected delight and the sweetest reward. FFF.

I am fortunate to have a loving and supportive extended family. I would like to thank Fred V. Murphy, the late Fayne Murphy, Matt Murphy, Fred Murphy, Julia Murphy, Paula Murphy, and Virginia Kirk. Ted Naos was so supportive of my academic career, and I am sad he did not live to see the second book, but I am so grateful for Barbara Naos. My father, John Murphy, still asks me when I plan to go to law school, but I hope my turn to legal history has satisfied him a bit. In the time it took me to write this book, my mother, Frances Lewis, retired from dentistry and has been volunteering as a docent, first at the Walters Art Museum and now at the American Visionary Art Museum. I am inspired by her passion for art and her bravery to embark on a new career. My parents took me on my first bus ride and were endlessly supportive of this book when all I had were vague ideas and source fragments. There would be no book without my sister, Maggie Murphy. Along with the password to the legal database that unlocked every tort lawsuit in this book, she gave me the key to her condo in Washington, DC, every summer. And even though she thinks I am dramatic and ridiculous (I am), her unconditional love and support sustain me always.

Notes

Abbreviations Used in Notes

BECTD	Birmingham Electric Company Transportation Department, Alabama State Archives
Davis v. State-Georgia	*Davis v. State*, Georgia Archives
Greyhound-Chicago	Greyhound Collection, Chicago History Museum
LC	Library of Congress
NARA	National Archives and Records Administration
Racial Situation, NARA	"Racial Situation: Tabulation of Racial Incidents"
RG	Record Group
WRHS	Western Reserve Historical Society

Introduction

1. "Virginia Supreme Court to Take Brazen Stand on Jim Crow," *Baltimore Afro-American*, June 16, 1945, 1. See also trial transcript, Morgan v. Commonwealth, 184 Va. 24 (1945), Supreme Court of Virginia Law Library, Richmond, Virginia.

2. *Morgan*, 328 U.S. 373.

3. Robinson, *Montgomery Bus Boycott*; McGuire, *Black Women*; Theoharris, *Rebellious Life*.

4. Tetrault, *Myth of Seneca Falls*, 120.

5. See, for example, Barnes, *Journey from Jim Crow*; Bay, *Traveling Black*. The major exception is Kelley, who, in a pioneering book chapter, "Congested Terrain," acknowledged that Black women were twice as likely to be arrested on Birmingham buses as men. R. D. G. Kelley, *Race Rebels*, 55–75.

6. Gregory, *Southern Diaspora*, 330, table A.1; Hine, "Black Migration," 127–46.

7. Carl W. Stocks, "America Moves by Bus Across the Continent," January 6, 1929, *New York Times*, 160.

8. For the growing literature on Black travel, see B. L. M. Kelley, *Right to Ride*; Pryor, *Colored Travelers*; Ortlepp, *Jim Crow Terminals*; Sorin, *Driving While Black*; Bay, *Traveling Black*.

9. Sanders, *Forgotten Migration*.

10. See Green, *Negro Motorist Green Book*; Bay, *Traveling Black*, 141–47.

11. Catsum, *Freedom's Main Line*; Arsenault, *Freedom Riders*; Hollars, *Road South*.

12. For recent works in Black legal history, see, for example, Smith, *Emancipation*; Welke, *Recasting American Liberty*; Welch, *Black Litigants*; Milewski, *Litigating*

Across the Color Line; Goluboff, *Lost Promise*; Devlin, *Girl Stands at the Door*; Burnham, *By Hands Now Known.*

13. Parker, *Department Stores.*

14. Bus drivers either were outfitted with weapons or used their accoutrements as weapons. For billy clubs, see "Says Kentucky Agent Made Her Leave Bags, Threatened Her with Club: Goes to Law," *Cleveland Call and Post*, August 8, 1942, 13A; for ticket punchers, see Charles O. Lightfoot, Camp McCain, Mississippi, to NAACP, June 17, 1943, Camp McCain, Mississippi, box 153, folder 5, National Association for the Advancement of Colored People Papers, pt. 2, series B, Manuscript Division, Library of Congress, Washington, DC (hereafter cited as NAACP-LC); for guns, see "Sister of Slain Soldier Asks Stimson for Problem," *Pittsburgh Courier*, September 5, 1942, 1; and for fists, see memo, "Leah Davis, Mary Miller, and Eleanor Anderson, New York City," May 1944, box 185, folder 3, NAACP-LC. For a discussion of weapons used on Black women on chain gangs, see LeFlouria, *Chained in Silence*, 71.

15. For an excellent discussion of Black women as both passengers and workers in the railroad industry, see Thaggert, *Riding Jane Crow*, and as both customers and workers in department stores, see Parker, *Department Stores.*

16. Lewis, *In Their Own Interests*; Gilmore, *Gender and Jim Crow*; Hunter, *To 'Joy My Freedom*; Dailey et al., eds., *Jumpin' Jim Crow*; Korstad, *Civil Rights Unionism*; Ortiz, *Emancipation Betrayed*; B. L. M. Kelley, *Right to Ride.*

17. See Welke, *Recasting American Liberty*; B. L. M. Kelley, *Right to Ride*; Pryor, *Colored Travelers.*

18. Few historians have analyzed the history of the bus industry in the United States. When they have discussed these companies, such as Greyhound and Trailways, they have largely focused on the postwar Black Freedom struggle, especially the Ride of Reconciliation in the 1940s and the Freedom Rides in the 1960s. See, for example, Catsam, *Freedom's Main Line*; Arsenault, *Freedom Riders.* Scholars have not sufficiently examined the *development* of these bus corporations and critically analyzed how white leaders and public relations executives branded their companies. Public historians have documented the cultural history of Greyhound and other bus companies, but they have not grappled with the ways that these bus lines constructed their racial practices within the precise contexts of racial segregation, imperialism, and migrant policing at the Southwest border. For a general history of buses, see C. Jackson, *Hounds of the Road*; Walsh, *Making Connections*; Hixson, *Pick of the Litter*; Gabrick, *Go the Greyhound Way.*

19. Many bus founders and executives were connected to the railroad industry. For example, Robert Budd served as the president of the Greyhound Management Company in the 1930s. His father, Ralph Budd, had worked on railroads in Panama, China, and Siberia and became president of the Great Northern Railroad. Marcus Dow, a Greyhound executive, had served as a claims agent for New York Central Lines. See "Ralph Budd Dies; Led 2 Railroads," *New York Times*, February 3, 1962, 16; "Dow's Promotion Brings More Shifts for Officials," *Buffalo Evening News*, March 7, 1913, 14; and "Four Railroads Have Alliances with Greyhound," *St. Louis Post Dispatch*, November 24, 1934, 2C.

20. Thaggert, *Riding Jane Crow.*

21. Thaggert, *Riding Jane Crow*, 4.

22. Bay, *Traveling Black*, 22–31.

23. Bay, *Traveling Black*, 40–41.

24. Bay, *Traveling Black*, 31; Pryor, *Colored Travelers*, 79–81.

25. Bay, *Traveling Black*, 152.

26. The most extensive discussion of Black women in the railroad industry can be found in Thaggert, *Riding Jane Crow.*

27. For a discussion of Indigenous Americans' discrimination on buses, see William Arapahoe, Miami, Florida, to Department of Justice, Washington, DC, December 14, 1937, Department of Justice Papers, RG 60, Entry A1, Class 90-0-2, Indian Matters, Litigation Files, 1928–1985, box 12, folder: file 90-2-0-173, National Archives II, College Park, Maryland; for a discussion of Mexican migrants' discrimination on buses, see "Exposes Bus Segregation in Chicago," *Chicago Defender*, November 19, 1927, 1; "Mexican Cotton Pickers Contracts, Jailed," *Los Angeles Sentinel*, December 9, 1948, 27.

28. Woodward, *Strange Career of Jim Crow*, 93.

29. Murray, *Song in a Weary Throat*, 142.

30. "Employer and Employee as Comrades," *Bus Transportation*, October 1925, 495. See also "Encouraging Service with a Smile," *Bus Transportation*, August 1924, 348–49; "Substantial Citizens Drive Colonial Coaches," *Bus Transportation*, May 1929, 242–44; "Safety Authority Joins Greyhound," *Indianapolis Star*, June 16, 1929, 6.

31. This image was meant to be Booker T. Spicely (see chap. 5). In July 1944, bus driver Herman Lee Council murdered Booker T. Spicely on a Duke Power Company bus. He was tried but acquitted in a swift trial in September.

32. For the historiography on Black women and interracial police violence, see Wolcott, *Remaking Respectability*, 111–14; Hicks, *Talk with You*; 64–70; Simmons, *Crescent City Girls*, 251; Haley, *No Mercy Here*, 252; Murphy, *Jim Crow Capital*, 75–109; Fischer, *Streets Belong to Us*; Harris, *Tell Her Story.* For recent works on policing, see King, *Whose Harlem Is This, Anyway?*; Felkor-Kantor, *Policing Los Angeles*; Balto, *Occupied Territory*; Randolph, *Mississippi Law.*

33. For a discussion about the emergence of bus segregation in the South, see Woodward, *Strange Career of Jim Crow*, 116–17.

34. This is discussed in detail in *Mississippi Power & Light Co.*, 179 Miss. 588.

35. Murray, *States' Laws on Race and Color*, 15–16, 86–87, 117, 419–20, 482–83.

36. Bay, *Traveling Black*, 153–63.

37. For these cases, see "Negro Wins 'Jim Crow' Case at Danville," *Richmond Times-Dispatch*, January 15, 1937, 4; *Harris*, 213 N.C. 758; *Tri-State Transit Co.*, 181 Miss. 388 (1938); "Wins Test Case vs. Greyhound Bus," *Chicago Defender*, February 20, 1937, 5.

38. B. L. M. Kelley, *Right to Ride*, 137; Smith, *Managing White Supremacy*, 259.

39. My thinking about power and silence in the archives has been most shaped by Fuentes, *Dispossessed Lives*; LeFlouria, *Chained in Silence*, 17; Greene, *Box 25*, 9–11.

40. Fuentes, *Dispossessed Lives*, 5.

41. Farmer, "In Search," 289–93.

42. For examples of studies that distinguish between municipal and interstate lines, see Thornton, *Dividing Lines*. Of the forty-three lawsuits examined in this book, 45 percent were against a Greyhound line, whereas 55 percent were against municipal bus companies or regional lines.

43. Glymph, "Paper Tracings," 1–18.

44. Burnham, *By Hands Now Known*, 242, 244.

45. For the seminal study of the long civil rights movement, see Hall, "Long Civil Rights Movement." For critiques on the "long civil rights movement" as a framework, see Arnesen, "Reconsidering the Long Civil Rights Movement"; Schmidt, "Legal History."

Chapter 1

1. Hill, *Advertising to the American Woman*, 171–73.

2. For Noll, see *Fifteenth Census of the United States*, 1930, Somerset County, New Jersey, Enumeration District 18–39, sheet 10B; "Frank J. Noll, Sr., Bus Firm President," *Courier News*, February 26, 1974, 10.

3. "Sell Sarah," *Bus Transportation*, September 1932, 148–49.

4. See, for example, advertisement, *Bus Transportation*, September 1939, 16.

5. Haley, *No Mercy Here*, 4.

6. "Visits Hell," *Chicago Defender*, July 20, 1935, 3; "Chicago Woman Is Beaten by Bus Driver," *Baltimore Afro-American*, July 27, 1935, 6.

7. For a discussion of the national reach of the *Chicago Defender*, see Grossman, *Land of Hope*, 75–80.

8. Haley, *No Mercy Here*, 84, 58–118.

9. Haley, *No Mercy Here*, 91–92, 58–118.

10. For Wadsworth, see *Fifteenth Census of the United States*, 1930, Westchester County, New York, Enumeration District 60–172, sheet 8B.

11. "Who Rides Buses Most, Men or Women?" *Bus Transportation*, July 1932, 4–5.

12. "The Greyhound Story Is of Interest to Everyone," undated, box 4, folder 4, Greyhound Bus Company Papers, Abakanowicz Research Center, Chicago History Museum, Chicago, Illinois (hereafter cited as Greyhound-Chicago).

13. "Greyhound Story," box 4, folder 4, Greyhound-Chicago; "Eleven Months of Nite Coach Operations," *Bus Transportation*, June 1930, 287–88.

14. "Brief History of the Greyhound Lines," box 6, folder 6, Greyhound-Chicago.

15. "Motor Bus Expansion Big Feature of Year," *New York Times*, January 10, 1926, A4.

16. Ingram, *Dixie Highway*, 152.

17. These three decisions were *Buck v. Kuykendall*, *Bush v. Maloy*, and *Michigan Commission v. Duke*. For a discussion of these cases, see Walsh, *Making Connections*, 140.

18. "Buses Declared Common Carriers in Seven More States," *Bus Transportation*, December 1925.

19. "Motor Bus Expansion Big Feature of Year," *New York Times*, January 10, 1926, A4.

20. Arthur S. Genet, "A Profile of the Greyhound Bus Corporation," box 6, folder 6, Greyhound-Chicago.

21. "University Offers Course in Bus Economics," *Bus Transportation*, May 1929, 46.

22. Hixson, *Pick of the Litter*, 80; "Motor Bus Expansion Big Feature of Year," *New York Times*, January 10, 1926, A4.

23. "Editor's Corner: Valuable Lessons Learned at Cleveland," *Bus Transportation*, October 1934, 72.

24. "Bus Transportation Chalks Up Two Decades of Service," *Bus Transportation*, January 1942, 4–5.

25. See, for example, "Coffee Is Served," *Bus Transportation*, December 1932, 503; "Attracting the Passenger," *Bus Transportation*, September 1934, 308; "Pullmans *Plus* on the Highways," *Bus Transportation*, April 1934, 59–60; "Colors Do's and Don'ts for the City Operator," *Bus Transportation*, March 1938, 122.

26. "Pullmans *Plus* on the Highways," *Bus Transportation*, April 1934, 59–60.

27. Rankin Johnson, "Popular Appeal an Important Factor," *Transit Journal*, September 1935.

28. "Motor Bus Expansion Big Feature of Year," A4.

29. "Co-ordinated Bus Service Advancing Steadily," *Transit Journal*, January 1932, Special Collections, Library of Virginia, Richmond, Virginia.

30. Walsh, *Making Connections*, 89–101. See also "Just a Girl, but She Built Up Iowa's Biggest Bus Line," *Des Moines Register*, September 16, 1923, 53; "Woman Running Bus Lines Fights Railways to Stay in Business," *Minneapolis Journal*, October 12, 1923, 43; "Bus Queen," *Niles Daily Star*, July 18, 1925, 1.

31. "No Jim Crow for Them," *Baltimore Afro-American*, July 22, 1921, 1; "Jim Crow Car Is Empty," *Baltimore Afro-American*, September 2, 1921, 1.

32. "Bus Company Offers Positions for Three," *New York Amsterdam News*, July 15, 1931, 7. See also "Citizens Open War on Jim Crow Motorbuses," *Chicago Defender*, June 18, 1927, 1.

33. "Woman Heads Winston Salem Bus Transportation Company," *Atlanta Daily World*, July 24, 1959, 2.

34. "Operates 31 Busses," *Baltimore Afro-American*, September 18, 1926, A19. See also "Certificate of Incorporation of Safe Bus Incorporation," 27967, May 1926 (in author's possession).

35. Korstad, *Civil Rights Unionism*, 80.

36. For a good discussion of Black-owned department stores and their fleeting existence, see Parker, *Department Stores*, 48–49.

37. Amalgamated Transit Union Staff, "From Rags to Riches," 55.

38. "Brief History of Greyhound Lines," box 6, folder 6, and "Supplementary Information for Salesmen-Confidential," box 2, folder 2, both in Greyhound-Chicago.

39. "She Wanted Repairs, Not Damages," *Bus Transportation*, May 1932, 218–19.

40. See, for example, *Highway Traveler*, April–May 1934; *Highway Traveler*, February–March 1935; *Highway Traveler*, February–March 1937; *Highway Traveler*, August–September 1937; *Highway Traveler*, August–September 1938.

41. *Selling the Bus Passenger*, in Greyhound Collection, Manuscript Division, Western Reserve Historical Society, Cleveland, Ohio (hereafter referred to as WRHS).

42. A discussion of the *Highway Traveler*'s treatment of Bahamian, Cuban, Indigenous, and Mexican people is beyond the scope of this book. But for examples, see "Florida's Primitive People," *Highway Traveler*, February–March 1938, 26; "So You Are Going to Florida," *Highway Traveler*, December 1935, 28–30; "Havana, Paris of America, Welcomes You," *Highway Traveler*, February–March 1936, 14–16; A New Highway to Mexico City," *Highway Traveler*, February–March 1936, 12–14; "Texas—for a Different Kind of Winter Vacation," *Highway Traveler*, December 1936.

43. Even though the historian Mia Bay argues that Greyhound was mainly focused on surviving financially in the late 1920s and early 1930s, an investigation into the company's periodicals demonstrates a deliberate strategy to install white supremacy in its company culture. See Bay, *Traveling Black*, 172–73.

44. "Interesting American Cities: Jackson, Mississippi, by a Chicagoan," *Highway Traveler*, March 29, 1929, 11, box 3, folder 4, Greyhound-Chicago.

45. Buses were central to colonial development in Africa. In South Africa in the 1920s, colonial leaders introduced buses but excluded Indigenous Black riders. A few years later, Black South Africans created their own "second-class buses" which were crudely composed of old car and truck chassis. See "The Motor Bus Has Invaded South Africa," *Bus Transportation*, December 1922; "Buses Emerging from the Jitney Era in Union of South Africa," *Bus Transportation*, December 1926.

46. Few historians have analyzed the history of King Sobhuza. For an analysis of his rule, see Kuper, *Sobhuza II*.

47. For a discussion about the ways that white European men depicted enslaved women's perceived loose sexuality, see Morgan, *Laboring Women*; Camp, *Closer to Freedom*. For a discussion of how Black women reformers encouraged women to dress properly to avoid assault, see Wolcott, *Remaking Respectability*.

48. Skwiot, *Purposes of Paradise*.

49. *Highway Log*, October 1930, box 3, folder 5, Greyhound-Chicago.

50. Parker, *Department Stores*, 26; Glymph, "Paper Tracings," 13; W. Johnson, *River of Dark Dreams*, 136.

51. For evidence of Black women working as maids, cooks, and cleaners in bus stations, see "Keeping the Driver on His Toes," *Bus Transportation*, May 1931, 581–82; "Maid Charges Radio Firm's Agent Struck Her; Files Suit for $5,000," *Baltimore Afro-American*, March 28, 1936, 21; "Figure of Black Women Greyhound Workers in Florida," Greyhound Collection, WRHS.

52. See "Safe Bus Company Hires 100, Serves 400,000 Negroes," *Pittsburgh Courier*, May 21, 1938, 12; "Bus Company, CIO End Brief Strike," *Atlanta Daily World*, July 2, 1947, 3.

53. These two women included Mary Miller Burns in 1959 and Delphine Morgan in 1960. See "Woman Heads Winston Salem Bus Transportation Company," *Atlanta Daily World*, July 24, 1959, 2. For a discussion of some of the surprising professional gains of women in the 1950s, see Meyerowitz, "Beyond the Feminine Mystique."

54. Williams-Forson, *Building Houses out of Chicken Legs*; Thaggert, *Riding Jane Crow*, 96–120.

55. Bates, *Pullman Porters and the Rise of Black Protest Politics in Black America*, 20–26.

56. Thaggert, *Riding Jane Crow*, 5; Chateauvert, *Marching Together*.

57. "Said a Southern Operator to a Northern Operator," *Bus Transportation*, August 1935, 314–15.

58. For a discussion of the performative aspects of racial segregation, see Berrey, *Jim Crow Routine*.

59. Arnesen, *Brotherhoods of Color*, 157–66. Information about redcaps can be found in their union organ, *Bags and Baggage*.

60. "And Now, Porter Service for Buses," *Bus Transportation*, August 1932; "Pullmans Plus on the Highway," *Bus Transportation*, April 1934, 130–31.

61. Goings, *Mammy and Uncle Mose*; McEyla, *Clinging to Mammy*; Parker, *Department Stores*, 26.

62. "Prizes Were Won, Everyone Had Fun," August 23, 1958, *Virginia Transit Company Journal*, Special Collections, Library of Virginia, Richmond, Virginia.

63. "Printing Tickets as Sold," *Bus Transportation*, November 1930, 598.

64. For example, in Washington, DC, a husband-and-wife team ran the W. M. & A. Bus Lines. The man was the president, and the woman served as the secretary-treasurer. And the British Columbia Motor Transportation Company hired a white woman to serve as the traffic manager. See "A Family Job," *Bus Transportation*, July 1936, 296; "A Man-Sized Job . . . and a Woman Swings It," *Bus Transportation*, April 1938, 170–71.

65. "Something New: Conductorettes," *Bus Transportation*, April 1933, 159–60.

66. "Laura E. Herb, Escorted Tours," *Bus Transportation*, February 1936, 79.

67. For examples of bus company agents enforcing Jim Crow in the early period, see "Exposes Bus Segregation in Chicago," *Chicago Defender*, November 19, 1927, 1; "More Bus Segregation," *Chicago Defender*, December 24, 1927, A2; "Jim Crow Bus," *Chicago Defender*, September 28, 1929, A2.

68. "Real Courtesy Builds Business for Pickwick," *Bus Transportation*, December 1926, 667.

69. "Every Bus a Ticket Office," *Bus Transportation*, December 1926, 669.

70. "Personnel Work & the Bus Operator," *Bus Transportation* 6, December 1927, 668–72.

71. "Copeland Assails Careless Autoists," *New York Times*, November 23, 1922, 16.

72. Schrader, *Badges Without Borders*; Guariglia, *Police and the Empire City*, 71.

73. "Enright Admits Crime Wave in City," *Brooklyn Daily Eagle*, December 19, 1920, 5. For a discussion of Enright, see Guariglia, *Police and the Empire City*, 193–94.

74. For a discussion of how policing in Mississippi was a white man's job, see Randolph, *Mississippi Law*, 5.

75. "City's 'Finest' Enthrall Visitors," *Daily News*, May 3, 1923, 6.

76. Taylor, *Fight the Power.*

77. Marcus Dow, "You and Your Driver," *Greyhound Traveler*, September 1929, box 3, folder 4, Greyhound-Chicago.

78. Hixson, *Pick of the Litter*, 89.

79. "Greyhound Line Wins Safety Award," *Abilene Reporter News*, February 12, 1953, 2-A.

80. For a discussion of the similar eligibility requirements and policing tactics in the US Border Patrol, see Hernández, *Migra!*; Bavery, *Bootlegged Aliens*, 12–54.

81. "Employer and Employee as Comrades," *Bus Transportation*, October 1925, 495. See also "Company Dinners Are Paying Investments," *Bus Transportation*, May 1925, 218–19; "Employer and Employee as Comrades," *Bus Transportation*, October 1925, 495; "Encouraging Service with a Smile," *Bus Transportation*, August 1924, 348–49.

82. "Substantial Citizens Drive Colonial Coaches," *Bus Transportation*, May 1929, 242–44. See also "How Employees Are Selected and Trained in Watertown," *Bus Transportation*, September 1923, 421–23.

83. "The Uniformed Driver Is a Business Builder," *Bus Transportation*, November 1925.

84. "Uniformed Driver Is a Business Builder."

85. See, for example, McGirr, *War on Alcohol*; Murphy, *Jim Crow Capital.*

86. "90 Day Trial Clinch Changed to Buses," *Bus Transportation*, December 1931, 620.

87. Canaday, *Straight State.*

88. Pryor, *Colored Travelers*; Hobbs, *Chosen Exile*, 28–70.

89. For examples of bus drivers making racial revelations and then changing their behavior, see "Exposes Bus Segregation in Chicago," 1; "Puzzled D.C. Bus Driver Hauls Chicago Eye Special," *Baltimore Afro-American*, December 8, 1928, 3; Eugene Watts, Greenwich, Connecticut, to NAACP, New York City, April 9, 1932, box 282, folder 16, NAACP-LC.

90. Snorton, *Black on Both Sides*; Woolner, *Famous Lady Lovers.*

91. My thinking on this issue is deeply indebted to Haley, *No Mercy Here*, 56–57, 17–57.

92. Irene F. Davis, Philadelphia, to Mr. J. Cummings, Philadelphia, December 31, 1931, box 282, folder 13, NAACP-LC.

93. J. Cuming, Philadelphia, to Irene F. Davis, Philadelphia, January 5, 1932, box 282, folder 13, NAACP-LC.

94. Hill, *Advertising to the American Woman*, 172.

95. Hill, *Advertising to the American Woman*, 170–71.

96. Rabinovitch-Fox, "Baby, You Can Drive My Car," 372–400.

97. For a discussion of the New Woman, see Freedman, "New Woman," 372–93.

98. Hill, *Advertising to the American Woman*, 172.

99. Marchand, *Advertising the American Dream*, 7.

100. "The Greyhound Story Is of Interest to Everyone," undated, box 4, folder 4, Greyhound-Chicago.

101. Marchand, *Selling the American Dream.*

102. "Either Way You Look at It: Florida Motor Lines," *Bus Transportation*, September 1937, 13.

103. See, for example, "Miss SchoolMa'am Is a Prospect," *Bus Transportation*, April 1933, 162–63; "School Marms," *Bus Transportation*, May 1936, 208; "Mass Market for Mass Transportation," *Transit Journal*, February 1932; "At the Ticket Window," *Bus Transportation*, March 1939, 121.

104. Lines emphasized that these vehicles could transport collapsible baby carriages, which were very convenient for women traveling with small children. See "Baggage: A Problem of Increasing Importance," *Bus Transportation*, May 1934, 160–61.

105. Advertisement, *Bus Transportation*, September 1939, 16.

106. "Attracting the Passenger," *Bus Transportation*, September 1934, 308. See also "Colors Do's and Don'ts for the City Operator," *Bus Transportation*, March 1938, 122.

107. "These Women and Their Damn White Gloves" *Bus Transportation*, October 1938.

108. See, for example, "Exposes Bus Segregation in Chicago," 1; "More Bus Segregation," *Chicago Defender*, December 24, 1927, A2.

109. "Says Kentucky Agent Made Her Leave Bags, Threatened Her with Club: Goes to Law," *Cleveland Call and Post*, August 8, 1942, 13A. For Johnson in the census, see *Sixteenth Census of the United States*, 1940, Franklin County, Ohio, Enumeration District 93–244, Sheet 2A.

110. Elizabeth Mimms and William Mimms, Kansas City, Kansas, to Roy Wilkins, New York City, April 13, 1932, box 282, folder 15, NAACP-LC. For the Mimms in the census, see *Sixteenth Census of the United States*, 1940, Wyandotte County, Kansas, Enumeration District 106–14, sheet 15B.

111. Gertrude Pryor, Leavenworth, Kansas, to NAACP, New York City, April 11, 1932, box 282, folder 16, NAACP-LC.

112. Thaggert, *Riding Jane Crow*; Hale, *Making Whiteness*, 129.

113. *Selling the Bus Passenger*, WRHS.

114. Haley, *No Mercy Here*, 94–96.

115. Hine, "Black Migration."

116. Hazel Crosby Cizek, "What! No Towels? The Theme Song of the Bus Traveler," *Bus Transportation*, January 1935, 3.

117. "Still No Towels (and No Soap Either)," *Bus Transportation*, March 1936, 15–116.

118. For Ada Montgomery, see *Sixteenth Census of the United States*, Allegheny County, Pennsylvania, 1940, Enumeration District 69–109, sheet 5B; Pittsburgh City Directory, 1934, p. 1408.

119. Ada Montgomery, Pittsburgh, to NAACP, New York City, July 8, 1935, box 183, folder 1, NAACP-LC.

120. Leila Payne, New York City, to Walter White, New York City, September 19, 1941, box 185, folder 1, NAACP-LC.

121. Haley, *No Mercy Here*, 4, 57.

122. For a discussion of how this applied to department stores, see Parker, *Department Stores*, 20–21.

Chapter 2

1. Grossman, *Land of Hope*, 66–97. For the Johnson Family in Opelousas, see *Thirteenth Census of the United States*, 1910, St. Landry Parish, Louisiana, Enumeration District 102, sheet 19A; for the Hooper Family in Beaumont, see *Fourteenth Census of the United States*, 1920, Jefferson County, Texas, Enumeration District 98, sheet 11B; for New Orleans, see *Fifteenth Census of the United States*, 1930, Orleans Parish, Louisiana, Enumeration District 36–13, sheet 1B; for the Hooper Family in Chicago, see *Sixteenth Census of the United States*, 1940, Cook County, Illinois, Enumeration District 108–167, sheet 7B.

2. For the bus driver, John Weatherod, see *Fifteenth Census of the United States*, 1930, Stephens County, Texas, Enumeration District 215–7, sheet 10B.

3. "Local Woman to Sue Bus Line for Throwing Her Off," *Chicago Defender*, July 29, 1939, 22.

4. Reagon, "African Diaspora Women," 167–79.

5. For a discussion of gender and the Great Migration, see Grossman, *Land of Hope*; Trotter, *Great Migration*; Baldwin, *Chicago's New Negroes*; Purnell et al., *Strange Careers*; Klanderud, *Struggle for the Street*.

6. Marchand, *Advertising the American Dream*, 63–65.

7. Moten, *Continually Working*.

8. For a good discussion of the Black press and gender, especially manhood, see D'Weston, *Let Us Make Men*.

9. Even though Black women played a vital role in local NAACP chapters, it was not until Ella Baker became a paid branch director in the 1940s that she pointed out gender dynamics and sexism to the NAACP's male leadership in New York and Washington, DC. For a discussion of the NAACP in the 1930s and 1940s, see Sullivan, *Lift Every Voice*, 190–237; Ransby, *Ella Baker*, 153–98.

10. For a discussion of African Americans and automobiles, see Sorin, *Driving While Black*; Bay, *Traveling Black*, 107–50.

11. Randolph, *Mississippi Law*, 52.

12. For a discussion of Black women passengers and trains, see Thaggert, *Riding Jane Crow*.

13. "Bus Travel Down 30%, Railways Say," *New York Times*, August 23, 1936, F1.

14. In this era, buses and trains were locked in competition for passengers. Some railroads were so threatened by the bus industry that they hired "investigators" to pose as riders on interstate buses and track the time of a bus trip with traffic. Whenever trains lowered their fares, Greyhound and other bus companies felt pressure to follow suit, whether it was offering reduced prices at the holidays, discounting trips to certain geographic regions, and, in 1937, slashing rates between 10 and 30 percent. See "Greyhound Lines Offers Low Round-Trip Fares," *Hartford Courant*, December 18, 1932, A11; "Bus Lines Planning Experimental Fare Cut, Disagree on Cause of Decline in Travel," *New York Times*, July 8, 1936, 13; "Advertising News

and Notes," *New York Times*, June 9, 1936, 34; "Bus Lines to Lower Fares," *New York Times*, February 27, 1937, 15.

15. Deutsch, *Building a Housewife's Paradise*, 52–53.

16. Stewart, *Migrating to the Movies*, 116.

17. For a discussion of Black consumption in the Great Migration, see R. Kelley, *Race Rebels*; Stewart, *Migrating to the Movies*; Baldwin, *Chicago's New Negroes*; Walker, *Style and Status*; Parker, *Department Stores*; Sorin, *Driving While Black*.

18. For an example of the unevenness of the bus industry in this era, see case file: 234008, February 5, 1929: Complaint against Nevin's Bus Company: Full citation: RG 60, DJ Central Files, box 4231, entry 112, folder: 234008, National Archives II, College Park, Maryland.

19. "Jim Crow Law Causes Tragedy on Motor Bus," *Chicago Defender*, January 26, 1929, 2. See also "Gas Kills Negro Bus Passenger," *St. Louis Globe Democrat*, January 13, 1929, 10b.

20. "Norfleet on Stand in Bus Hearing," *Commercial Appeal*, September 13, 1929, 16.

21. For a discussion of the *Chicago Defender*, see Michaeli, *The Defender*, 50–51.

22. "Exposes Bus Segregation in Chicago," *Chicago Defender*, November 19, 1927, 1. See also Bay, *Traveling Black*, 169–70.

23. "The Greyhound Limited," January 1929, *Highway Traveler*, Greyhound Collection, Western Reserve Historical Society.

24. "More Bus Segregation," *Chicago Defender*, December 24, 1927, A2.

25. "Ride Those Busses," *Chicago Defender*, July 20, 1929, A2.

26. Sullivan, *Lift Every Voice*, 151.

27. "Welfare Group Open Justice Drive," *Chicago Defender*, June 27, 1931, 2.

28. Memo, William Andrews, New York City, to Beatrice Marshall, New York City, July 21, 1931, box 282, folder 8, NAACP-LC.

29. "Alleged Bus Segregation Cases Before Commish," *Pittsburgh Courier*, April 2, 1932, 13.

30. Mrs. Woodson, Philadelphia, to NAACP National Office, New York City, April 18, 1932, box 282, folder 16, NAACP-LC.

31. Augusta Saunders, Los Angeles, California, to NAACP, New York City, April 1932, box 282, folder 16, NAACP-LC. For Augusta Saunders in the census, see *Sixteenth Census of the United States*, 1940, Los Angeles County, California, Enumeration District 106–14, sheet 13B.

32. Nerline Brown, Independence, to Roy Wilkins, New York City, August 15, 1932, box 282, folder 16, NAACP-LC. For the sisters in the census, see *Sixteenth Census of the United States*, 1940, Independence, Missouri, Enumeration District 4, sheet 10A.

33. Ida B. Richardson, New York City, to NAACP, New York City, April 7, 1932, box 282, folder 15, NAACP-LC. For Richardson in the census, see *Fifteenth Census of the United States*, 1930, New York City, Enumeration District 31–982, sheet 12A.

34. NAACP Special Legal Assistant to Charles Archer, Esquire, Attuck Theater Building, Norfolk, VA, January 19, 1932, box 282, folder 8, NAACP-LC; affidavit of Ida Meantineal, box 282, folder 15, NAACP-LC.

35. Affidavit of Nellie Middleton, March 22, 1932, box 282, folder 1, NAACP-LC.

36. For a discussion of African Americans and affidavits, see Penningroth, *Before the Movement*, 161–66.

37. E. Pauline Myers, Bowling Green, West Virginia, to NAACP, March 25, 1932, box 282, folder 15, NAACP-LC.

38. Ethel Brooks, Pittsburgh, to NAACP, New York City, April 21, 1932, box 282, folder 15, NAACP-LC.

39. Adele Grymes, Bridgeton, New Jersey, to NAACP, April 7, 1932, box 282, folder 16, NAACP-LC.

40. Augusta Saunders, Los Angeles, California, to NAACP, New York City, April 20, 1932, box 282, folder 16, NAACP-LC.

41. Mattie Bradshaw, West Virginia, to NAACP National Office, New York City, April 9, 1932, box 282, folder 16, NAACP-LC.

42. Greene, *Box 25*, 5.

43. Goldie Washington, Kansas City, Missouri, to NAACP, New York City, April 13, 1932, box 282, folder 15, NAACP-LC.

44. This is discussed in Bay, *Traveling Black*, 174–75.

45. John B. Walker, Cleveland, to Roy Wilkins, New York City, April 29, 1932, box 282, folder 16, NAACP-LC.

46. This is based on my investigation of the Greyhound Bus Papers and close reading of two periodicals: *Highway Traveler* and *Bus Transportation.*

47. "NAACP Refuses Greyhound Buses Conference Business," *Philadelphia Tribune*, April 28, 1932, 2.

48. Roy Wilkins, New York, to J. B. Walker, Cleveland, May 5, 1932, box 282, folder 16, NAACP-LC.

49. J. B. Walker to Roy Wilkins, June 27, 1932, box 282, folder 16, NAACP-LC.

50. "Press Release," July 1, 1932, box 282, folder 16, NAACP-LC.

51. For Rebecca Ferguson, see *Fifteenth Census of the United States*, 1930, Brooklyn County, New York, Enumeration District 24–549, sheet 5A.

52. Rebecca Ferguson, Sumter, to Max Koenig, New York, March 21, 1938, box 282, folder 11, NAACP-LC.

53. For a discussion of Black women's citizenship rights in the 1930s, see Chatelain, *South Side Girls*, 110–72; Parker, *Department Stores*, 54–115.

54. Lucille Lewis, New York, to NAACP, New York, August 5, 1935, box 283, folder 3, NAACP-LC.

55. George B. Murphy to Lucille Lewis, Elbert, West Virginia, August 11, 1938, box 283, folder 3, NAACP-LC.

56. "Bus Discrimination," *Chicago Defender*, September 20, 1941, 14. For Viola Barnes in the census, see *Sixteenth Census of the United States*, 1940, Cook County, Enumeration District 103–2654, sheet 14A.

57. For Alice Dixon Byrd, see *Thirteenth Census of the United States*, 1920, Virginia, Enumeration District 57, sheet 5B; for Francina Coleman, see *Fifteenth Census of the United States*, 1930, New York, Enumeration District 24, sheet 13A. See also "Abstract of Divorce Degree," Alice Dixon Byrd and Joshua Byrd, State File 1671, March 17, 1947.

58. For a discussion of African American divorce in the era of migrations, see Penningroth, "African American Divorce in Virginia and Washington, D.C., 1865–1930," 21–35.

59. "Statement of Facts," January 1944, box 185, folder 3, NAACP-LC.

60. For a discussion of Konvitz's lifelong activism, see Daniels, *Rights, Liberties, and Ideals.*

61. F. F. Ernest, PR Department, Pennsylvania Greyhound Lines to Milton Konitz, November 29, 1943, and Lynwood C. Major, Cleveland, to Milton Konitz, New York City, February 19, 1944, both in box 185, folder 3, NAACP-LC.

62. "Boycott Greyhound Bus?" *Chicago Defender,* November 30, 1935, 16.

63. Charles Hamilton Houston, New York, to T. Gillis Nutter, Charleston, West Virginia, July 12, 1935, box 283, folder 1, NAACP-LC.

64. For Edna Reed, see *Seventeenth Census of the United States,* 1950, Westchester County, New York, Enumeration District 74–124, sheet 74.

65. Thurgood Marshall, New York City, to Great Eastern System Incorporated, Cleveland, Ohio, January 27, 1937, box 282, folder 11, NAACP-LC.

66. Great Eastern System, Inc., 400 Empire Building, Cleveland, Ohio, to Thurgood Marshall, NAACP, New York City, February 11, 1937, box 282, folder 11, NAACP-LC.

67. "Bus Victims Post Bonds; Gain Temporary Freedom," *Atlanta Daily World,* August 29, 1939, 2. For Odel Moore in the census, see *Fifteenth Census of the United States,* 1930, Allegheny County, Pennsylvania, Enumeration District 2–553, sheet 9A.

68. "Birmingham Police Jail Two Pittsburgh Women," *Pittsburgh Courier,* August 26, 1939, 1.

69. "Women Pulled Off Bus; Fined," *Baltimore Afro-American,* April 6, 1940, 1.

70. Thurgood Marshall, New York City, to Lewis S. Flagg, Brooklyn, July 16, 1940, and letter from L. N. Gregg, Greensboro, North Carolina, to Lewis S. Flagg, June 20, 1940, both in box 185, folder 1, NAACP-LC.

Chapter 3

1. *Fifteenth Census of the United States,* 1930, Detroit, Michigan, Enumeration District 82–114, sheet 6B. Interracial marriage was legal in Michigan in the 1930s, but very rare. I was surprised to discover that Paulina Stevens was married to a white man, but her husband, Fred Stevens, is listed as white in the census. He was born in New York to immigrant parents from Ireland.

2. "Greyhound Company Loses Bus Segregation Suit," *Baltimore Afro-American,* February 22, 1930, 1.

3. Judge Sample had previously ruled that an all-Black school in Ypsilanti, Michigan, had to be shut down because it was operating on the principle of racial segregation and he was a regular reader of the *Crisis,* the NAACP's monthly organ. See, for example, "Michigan Separate School Ordered Closed," *Chicago Defender,* May 10, 1919; George W. Sample, Ann Arbor, to W. E. B. Du Bois, New York City, October 19, 1922, in W. E. B. Du Bois Papers, series 1: Correspondence, University Archives, University of Massachusetts at Amherst.

4. "Judge Cites Constitution and Decides Against Bus Company," *Chicago Defender*, February 22, 1930, 1.

5. "Wins Decision Against Company," *Pittsburgh Courier*, March 8, 1930, 3.

6. McGuire, *At the Dark End of the Street*; Theoharis, *Rebellious Life of Mrs. Rosa Parks*.

7. For a discussion of African Americans' development of legal knowledge, see Eatmon, "Public Wrongs, Private Rights," 12.

8. *Sixteenth Census of the United States*, 1940, Wayne County, Michigan, Enumeration District 84–72, sheet 81-B.

9. Burnham, *By Hands Now Known*, xviii.

10. Roy Wilkins, New York City, to L. C. Blount, Detroit, March 26, 1932, box 282, folder 1, NAACP-LC.

11. This is based on a close reading of the NAACP Papers and Black newspapers. For major lawsuits from Black men, see, for example, "Sues Bus Company for Segregation in Michigan," *Chicago Defender*, January 21, 1928, 1; "Bus Company Is Hit in Suit of Kentuckian," *Chicago Defender*, March 13, 1932, 13; "Wins $3,500 Judgment from Greyhound Bus Company," *Chicago Defender*, February 4, 1939, 10.

12. See, for example, Hirsch, *Making the Second Ghetto*; Boyle, *Arc of Justice*.

13. King, *Whose Harlem Is This, Anyway?*; Felkor-Kantor, *Policing Los Angeles*; Balto, *Occupied Territory*.

14. Gross, *Colored Amazons*, Hicks, *Talk with You Like a Woman*.

15. For examples of Black respectability politics, see Wolcott, *Remaking Respectability*, Harris, *Sex Workers, Psychics, and Numbers Runners*.

16. Eatmon, "Wielding an Unlikely Weapon," 283.

17. Smith, *Emancipation*, 41–63.

18. Smith, *Emancipation*, 48.

19. Mack, *Representing the Race*, 54.

20. See, for example, Schweninger, *Appealing for Liberty*; Welch, *Black Litigants in the Antebellum American South*; Milewski, *Litigating Across the Color Line*; Masur, *Until Justice Be Done*, Penningroth, *Before the Movement*.

21. Penningroth, *Before the Movement*.

22. Smith, *Emancipation*, 6.

23. Charles Hamilton Houston, "The Need for Negro Lawyers," *Journal of Negro Education* 4, no. 1 (1935): 49–52.

24. Mack, *Representing the Race*, 64.

25. For a good discussion of Black migrant attorneys in the North, see Burnham, *By Hands Now Known*, 68.

26. For Laura Fischer in the census, see *Fifteenth Census of the United States*, 1930, Cincinnati, Ohio, Hamilton County, Enumeration District 31–204, sheet 13B.

27. Glen Branoski is listed in the census as "Joseph Branoski." See *Fourteenth Census of the United States*, 1920, Belmont, Ohio, Enumeration District 9, sheet 24-A.

28. "Bus Driver Faces Trial After Row with Negro Woman," *Richmond Palladium*, November 21, 1927, 1.

29. Even though Fischer was listed as married in the 1930 and 1940 census, by 1950 she is listed as divorced. It is likely that she was estranged from her husband. See *Sixteenth Census of the United States*, 1940, Hamilton County, Ohio, Enumeration District 91–272, sheet 4A; *Seventeenth Census of the United States*, 1950, Hamilton County, Ohio, Enumeration District 91–541, sheet 4.

30. "Indiana State News," *Chicago Defender*, September 20, 1941, 11; *Fifteenth Census of the United States*, 1930, Wayne County, Indiana, Enumeration District 89–41, sheet 1B. In 1921, the bar in Richmond had appointed Roscoe to serve as a special judge, where he oversaw a case involving three white men who were convicted of violating the new Prohibition laws. And during the 1920s, President Calvin Coolidge appointed him to the Virgin Island Commission. See Smith, *Emancipation*, 390.

31. "Bus Driver Faces Trial After Row with Negro Woman," 1.

32. For Anvedeo Vioni, see *Fifteenth Census of the United States*, Richmond City, Indiana, 1930, Enumeration District 89–40, sheet 10B.

33. "Bus Driver Faces Trial After Row with Negro Woman," 1.

34. "Bus Discrimination Given Setback by Indiana Judges," *Chicago Defender*, December 3, 1927, 2.

35. Mack, "Law, Society, Identity," 377–410; Thaggert, *Riding Jane Crow*, 63.

36. There are a few theories that might explain why Judge Pickett sided with Laura Fischer in this case. Judge Pickett was a Quaker, and his religious beliefs in equality might have influenced his ruling. Judge Pickett had also recently lived in Washington, DC, a city with a large population of African Americans, and that experience might have shaped his consciousness around these matters. Finally, racial politics in Indiana in the 1920s were contentious, vacillating between stirrings for civil rights against robust support for the Ku Klux Klan. A few years earlier, the state legislature had considered a bill to install racial segregation on all railroads, streetcars, buses, and steamships.

37. "Bus Discrimination Given Setback by Indiana Judges," *Chicago Defender*, December 3, 1927, 2.

38. "Bus Discrimination Given Setback by Indiana Judges," 2.

39. Burnham, *By Hands Now Known*, xvii.

40. Penningroth, *Before the Movement*.

41. For O'Hara, see *Sixteenth Census of the United States*, 1950, Vanderburgh County, Indiana, Enumeration District 93–25, sheet 9B.

42. "Seeks $500 Damages for Bus Discrimination," *Chicago Defender*, December 31, 1927, 4; "Is Candidate for Justice of the Peace," *Chicago Defender*, April 9, 1938, 3.

43. For a good discussion of Black citizenship rights in Michigan, see Finkleman, "Promise of Equality," 187–213.

44. "Judge Cites Constitution and Decides Against Bus Company," *Chicago Defender*, February 22, 1930, 1.

45. "Discrimination Charged in Proposed Suit Against Greyhound Bus," *New York Amsterdam News*, December 16, 1931, 2.

46. Thomas was a politically savvy attorney. The Mississippi native had graduated from Cornell University Law School. In 1921, he became one of the first Black

lawyers in the United States appointed to assistant US attorney in the Southern District of New York, where he specialized in immigration cases. See "James C. Thomas, New York Assemblyman, to Speak Here," *Atlanta Daily World*, February 27, 1955, 5; Smith, *Emancipation*, 400.

47. "Discrimination Charged in Proposed Suit Against Greyhound Bus," 2.

48. "2,000 Employees Insured," *New York Times*, February 15, 1931, 47.

49. "Ample Facilities Are Provided in Cleveland's Terminal," *Bus Transportation*, March 1932.

50. Phillips, *AlabamaNorth*, 129.

51. Hine, "Rape and the Inner Lives of Black Women," 913.

52. Philipps, *AlabamaNorth*, 130.

53. "Society," *Chicago Defender*, July 11, 1931, 7.

54. "Negroes Offered Prizes," *Commercial Appeal*, February 4, 1917, 18. For Iola Wimbs Ellis in the census, see *Fourteenth Census of the United States*, 1920, Shelby County, Tennessee, Enumeration District 149, sheet 6A; *Fifteenth Census of the United States*, 1930, Cuyahoga County, Ohio, Enumeration District 183–53, sheet 15A.

55. *Fifteenth Census of the United States*, 1930, Cuyahoga County, Ohio, Enumeration District 183–57, sheet 4B.

56. "State of Ohio, Cuyahoga County, in the Court of Common Please, No. 368,568, Iola Wimbs Ellis and Elemenoire Austin v. Greyhound," box 282, folder 15, NAACP-LC.

57. Smith, *Emancipation*, 415.

58. "Two Women Sue Greyhound Lines for Segregation," *Chicago Defender*, January 9, 1932, 4.

59. Chester Gillespie, Cleveland, to Roy Wilkins, New York City, April 1932, box 282, folder 15, NAACP-LC.

60. Smith, *Emancipation*, 417.

61. "Jane Hunter Sues Bus Company for Insult," *Atlanta Daily World*, June 1, 1934, 2.

62. The only record I have been able to locate for Willetta Brown is her marriage certificate. See "Marriage License 10768," Cuyahoga County, Cleveland, June 27, 1933.

63. "Bus Co. Sued," *Cleveland Call and Post*, January 26, 1935, 1.

64. Hine, "Rape and the Inner Lives of Black Women," 912–20.

65. McGuire, *At the Dark End of the Street*.

66. "Bus Co. Sued," 1.

67. "Cleveland: Social and Personal," *Cleveland Gazette*, May 4, 1935, 3.

68. "Armless Judge to Sit on Bench in Cleveland," *Washington Post*, November 7, 1915, 7. For Moylan in the census, see *Sixteenth Census of the United States*, 1940, Cuyahoga County, Ohio, Enumeration District 92–13, sheet 13A.

69. "Greyhound Lines Pay Damages of $250 Hastily," *Atlanta Daily World*, June 10, 1935, 1.

70. "Two Win Damage Suits in Bus Company Jim Crow Cases," *Baltimore Afro-American*, April 20, 1935, 10.

71. *Fifteenth Census of the United States*, 1930, Chicago, Illinois, Enumeration District 16–630, sheet 13A.

72. "Refused Bus Passage, Sues," *California Eagle*, June 16, 1933, 1.

73. "Dr. Charles Thompson Refused Service, Sues," Chicago Defender, November 22, 1930, 7; "Jim Crow Restaurant in Chi Loses Two Suits," *Pittsburgh Courier*, June 30, 1934, 2; "Chicago NAACP Halts Taking of Youth Back to Louisiana," *Baltimore Afro-American*, May 20, 1933, 21.

74. "NAACP Lawyers Win Signal Victory," *Pittsburgh Courier*, April 6, 1935, 1.

75. "Woman Sues Bus Line; Wins Damages for Jim Crow; Jury Gives Award in Court," *Chicago Defender*, March 30, 1935, 1.

76. "NAACP Lawyers Win Signal Victory," *Pittsburgh Courier*, April 6, 1935, 1.

77. For Jones in the census, see *Seventeenth Census of the United States*, 1950, Mahoning County, Ohio, Enumeration District 100–126, sheet 18.

78. For Jones's attorney in the census, see *Sixteenth Census of the United States*, 1940, Mahoning County, Ohio, Enumeration District 50–13, sheet 21A.

79. *Jones*, 1937 WL 2366.

80. *Higgins*, 141 Kan. 641.

81. Zena R. Higgins, Kansas City, to NAACP National Office, New York City, April 22, 1932, box 282, folder 1, NAACP-LC.

82. "Wins $500 in Suit Against Bus Company," *Plaindealer*, May 4, 1934, 1.

83. *Higgins*, 141 Kan. 641.

84. Bay, *Traveling Black*, 33.

85. Purnell et al., *Strange Careers*.

86. Marcus A. Dow, "You and Your Driver," *Greyhound Traveler*, September 1929, box 3, folder 4, Greyhound-Chicago.

87. See, for example, "On to Cleveland," *Pittsburgh Courier*, October 28, 1928, A5.

88. See, for example, "NAACP Will Not Use Bus Transportation," *New Journal and Guide*, April 18, 1936, 4.

89. Parker, *Department Stores*, 58–59.

90. These cases were brought by Alice Prince (1937), Edna Williams (1937), Esther Carroll and Emma Means (1939), Gertrude Herndon (1939), and Clara Wilson (1941). See "Denied Bus Seat, Sues," *New York Amsterdam News*, October 9, 1937, 24; "Woman Sues Bus Line for $20,000 for Maltreatment," *Chicago Defender*, November 6, 1937, 5; "Bus Company Faces Suit for $10,000," *Baltimore Afro-American*, December 23, 1939, 24; "Seeks $50,000 from Bus Lines," *Atlanta Daily World*, April 2, 1939, 1.

91. "Seeks $50,000 from Bus Lines," 1.

92. "Seeks $50,000 from Bus Lines," 1.

93. Alexander Martin was a distinguished lawyer in the city. He was the first African American man to graduate from the Western Reserve Law School, and in 1924 he was appointed as a special assistant to the United States attorney general. In Cleveland, he worked to keep prisoners out of the death chamber. See Smith, *Emancipation*, 412; "Fleming's Counsel to Play Last Court Card," *Pittsburgh Courier*, May 31, 1939, 1.

94. Bay, *Traveling Black*, 233–39.

95. *Morgan*, 184 Va. 24.

96. For Sarah Prendes in 1930, see *Fifteenth Census of the United States*, 1930, Genesee County, Michigan, Enumeration District 25–22, sheet 13A. For Sarah Love in the 1940 census, see *Sixteenth Census of the United States*, 1940, Jackson County, Michigan, Enumeration District 2231, sheet 5A.

97. Sarah M. Love, Jackson, Michigan, to Walter White, New York City, November 19, 1940, box 185, folder 1, NAACP-LC.

98. "Head of Terminal: Manfred Burleigh," *Courier-Journal*, April 28, 1937, 16.

99. See Sarah M. Love, Jackson, to L. H. Ristow, Cleveland, November 6, 1940, box 185, folder 1, NAACP-LC.

100. Thurgood Marshall, New York, to Dr. James McClendon, Detroit, November 25, 1940, box 185, folder 1, NAACP-LC.

101. For Morris, see *Sixteenth Census of the United States*, 1940, Wayne County, Michigan, Enumeration District 84–25, sheet 5A.

102. "Woman Awarded $250 in Damages for Humiliation While Riding on Bus," 1. See also "Woman Wins $250 in Bus Lawsuit," *Detroit Free Press*, July 27, 1941, 2.

103. Melba Goss's grandparents had raised her in Kentucky. Her grandfather labored as a blacksmith, while her grandmother worked as a laundress. For her family, see *Sixteenth Census of the United States*, 1940, Pulaski County, Kentucky, Enumeration District 100–2, sheet 8A.

104. Harris was a native of Alabama. His family operated a prominent funeral home, and he migrated to Cincinnati. Bush was a native of Ohio. For Walter W. Harris, see *Sixteenth Census of the United States*, 1940, Hamilton County, Ohio, Enumeration District 91–144, sheet 3A; for Myron Bush, see *Seventeenth Census of the United States*, 1950, Hamilton County, Ohio, Enumeration District 91–297, sheet 4.

105. Melba Goss, "Melba Goss v. Greyhound," box 185, folder 2, NAACP-LC.

106. Goss, "Melba Goss v. Greyhound."

107. "Cincinnati Woman Brings Suit Against 'Greyhound,'" *Cleveland Call and Post*, November 14, 1942, 1.

108. Goss v. Southeastern Greyhound Lines (1942).

109. "Cincinnati Woman Brings Suit Against 'Greyhound,'" 3.

Chapter 4

1. For the Shankles, see the *Seventeenth Census of the United States*, 1950, Calesia, Louisiana, Enumeration District 10–39, sheet 10.

2. The state of Louisiana never had a formal policy of barring African Americans from serving on a jury. In three parishes in Louisiana, a handful of Black men were able to serve on a jury. For more information, see Milewski, *Litigating Across the Color Line*, 117.

3. *Shankle*, 8 So.2d 714.

4. Hunter, *Bound in Wedlock*, 4–5.

5. *Shankle*, 8 So.2d 714. Judge John Hugo Dore presided over two other cases involving African American women: *Valdry*, 5 So.2d 173, and *Grant*, 15 So.2d 123.

6. Penningroth, *Before the Movement*, 165.

7. Carter, *Scottsboro*.

8. Milewski, *Litigating Across the Color Line*, 14.

9. Welch, *Black Litigants in the Antebellum American South*; Milewski, *Litigating Across the Color Line*; Goluboff, *Lost Promise of Civil Rights*; Devlin, *Girl Stands at the Door.*

10. See, for example, "Bus Discrimination Given Setback by Indiana Judges," *Chicago Defender*, December 3, 1927, 2; "Seeks $500 Damages for Bus Discrimination," *Chicago Defender*, December 31, 1927, 4; "Greyhound Company Loses Bus Segregation Suit," *Baltimore Afro-American*, February 22, 1930, 1; "Judge Cites Constitution and Decides Against Bus Company," *Chicago Defender*, February 22, 1930, 1; "Two Win Damage Suits in Bus Company Jim Crow Cases," *Baltimore Afro-American*, April 20, 1935, 10.

11. "Kentuckians Work to Stop Bus Segregation," *Chicago Defender*, February 25, 1928, 2.

12. "Honeymooning Through Kentucky and Tennessee," *Greyhound Traveler*, December 1929.

13. For William D. Butts, see *Sixteenth Census of the United States*, 1940, Newport New City, Virginia, Enumeration District 113–19, sheet 2A.

14. "Echoes of 5-Year-Old Bus Case Heard," *New Journal and Guide*, October 30, 1937, 11.

15. *Kinchlow*, 66 App. D.C. 382.

16. For Campbell W. Gray in the census, see *Sixteenth Census of the United States*, 1940, Norfolk City, Virginia, Enumeration District 114–135, sheet 7A.

17. For Isabella Smith, see *Sixteenth Census of the United States*, 1940, Philadelphia County, Pennsylvania, Enumeration District 51–1309, sheet 9A.

18. "Pennsylvania Woman Sues Greyhound Bus Line for Jim Crow," *Baltimore Afro-American*, October 6, 1934, 1.

19. "Make Greyhound Bus Company Behave," *Baltimore Afro-American*, October 13, 1934, 4.

20. See, for example, Roy Wilkins to Herman Cruse, February 17, 1933, box 282, folder 9, NAACP-LC; Dr. C. Herbert Marshall, Washington, DC, to Thurgood Marshall, New York City, September 29, 1941, box 185, folder 1, NAACP-LC.

21. *Patillo*, 120 Tex.Crim. 568.

22. Murray, *States' Laws on Race and Color*, 455–56.

23. Roy Wilkins, New York City, to West Publishing Company, St. Paul, Minnesota, April 19, 1932, box 282, folder 16, NAACP-LC.

24. "Appeal Will Test Texas Jim Crow Bus Case," *New Journal and Guide*, July 11, 1931, 3.

25. Catharine A. Blaine, "Form B: for Use of Widows of Soldiers Who Are Indigent Circumstances," May 1907, form: 981–713–3M.

26. The first Black client that Blain had represented was Luberta Jacobs. In December 1930, Luberta Jacobs and her husband, Phil, were driving their automobile in Beaumont, Texas. It was dark, and their car unexpectedly drove into a large ditch; both Luberta and Phil sustained injuries. This prompted the couple to sue the Dixie Gas & Fuel Company, alleging that this company was responsible for the ditch. During the trial, Luberta Jacobs's injuries were so severe that she had to

be carried into the courthouse on a stretcher. She sued for injuries, as well as the loss of work. The jury initially awarded her a staggering $8,000 in damages, but then the Dixie Gas & Fuel Company appealed the decision, and the Court of Appeals in Texas argued that there should be a new trial. Despite the changed outcome, the fact that a jury initially granted such a large sum to Jacobs indicates that white Texans in Beaumont were willing to grant an African American woman damages for the injuries that she sustained. And the fact that William Blain, a white lawyer only a generation removed from slavery, represented two African American women in personal injury cases that traveled to the appellate level offers a new narrative for thinking about race relations in the Jim Crow South. See *Dixie Gas & Fuel Co.*, 47 S.W.2d 457.

27. See Milewski, *Litigating Across the Color Line*, 151–52; Penningroth, *Before the Movement*, 163.

28. See "Helen Elizabeth Grinage," *The Bison*, 1929, 47.

29. For Helen Willis in the census, see *Sixteenth Census of the United States*, 1940, Danville County, Virginia, Enumeration District 106–8A, sheet 18A. For John C. Carter, see *Fourteenth Census of the United States*, Danville County, Virginia, Enumeration District 39, sheet 9B.

30. "Helen Willis Bus Ride Is Within Law," *Danville Register and Bee*, January 14, 1937, 1.

31. "Negro Wins 'Jim Crow' Case at Danville," *Richmond Times-Dispatch*, January 15, 1937, 4; "'White Only' Buses Banned in Virginia," *Pittsburgh Courier*, January 23, 1937, 1; "Woman Wins J.C. Bus Case," *Afro-American*, January 23, 1937, 2; "Legal Extraction of Jim-Crow's Teeth," *New Journal and Guide*, January 23, 1937, A8.

32. "Testimony of J. B. Harris," in *State v. Harris*, 213 N.C. 758 (1938), located in the Supreme Court of North Carolina Law Library, Raleigh, North Carolina. I am grateful for Thomas P. Davis and James B. Fish at the Supreme Court of North Carolina Law Library for locating and digitizing this case for me.

33. Berrey, *Jim Crow Routine*, 46–47.

34. "Wins N. C. Bus Jim Crow Case," *New Journal and Guide*, June 25, 1938, 1.

35. "Ed Alston Fights Against Execution," *Durham Herald-Sun*, May 25, 1938, 3.

36. *State*, 213 N.C. 758.

37. *State*, 213 N.C. 758. See also "Jim Crow Bus Question Goes to North Carolina Court," *Philadelphia Tribune*, April 12, 1928, 5.

38. "The Bus Case Reversal," *Carolina Times*, June 25, 1938, 4.

39. For Garner, see *Fifteenth Census of the United States*, 1930, Hinds County, Mississippi, Enumeration District 25–6, sheet 21B.

40. "Direct Examination of Jessie Lee Garner," in *Mississippi Power & Light Co. v. Garner*, 179 Miss. 588 (1937), Mississippi Department of Archives and History, Jackson, Mississippi. I am so grateful to Stephen Parks, the law librarian of Mississippi, for locating and digitizing this case for me.

41. "Direct Examination of W. W. Bean," in *Mississippi Power & Light Co. v. Garner*, 179 Miss. 588 (1937), Mississippi Department of Archives and History, Jackson, Mississippi.

42. *Mississippi Power & Light Co.*, 179 Miss. 588.

43. "Negro Woman Gets $1,000 in Suit against Jim Crow Buses," *Kansas American*, October 15, 1937, 1.

44. *Mississippi Power & Light Co.*, 179 Miss. 588.

45. *Mississippi Power & Light Co.*, 179 Miss. 588.

46. Eatmon, "Wielding an Unlikely Weapon," 267–68. See also Milewski, *Litigating Across the Color Line*; Eatmon, "Public Wrongs, Private Rights"; Penningroth, *Before the Movement.*

47. Milewski, *Litigating Across the Color Line*, 144–46; Welke, *Recasting American Liberty.*

48. Milewski, *Litigating Across the Color Line*, 145.

49. Milewski, *Litigating Across the Color Line*, 150.

50. See, for example, *Interurban Transp. Co.*, 194 Ark. 321; *Dunn Bus Service*, 140 Fla. 341; *Panhandle Stages*, 171 S.W.2d 911; *Alabama Power Co.*, 31 Ala. App. 438.

51. For white couples, see, for instance, *Buckley*, 254 A.D. 702; *Morris*, 120 N.J.L. 261.

52. The only known case is *Shankle*, 8 So.2d 714.

53. See, for example, *Waters*, 258 A.D. 755. A full investigation of bus tort lawsuits across racial and gender lines is beyond the scope of this book. But even a cursory search in Westlaw Campus Research reveals the dominance of women in bus injury lawsuits. Even though historians have conducted excellent research on women and tort law in railroads, there is also a rich body of material for a study of tort lawsuits on buses and automobiles. For a discussion of white women and torts, see Welke, *Recasting American Liberty*; Schlanger, "Injured Women Before Common Law Courts," 79–140.

54. *Hughes*, 188 So. 473, accessed in Baton Rouge Clerk Court. I am grateful to Bryan Hastings for locating and digitizing this case for me.

55. For information about scientific racism perpetrated against African Americans during slavery and Reconstruction, see Owns, *Medical Bondage*; Downs, *Sick from Freedom*; Long, *Doctoring Freedom.*

56. Milewski, *Litigating Across the Color Line*, 145.

57. Milewski, *Litigating Across the Color Line*, 10, 151.

58. Milewski, *Litigating Across the Color Line*, 10, 162, 150.

59. Milewski, *Litigating Across the Color Line*, 158.

60. Ayers, *Promise of the New South*, 247–48.

61. Milewski, *Litigating Across the Color Line*, 149.

62. For Johnson in the census, see *Fourteenth Census of the United States*, 1920, Monroe City, Louisiana, Enumeration District 93, sheet 25A.

63. For Norman Coon in the census, see *Fifteenth Census of the United States*, 1930, Monroe City, Louisiana, Enumeration District 37–9, sheet 16-B.

64. "Testimony Concluded in Case Against City," *Monroe News Star*, September 26, 1934, 9.

65. *Johnson*, 164 So. 456.

66. *Missouri Pacific Transp. Co.*, 199 Ark. 225.

67. For the Martin family, see *Sixteenth Census of the United States*, 1940, Madison County, Mississippi, Enumeration District 45-3B, sheet 12A.

68. "Weather," *Daily Clarion Ledger*, August 13, 1936, 1.

69. For Dick McCool, see *Sixteenth Census of the United States*, 1940, Madison County, Mississippi, Enumeration District 45-1B, sheet 5B; for J. Paul White, see *Fifteenth Census of the United States*, 1930, Madison County, Mississippi, Enumeration District 45-2, sheet 7A.

70. *Tri-State Transit Co.*, 181 Miss. 388.

71. *Tri-State Transit Co.*, 181 Miss. 388.

72. Penningroth, *Before the Movement*, 154.

73. "Poor Have Rights That Can't Be Denied," *Commercial Appeal*, March 13, 1938, 2.

74. "First Dipping Vat Case in Years in High Court," *Daily Clarion-Ledger*, March 8, 1938, 2.

75. "Mississippi Murder Trial Shocks Supreme Court," *New Journal and Guide*, January 18, 1936, 1. For a good discussion of Judge Griffith and *Brown v. Mississippi*, see Randolph, *Mississippi Law*, 43–46.

76. Cortner, *"Scottsboro" Case in Mississippi.*

77. "Linnie Eaddy, Direct Examination," in *Eaddy v. Greensboro-Fayetteville Bus Lines*, 191 S.C. 538 (1939), accessed through the State Supreme Court of South Carolina Law Library, Columbia, South Carolina.

78. *Eaddy*, 191 S.C. 538.

79. *Shankle*, 8 So.2d 714.

80. Oral History of Jennie Bibbs Didlick, interviewed by Emily Parker, August 8, 1986, number: 1986OH243 KH 370, "Blacks in Lexington Oral History Project," Louie B. Nunn Center for Oral History, University of Kentucky Libraries; "Awarded $100 After Driver Put Her Off Jim Crow Bus," *Atlanta Daily World*, December 5, 1940, 1; *Didlick v. Southern Greyhound Company*, November 22, 1940.

81. For the Bibbs family, see *Fourteenth Census of the United States*, 1920, Fayette County, Kentucky, Enumeration District 58, sheet 3A. At the time of his death, Bob Bibbs was employed as a janitor. See "Death Certificate: Benjamin Bibbs," Commonwealth of Kentucky: State Board of Health, July 4, 1930, file 16496.

82. For Grant in the census, see *Fifteenth Census of the United States*, 1930, Baton Rouge, Louisiana, Enumeration District 17-36, sheet 6A.

83. *Grant*, 15 So.2d 123.

84. For a similar case, see *McFarland*, 11 So.2d 19.

85. For Peterson in the census, see *Sixteenth Census of the United States*, 1940, Memphis City, Tennessee, Enumeration District 98-304, sheet 12B.

86. For Latting in the census, see *Sixteenth Census of the United States*, 1940, Memphis City, Tennessee, Enumeration District 98-28A, sheet 13A.

87. For George B. Coleman in the census, see *Sixteenth Census of the United States*, 1940, Memphis City, Tennessee, Enumeration District 98-122, sheet 12B.

88. "Wins Test Case vs. Greyhound Bus," *Chicago Defender*, February 20, 1937, 5.

89. "Divorce Action Is Reviewed in Appeals Court," *Jackson Sun*, May 24, 1937, 9, "Appeals Court Reverses Case from Madison," *Jackson Sun*, June 15, 1936, 12; "Court of Appeals Gives 3 Reversals," *Nashville Tennessean*, June 16, 1937, 8.

90. "Wins Test Case vs. Greyhound Bus," *Chicago Defender*, February 20, 1937, 5.

91. Mack, *Representing the Race*, 85.

92. For Owens in the census, see *Fifteenth Census of the United States*, 1930, Shreveport City, Louisiana, Enumeration District 916, sheet 25-A.

93. *Owens*, 191 So. 581.

94. *Valdry*, 5 So.2d 173.

95. *Hughes*, 188 So. 473.

96. *Hughes*, 188 So. 473.

97. "I'll Be Suing You," *Bus Transportation*, August 1940; "Judge, I Didn't Know," *Bus Transportation*, April 1943.

98. Penningroth, *Before the Movement*, xxv.

Chapter 5

1. Norma L. Green is also known as Nora L. Green. For her birth and work, see *Fourteenth Census of the United States*, 1920, Randolph, West Virginia, Enumeration District 160, sheet 1A; *Sixteenth Census of the United States*, Petersburg, Virginia, 1940, Enumeration District 27–4, sheet 6A.

2. Delmont, *Half American*.

3. Telegram from F. D. Patterson, Tuskegee Institute, Alabama, to Walter White, DC, September 16, 1942, box 194, folder 8, NAACP-LC; "Protest Beating of Tuskegee Army Nurse," *Atlanta Daily World*, September 24, 1942, 1.

4. Marjorie McKenzie, "Against the Lean Years," *Afroamerican Woman's Journal: The Negro Woman Serves America Issue* 3, no. 2 (1943): 7.

5. Murray, *States' Laws on Race and Color*, 15–16, 86–87, 117, 419–20, 482–83.

6. "Transportation Problem," *New York Times*, February 22, 1942, E6.

7. Undated newspaper clipping, "County Fair, Conventions, Banned by ODT," box 153, folder 4, NAACP-LC.

8. "Intercity Buses at War: The Story of Highway Passenger Transportation," box 6, folder 7, Greyhound-Chicago.

9. Walsh, *Making Connections*, 33.

10. "New Virginia Speed Law to Cut Bus Service on Highways," *New Journal and Guide*, October 10, 1942, A2.

11. For the historiography outlining Black women's limited opportunities in the Southern wartime economy, see Anderson, "Last Hired, First Fired"; Boris, "'You Wouldn't Want One of 'Em Dancing with Your Wives,'" 77–108; Green, "'Where Would the Negro Women Apply for Work?,'" 95–117; Kruse and Tuck, *Fog of War*.

12. See, for example, Hine, *Black Women in White*; Threat, *Nursing Civil Rights*; Bolzenius, *Glory in Their Spirit*.

13. See, for example, Phillips, *War! What Is It Good For?*, 64–111; Gergel, *Unexampled Courage*; Bay, *Traveling Black*; Guglielmo, *Divisions*; Burnham, *By Hands Now Known*; Delmont, *Half American*.

14. For a discussion about how Black women in Georgia on chain gangs engaged in similar types of resistance, see LeFlouria, *Chained in Silence*, 86.

15. "1,300 Ask Jobs for Women in Plane Plant," *Chicago Defender*, April 17, 1943, 6.

16. Nelson, "Organized Labor and the Struggle for Black Equality," 952–88.

17. Anderson, "Last Hired, First Fired," 88.

18. Green, "'Where Would the Negro Women Apply for Work?,'" 97.

19. Green, "'Where Would the Negro Women Apply for Work?,'" 97.

20. Bolzenius, *Glory in Their Spirit*, 10.

21. Anderson, "Last Hired, First Fired," 86; Green, "'Where Would the Negro Women Apply for Work?,'" 98.

22. Green, "'Where Would the Negro Women Apply for Work?,'" 103; Boris, "You Wouldn't Want One of 'Em Dancing with Your Wives," 86.

23. Bolton, *Home Front Battles*, 65–90.

24. Anderson, "Last Hired, First Fired," 91.

25. Anderson, "Last Hired, First Fired," 83.

26. "3,000 Jamaicans Imported to Work in Conn. Tobacco Crop," *Afro-American*, August 21, 1943, 17.

27. For an article praising Black migrants, see "Leaves for New Job," *Birmingham Daily World*, December 22, 1941, 4. For articles discussing Black women's wartime accomplishments outside the South, see "Curtiss-Wright to Hire Negro Women," *Birmingham Daily World*, March 6, 1942, 4; "Negro Women Best Shipyard Welder," *Birmingham Daily World*, March 19, 1943, 4; "Women Get Jobs of Men in D.C.," *Birmingham Daily World*, April 9, 1943, 4; "Building Flying Fortresses for Allied Defense," *Birmingham Daily World*, July 30, 1943, 4; "Negro Women to Be Found in All Key Industries," *Birmingham Daily World*, February 4, 1944, 4; "Race Women Get Opportunity as Streetcar Conductors," *Birmingham Daily World*, April 24, 1944, 4; "They Claim to Riveting Championship," *Birmingham Daily World*, May 25, 1944, 4.

28. Phillips, *War! What Is It Good For?*, 64–70.

29. See, for example, "Women Employees," *Highway Traveler*, undated, Greyhound Collection, WRHS; "The Story of Highway Passenger Transportation," *Highway Traveler*, undated, Greyhound Collection, WRHS.

30. "Telling the Story in Birmingham," *Transit Journal*, November 1942.

31. "Jackson," *Chicago Defender*, March 4, 1944, 17B.

32. Thornton, "Segregation and the City," 55.

33. Dailey, "Sexual Politics of Race in World War II America," 157–58.

34. Kelley, "Congested Terrain," 56, 60, 61.

35. Ransby, *Ella Baker and the Black Freedom Movement*, 125–28.

36. Sosna, introduction, xvi.

37. Mrs. Myrtle Smith, Anniston, Alabama, to the editor of the *Pittsburgh Courier*, April 5, 1943, box 153, folder 5, NAACP-LC. For the bus driver, see "World War II Draft Card," Lewis William McCurry, Honorable Discharge, February 10, 1946.

38. Cronenberg, *Forth to the Mighty Conflict*, 2–3.

39. His uncle was the novelist Thomas Dixon, who wrote *The Clansmen*, which became the racist film *Birth of a Nation*.

40. Thornton, "Segregation in the City," 57.

41. "Alabama's Governor Frank Dixon Gives His Views on the South's Race Attitudes," *Chicago Defender*, August 8, 1942, 6; "Alabama Governor Times Injunction of Race Issue," *Atlanta Daily World*, July 28, 1942, 2; "Governor Dixon," *Alabama Daily World*, December 15, 1942, 3; Thornton, "Segregation in the City," 57.

42. "Bus Driver Beats Expectant Mother," *New York Amsterdam News*, June 13, 1942, 3.

43. "Alabama Cop Beats, Jails Woman Bus Rider," *Baltimore Afro-American*, December 19, 1942, 12.

44. "Telling the Story in Birmingham," *Transit Journal*, November 1942.

45. "MECTD Traffic Report, 1942," box 10, folder 13, Birmingham Electric Company Transportation Department (BECTD) comments, undated, box 10, folder 13, Cooper Green Papers, Alabama State Archives, Birmingham Alabama, (hereafter cited as BECTD-Alabama).

46. Birmingham Electric Company Transportation Department (BECTD) comments, undated, box 10, folder 13, BECTD-Alabama.

47. Thornton, *Dividing Lines*, 153.

48. "Streetcar Friction to Get NAACP Attention," *Birmingham Daily World*, April 16, 1942, 2. See also "Transportation Number 1 Problem in B'ham," *Birmingham Daily World*, July 9, 1943, 3.

49. "Negro Killed by Bus Driver," *Decatur*, August 17, 1942, 8.

50. Grover E. Chandler, Enlistment Record, November 1943, Camp Shelby, Mississippi, Enlistment Number 34876412.

51. "Sister of Slain Soldier Asks Stimson for Problem" *Pittsburgh Courier*, September 5, 1942, 1; Delmont, *Half American*, 144.

52. "Negro Shot by Bus Driver," *Weekly Review*, August 22, 1942, 1.

53. "The Race Issue Must Not Be Alabama's Shame . . . by Reason of Color," *Pittsburgh Courier*, August 22, 1942, 5.

54. American Negro Nurses, Tuskegee, to Attorney General Francis J. Biddle, Washington, DC, September 18, 1942, Department of Justice Class 144, RG 60, stack 20, row 17, compartment 48, shelf 3, box 2, National Archives II, College Park, MD.

55. Almeria Plaskett Roberts to parents, September 17, 1942, box 194, folder 8, NAACP-LC.

56. For the Plaskett family, see *Twelfth Census of the United States*, 1920, Bucks County, Pennsylvania, Enumeration District 1245, sheet 7B.

57. "Tuskegee Army Nurse Severely Beaten by Alabama Police," *Detroit Tribune*, October 10, 1942, 3.

58. Chautevert, *Marching Together*, 178; *Aframerican Woman's Journal*, 1942.

59. "Protest Beating of Tuskegee Army Nurse," *Atlanta Daily World*, September 24, 1942, 1. See also telegram, Walter White to Fredrick Patterson, September 16, 1942, box 194, folder 8, NAACP-LC.

60. See, for example, "An Afro-American Soldier," Camp Polk, LA, to Walter White, New York City, May 7, 1943, box 153, folder 5, NAACP-LC; "How Savannah (GA) Sabotages the War Effort," *Baltimore Afro-American*, June 12, 1943, 1;

Frank Yerby, "Health Card," *Harper's Magazine*, 1944. See also Parascandola, "'Quarantining Women,'" 431–59.

61. Audrey Riley, Mississippi, to the NAACP, New York City, June 3, 1943, in Correspondence, December 1940–November 1943, NAACP Papers, Proquest History Vault.

62. Milton R. Konvitz, New York City, to Truman K. Gibson, Washington, DC, June 16, 1943, in Correspondence, December 1940–November 1943, NAACP Papers, Proquest History Vault.

63. For information on his discharge, see Theodore Riley, Application for Headstone, Discharge August 17, 1943, Pension Number: XC-03-403-127.

64. "Soldier's Fair Wife to Sue Dixie Bus Company," *Afro-American*, July 3, 1943, 15.

65. For Zelma Barnes, see *Sixteenth Census of the United States*, Cuyuhoga County, Ohio, 1940, Enumeration District 94–459, sheet 11A. For Phrania Henderson, see *Sixteenth Census of the United States*, Cuyuhoga County, Ohio, 1940, Enumeration District 92–408, sheet 15B. For their marriage license, see Marriage Record, license 87562, August 16, 1941. For his enlistment record, see "Zelma E. Barnes," US Department of Veterans Affairs, BIRLS Death File, page 1, enlistment date, April 28, 1944, discharge date, March 30, 1946.

66. "Jail Soldier's Wife, Baby After Refusal to Take Back Seat on Southern Muny Bus," *Cleveland Call and Post*, August 19, 1944, 1A.

67. See also "Three Women Jim Crowed; Filed Suits," *New York Amsterdam News*, December 2, 1944, 7A.

68. "Bus Driver Shoots Negro Corporal," *Montgomery Advertiser*, March 28, 1943, 9.

69. Memo to Thurgood Marshall from Walter White, September 14, 1943, box 153, folder 5, NAACP-LC.

70. "City Bus Driver, Slayer of Negro Soldier, Released," *Alexandria Daily Town Talk*, March 15, 1944, 1.

71. "Dixie Driver of Bus Slays NY Soldier," *New York Amsterdam News*, April 1, 1944, 1A.

72. See, for example, Edward R. Dudley, Assistant Special Counsel, to Truman Gibson, Civilian Aide to Secretary of War, March 19, 1944, box 152, folder 8, NAACP-LC; "Fail to Hold Bus Driver in Killing," *Philadelphia Tribune*, March 25, 1944, 2; "War Official Declares Army Wil Continue Jim Crow Policy," *New York Amsterdam News*, April 15, 1944, A1; Thurgood Marshall, New York City, to Honorable Francis J. Biddle, Washington, DC, April 27, 1944, box 152, folder 8, NAACP-LC.

73. "Is Southern Jim Crow Enforced by the Army?," *Pittsburgh Courier*, June 10, 1944, 6.

74. "Tuskegee Aid in Army Slain by White Bus Driver," *Chicago Defender*, July 22, 1944, 1.

75. "Bus Driver Kills Negro Soldier," *Gazette and Daily*, July 14, 1944, 2.

76. "Tuskegee Aid in Army Slain by White Bus Driver," *Chicago Defender*, July 22, 1944, 1.

77. "The Law Is Supreme," *News and Observer*, July 15, 1944, 4. Spicely's relatives reached out to the NAACP for assistance. Robert Spicely, a worker in the Tuskegee Cafeteria, asked how much it would cost for the NAACP to get involved in the case. Ruth Ida Spicely, the sister of the victim, wrote to the NAACP and enclosed sixty-seven dollars. She noted that this was "contributions from my co-workers and employees who wishes to contribute something to aid in the persecution for the slayer of my brother." See Robert A. Spicely, Tuskegee Institute Cafeteria, to Charles Houston, New York City, July 20, 1944, box 152, folder 10, NAACP-LC; Ruth Ida Spicely, Philadelphia, to NAACP Legal Defense and Education Fund, New York City, September 9, 1944, box 152, folder 10, box 152, NAACP-LC.

78. "Bus Driver Cleared in Death of Negro," *Selma Times Journal*, September 17, 1944, 1.

79. See, for example, "Soldier's Fair Wife to Sue Dixie Bus Company," 15; "Jail Soldier's Wife, Baby After Refusal to Take Back Seat on Southern Bus," 1A.

80. Letter from Walter White, New York City, to Honorable Robert Patterson, Washington, DC, September 21, 1944, Box 194, Folder 2, NAACP-LC.

81. September 1, 1944, Action: Federation for Constitutional Liberties, box 194, folder 2, NAACP-LC. See also "South Raves as Order Ends Jim Crow," *Pittsburgh Courier*, September 2, 1944, 1.

82. For Roberta McKenzie and Gladys Blackmon, see Electronic Army Serial Number Merged File, 1938–1946, NAID 1263923, Records of the National Archives and Records Administration, 1789-ca. 2007, RG 64, box 00171, reel 17.

83. Affidavits of Roberta McKenzie and Gladys Blackmon, December 23, 1943, box 194, folder 3, NAACP-LC.

84. War Department, Section 2, Siebert, Alabama, to Walter White, New York City, December 24, 1944, box 194, folder 3, NAACP-LC.

85. Thurgood Marshall, New York City, to William H. Hastie, Washington, DC, January 13, 1945, box 194, folder 3, NAACP-LC.

86. Middle-class Black Southerners banded together to take preventive action against mounting violence on buses. Black lawyers knew firsthand how intransigent bus companies could be, having spent the 1930s representing African Americans in lawsuits. In December 1942 in Memphis, Augustus L. Latting, a prominent lawyer, joined forces with J. A. Beauchamp, the secretary of the Boy Scouts, to create a club to "improve the seating situation on street cars and buses" and to foster interracial cooperation to prevent misunderstandings on the buses. Latting was the attorney who had previously defended Marie Peterson in 1937, when she sued the Dixie Greyhound Lines to recover her fur coat and won. By forming this committee, Latting and Beauchamp exercised a dose of precaution, rightly anticipating that bus conflicts would only worsen throughout the war. "Victory Clubs Formed to Stop Racial Trouble," *Baltimore Afro-American*, December 19, 1942, 19. In Augusta, a committee from the Negro Business and Civic League met with officials from the Georgia Power Company in 1943 to discuss the abuses that African American passengers had recently experienced. See "Augusta Bus Bias Assailed," *Chicago Defender*, February 13, 1943, 9.

87. Simmons, *Crescent City Girls*, 5.

88. "Augusta Girl Is Attacked by Bus Operator," *Atlanta Daily World*, February 25, 1943, 1. For the Harris family, see *Sixteenth Census of the United States*, 1940, Richmond County, Georgia, Enumeration District 121–34, sheet 8A. For a discussion of Black girls and criminality, see Simmons, *Crescent City Girls*; Chatelain, *South Side Girls*.

89. "High School Girl, 16, Arrested in Bus Disorder," *New Journal and Guide*, April 10, 1943, 2.

90. For Dorothy Foster, see *Sixteenth Census of the United States*, 1940, Spartanburg County, South Carolina, Enumeration District 42–77, sheet 22A; for Mildred McGowan, see *Sixteenth Census of the United States*, 1940, Spartanburg County, South Carolina, Enumeration District 42–63, sheet 63-A.

91. "S.C. Bus Company Sued for Girls' Beating," *Afro-American*, April 1, 1944, 16.

92. See, for example, "2 Race Ministers, 1 Woman File Civil Liberties Suit," *Atlanta Daily World*, October 1, 1942, 1; "Mother, Attacked by Bus Driver, Is Awarded $275," *Pittsburgh Courier*, November 27, 1943, 3; "$400 Awarded to 4 Negroes Put Off the Bus," *Knoxville News Sentinel*, August 2, 1943, 2.

93. "Bus Driver Held in Club-Slugging of Race Woman," *Chicago Defender*, October 23, 1943, 3.

94. "Heavy Migration of Race to Cities Puzzles Southern Plantation Owners," *Birmingham Daily World*, March 13, 1942, 2.

95. "Racial Situation: Tabulation of Racial Incidents, December 31, 1945," *Records of Headquarters Army Service Forces*, RG 160, box 69, file 291.2, National Archives, College Park, Maryland (hereafter cited as "Racial Situation," NARA).

96. "Racial Situation," NARA.

97. "Racial Situation," NARA.

98. "Racial Situation," NARA.

99. "Racial Situation," NARA.

100. "Racial Situation," NARA.

101. "Racial Situation," NARA. For a discussion about the need for more examinations of power relations between Black and white women, see Fuentes, *Dispossessed Lives*, 1–2.

102. "Racial Situation," NARA.

103. Haley, *No Mercy Here*, 35.

104. "Racial Situation," NARA.

105. "Nazi-Like Bus Driver Assaults Woman, Has Soldiers Jailed," *Norfolk Journal and Guide*, October 7, 1944, C1.

106. "Put 8 Soldiers on Chain Gang in South Carolina," *New York Amsterdam News*, October 21, 1944, 1B.

107. "Negroes in the Army," *New Republic*, December 25, 1944, 871–72.

108. "Put 8 Soldiers on Chain Gang in South Carolina," 1B.

109. A discussion of World War II bus violence in the Jim Crow South underscores the importance of highlighting the experiences of both women and men.

110. For Charlotte Wright, see *Sixteenth Census of the United States*, 1940, Baldwin County, Georgia, Enumeration District 3–4, sheet 4A. I also consulted the previous two censuses to determine how many children she had.

111. "Notice: Change Bus Schedule for Southern Stages, Inc." *Macon Evening News*, April 9, 1935, 5.

112. *Davis v. State*, trial transcript, in RCB-11019, RGSGS 092-01-003, Supreme Court, Clerk of Court Criminal Appeal Case Files, 1917–1946, case file 1976-0029A, Georgia Archives, Morrow, Georgia (hereafter cited as *Davis v. State*-Georgia).

113. *Davis v. State*-Georgia. For Carter S. Baldwin in the census, see *Seventeenth Census of the United States*, 1950, Baldwin County, Georgia, Enumeration District 5-11, sheet 79.

114. For Azilee Whittle in the census, see *Seventeenth Census of the United States*, 1950, Clarkesville County, Georgia, Enumeration District 68-2, sheet 7.

115. *Davis v. State*-Georgia.

116. Freedmen, *Redefining Rape*.

117. *Davis v. State*-Georgia. See also *Davis*, 202 Ga. 13.

Chapter 6

1. *Mack v. Dixie Greyhound Lines, Inc.*, Case 2348, Records of the United States District Court, Eastern District of Missouri-St. Louis, Civil Case Files, 1938–2000, ID 56278, RG 21, National Archives at Kansas City, Kansas City, Missouri. I wish to thank the archivist, Stephen Spence, for locating this case and digitizing it for me. See also "Trial of 25,000 'Jim Crow' Bus Suit Opens Here," *St. Louis Star and Times*, February 15, 1944, 3. Her attorneys were Clyde Cooper, Virgil Green, and T. J. Crowder. For Cooper in the census, see Claude F. Cooper, 1940 census, *Sixteenth Census of the United States*, 1940, Blytheville, Arkansas, Enumeration District 47-14, sheet 14A. For Green, see *Sixteenth Census of the United States*, 1940, Blytheville, Arkansas, Enumeration District 47-14, sheet 4B. For Crowder, see *Sixteenth Census of the United States*, 1940, Blytheville, Arkansas, Enumeration District 47-14, sheet 20B.

2. "Trial of 25,000 'Jim Crow' Bus Suit Opens Here," 3. For Miller in the census, see Joseph C. Miller, *Seventeenth Census of the United States*, 1950, Enumeration District 92-240, sheet 2.

3. "Negro Wins Bus Suit," *New York Times*, February 18, 1944, 19. See also "$1,500 Judgement Given Teacher in Jim Crow Bus Case," *Chicago Defender*, February 26, 1944, 5.

4. "Negro Wins Bus Suit," 19; "Colored Woman Wins Civil Rights Verdict," *St. Joseph News-Press*, February 17, 1944, 7; "Negress Wins Judgement," *Lansing State Journal*, February 17, 1944, 24.

5. For Mack in the census, see Maggie Mack, *Sixteenth Census of the United States*, 1940, Caruthersville City, Missouri, Enumeration District 78-120, sheet 20A. For her birth, see Maggie Mack, *Fourteenth Census of the United States*, 1920, Panola County, Mississippi, Enumeration District 72, sheet 20A. For the bus driver, Walter Ramsey, see *United States City Directory*, Memphis, Tennessee, 1940, p. 742.

6. No historian has yet to examine Black women's bus experiences during World War II in the Jim Crow North. For the historiography on Black women in World War II, see Anderson, "Last Hired, First Fired," 82–97; Ervin, *Gateway to Equality*,

97–120; Turk, "'Fair Chance to Do My Part of Work,'" 209–44; Shockley, *"We Too, Are Americans,"* 11; Sims-Wood, "'We Served America, Too!"; Kimble, "I Too, Serve America," 95–117; Bolzenius, *Glory in Their Spirit.*

7. George E. DeMar, "Negro Women Are American Workers, Too," *Opportunity*, April 1943, 77.

8. On the eve of World War II, approximately 1,780,962 African American women were in the paid labor force, working primary in jobs related to personal service, agriculture, and some clerical and professional positions. Approximately one in three African American women held a paid labor position outside their homes, while the proportion for white women was one in five. By 1944, toward the end of the war, Black women's paid employment increased to two in five, while for white women, it was one in three. For these statistics, see *Negro Women War Workers*, 19, ii.

9. Honey, *Bitter Fruit*, 12.

10. Shockley, *"We Too, Are Americans,"* 12.

11. *Negro Women War Workers*, 2.

12. *Negro Women War Workers*, 2. One of the reasons why navy yards employed so many Black women workers was that a training program offered through the National Youth Administration (NYA) instructed Black women in gas welding, sheet metalwork, aircraft riveting, and radio construction. See "NYA Women Trainees Get Navy Yard Jobs," *Philadelphia Tribune*, February 20, 1943, 4.

13. Delmont, *Half American*, 60.

14. "25 Detroiters Take Job Complaints to WMC," *Atlanta Daily World*, November 28, 1942, 1.

15. Anderson, "Last Hired, First Fired," 86.

16. Ervin, *Gateway to Equality*.

17. Gregory, *Southern Diaspora*, 330, table A.1. For a discussion of African American women's migration to California during World War II, see Lemke-Santangelo, *Abiding Courage*.

18. "Workers Attempting to Migrate to New Jersey Jailed in Florida," *Atlanta Daily World*, June 8, 1944, 1.

19. "Women Do Vital War Work at Edgewood Arsenal," *Pittsburgh Courier*, January 16, 1943, 11.

20. "Afro Finds 300 Women Making Gas Masks," *Baltimore Afro-American*, May 3, 1941, 8.

21. "Only 11% Use Buses," *Bus Transportation*, March 1943, 33.

22. "Newark Booms with War Work," *New York Amsterdam News*, November 21, 1942, 13.

23. Hortense Johnson, "What My Job Means to Me," *Opportunity*, April 1943.

24. "Bus Service Extended to Roberts Park," March 13, 1943, *Norfolk Journal and Guide*, B2.

25. "Southern White Seamen Jailed after 'Nasty Words' on the Bus," *New York Amsterdam News*, April 22, 1944, 1A.

26. *Negro Women War Workers*, 19.

27. Anderson, *Last Hired, First Fired*, 91.

28. For examples of Black women seizing on their government war work to make claims for citizenship rights during the Civil War and Reconstruction, see Masur, *Example for All the Land*; Masur, "Patronage and Protest in Kate Brown's Washington," 1047–71. For efforts to reclaim that citizenship, see Eric Yellin, *Racism in the Nation's Service*.

29. "Domestic Help Shortage Acute," *Birmingham Daily World*, June 5, 1942, 4.

30. "Leaves for New Job," *Birmingham Daily World*, December 22, 1941, 4. For Theresa Nash in the census, see *Sixteenth Census of the United States*, 1940, Jefferson County, Alabama, Enumeration District 37–152, sheet 10B.

31. "Want a Job? Uncle Sam Is Hard Up for Stenographers," *Cleveland Call and Post*, September 5, 1942, 15.

32. "A Young War Worker Goes to Washington . . . Adjustment Made Easier Through Information," *Pittsburgh Courier*, January 23, 1943, 10.

33. "D.C. War Worker Disgusted with the Capital," *Chicago Defender*, March 6, 1943, 14.

34. "Charge War Department Jim Crows Its Girls," *Chicago Defender*, July 18, 1942, 2.

35. "Bus Trouble in Capital," *Cleveland Call and Post*, March 6, 1943, 11B.

36. "Affidavit of Mildred I. Turpin," January 8, 1943, box 191, folder 2, NAACP-LC.

37. "2 Girls Jailed for Flouting Jim-Crow Bus Rule," *New York Amsterdam News*, January 23, 1943, 24; "2 Jailed for Violating VA. Bus Jim Crow," *Chicago Defender*, January 16, 1943, 8.

38. "Kick the Rascals Out—an Editorial," *Baltimore Afro-American*, January 23, 1943, 6.

39. She had previously labored as a domestic servant. See Lola Walters, *Sixteenth Census of the United States*, 1940, Newark, New Jersey, Enumeration District 25191, sheet 4A.

40. Lola E. Walters, Washington, DC, to Thurgood Marshall, New York City, May 2, 1944, box 185, folder 3, NAACP-LC.

41. J. E. Donahue, Cleveland, to Milton Konvitz, New York, August 18, 1944, box 185, folder 3, NAACP-LC.

42. "Filling Men's Shoes," *Bus Transportation*, October 1942, 471; "Women Can't Drive?," *Bus Transportation*, November 1942, 511; "So They Took Women . . . and Like 'Em," *Bus Transportation*, April 1943, 23; "Training . . . Key to Help Shortages," *Bus Transportation*, April 1943, 36; "Remanning with Women," *Bus Transportation*, May 1943, 26–27.

43. "Women in the Transportation Industries," Women's Bureau Department Papers, History Vault-Proquest.

44. See "In Capable Hands," *Bus Transportation*, September 1939, 1; "They Did It Before, They Can Do It Again," *Bus Transportation*, January 1943, 28–31.

45. See "In Capable Hands," *Bus Transportation*, October 1942, 471; "Women Can't Drive?," *Bus Transportation*, November 1942, 511–12; "Training: Key to the Skilled Help Shortage," *Bus Transportation*, March 1943, 38–40; "Help Wanted . . . Female," *Bus Transportation*, September 1943, 58–59; "So They Took Women . . . and Like 'Em!," *Bus Transportation*, April 1943, 23–25.

46. "Office of Defense Transportation: Office of War Information," History Vault-Proquest.

47. For a discussion of wartime Michigan, see Sugrue, *Origins of the Urban Crisis*, 17–32.

48. "Mother Practices Driving DSR Bus," *Detroit Evening Times*, January 24, 1943, 3. For Lois Wright in the census, see *Sixteenth Census of the United States*, 1940, Wayne County, Michigan, Enumeration District 84–405, sheet 4B; *Seventeenth Census of the United States*, 1950, Wayne County, Michigan, Enumeration District 85–1871, sheet 75.

49. For a discussion of Black women's exercise and citizenship, see Purkiss, *Fit Citizens*, 132–41.

50. "First Woman Bus Driver Takes Over," *New York Amsterdam News*, January 30, 1943, 1.

51. "Bus, Streetcar Employers in Many Cities Relax Job Policy," *New Journal and Guide*, March 6, 1943, B1.

52. "Queens Bus Company to Employ Women," *New York Amsterdam News*, September 18, 1943, 16. For a discussion of the push for Black bus drivers in New York City, see Biondi, *To Stand and Fight*, 22.

53. "First Negro Woman Qualifies as CTS Bus Driver," *Cleveland Call and Post*, April 22, 1944, 1A.

54. "Akron FOL Wins Jobs for Women at Palmer Match," *Cleveland Call and Post*, February 6, 1943, 1B.

55. "Bus Company Has No Jobs for 'Colored,'" *Cleveland Call and Post*, August 12, 1944, 1A.

56. Maya Angelou, as quoted in Emily Yellin, *Our Mother's War*, 206–7.

57. "D.C. Bus Firm Insists on Barring Negro Drivers," *Chicago Defender*, November 28, 1942, 3.

58. "Girls Take Men's Jobs in Virginia," *Baltimore Afro-American*, August 15, 1942, 16.

59. "Full Employment Emphasized at Bennett Home-Making Institute," *New Journal and Guide*, March 30, 1946, 3.

60. Smith, *Managing Race Relations*, 257–60.

61. For Sarah Morris, see *Fifteenth Census of the United States*, Norfolk City, Virginia, Enumeration District 114–29, sheet 7B.

62. "Marriage License of Sarah Morris and Vernon Davis," Norfolk, Virginia, April 7, 1943, Clerk #1026.

63. For Horner in the census, see *Sixteenth Census of the United States*, 1940, Norfolk City, Virginia, Enumeration District 114–48, sheet 14A.

64. "Testimony of Sarah B. Davis," in Davis v. Commonwealth, 182 Va. 760 (1944), accessed in the Supreme Court of Virginia Law Library, Richmond, Virginia.

65. "Fine Upheld in Race Case," *Ledger Star*, July 23, 1943, 16. For the judge, see *Sixteenth Census of the United States*, 1940, Norfolk City, Virginia, Enumeration District 114–25, sheet 4A.

66. "Court News," *Ledger-Star*, July 23, 1943, 20.

67. For the Randolph family, see *Fifteenth Census of the United States*, Virginia, 1930, Alexandria County, Virginia, Enumeration District 101–6, sheet 8A.

68. "Grant Review in Race Case," *Daily Press*, Newport News, Virginia, April 27, 1944, 2.

69. "Jim Crow Case Before High Court," *Evening Herald Courier*, December 1, 1943, 7; "Court to Study Jim Crow Law," *Arizona Republic*, December 1, 1943, 6; "Court to Act on Jim Crow Appeal," *San Francisco Examiner*, December 1, 1943, 8.

70. For Walter Davis, see *Sixteenth Census of the United States*, 1940, Norfolk City, Virginia, Enumeration District 114–81, sheet 61A. See also "Court Opens Way to Ruling on 'Jim Crow,'" *Richmond News Leader*, November 30, 1943, 1.

71. "To Lessen Race Friction," *Richmond Times-Dispatch*, November 13, 1943, 4.

72. "Anti-Segregation Crusaders Seek United State Support," *Afro-American*, December 18, 1943, 9.

73. Mack v. Dixie Greyhound Lines, Inc., 2348, MO 1943 (found in Records of the United States District Court, Eastern District of Missouri-St. Louis, Civil Case Files, 1938–2000, ID 56278, RG 21, National Archives at Kansas City, Kansas City, Missouri).

74. "'Jim Crow' Case," *Richmond Times Leader*, March 6, 1944, 15.

75. "Grant Review in Race Case," *Daily Press*, Newport News, Virginia, April 27, 1944, 2; *Randolph*, 183 Va. 420.

76. "Grant Review in Race Case," 2; "'Jim Crow' Tests Before State Court," *Norfolk Journal and Guide*, May 6, 1944, A6. See also "'Jim Crow' Case May Be Decided," *Richmond News Leader*, April 29, 1944, 4; "Girl Upheld in Suit for False Arrest," *Bee*, May 1, 1944, 4.

77. Marriage Certificate, Ethel Ward and Alvin B. New, Pima County, Arizona, November 14, 1942.

78. "Va. Court Rules Law Applies to Both Races," *Richmond News Leader*, June 22, 1944, 1.

79. *Davis*, 182 Va. 760.

80. VA Appeals Court Reverses Segregation Law Conviction," *Pittsburgh Courier*, July 1, 1944, 1.

81. For Irene Amos's household, see *Fifteenth Census of the United States*, 1930, Baltimore City, Enumeration District 4–572, sheet 13A.

82. Tushnet, *Making Civil Rights Law*.

83. "Direct Examination of Barbara Lewis," in Lewis v. Commonwealth, 184 Va. 69 (1945), accessed in the Supreme Court of Virginia Law Library, Richmond, Virginia.

84. *Lewis*, 184 Va. 69.

85. For Diguad, see *Sixteenth Census of the United States*, 1940, Campbell County, Virginia, Enumeration District 111–25, sheet 12B.

86. "Girl Kicked Off Bus, Fined $200, Gets 6 Months in VA," *Baltimore Afro-American*, October 21, 1944, 3.

87. "Fights 'Virginia' Justice: The Incident in Review," *New York Amsterdam News*, October 21, 1944, 3B.

88. "Embittered GIs Come to Rescue," *New York Amsterdam News*, January 6, 1945, A1.

89. Hurt, *Great Plains During World War II*, 158–262.

90. William S. Diguid, Lynchburg, to Edward R. Dudley, New York City, January 15, 1945, NAACP Papers, History Vault.

91. "Lynchburg NAACP Supports Bus Appeal," *New Journal and Guide*, December 2, 1944, A15.

92. *Randolph*, 183 Va. 420.

93. "Error Granted in 'Jim Crow' Law Appeal," *Richmond News Leader*, January 17, 1945, 20.

94. "Case from Middlesex," *Richmond News Leader*, March 6, 1945, 5.

95. "Supreme Court to Meet Today," *Roanoke Times*, April 16, 1945, 2.

96. Milewski, *Litigating Across the Color Line*, 178–80.

97. *Lewis*, 184 Va. 79.

98. Hill, Martin, & Robeson to Nelle Morton, Chapel Hill, North Carolina, December 8, 1946, NAACP Papers, History Vault.

99. *Morgan*, 184 Va. 24, Brief on Behalf of the Commonwealth, accessed through the Supreme Court of Virginia Law Library, Richmond, Virginia.

100. *Morgan*, 184 Va. 24.

101. "Va. Racial Separation Law Upheld," *Richmond News Leader*, June 8, 1945, 3.

102. "Lewis Case Set for Trial July 23," *Afro-American*, July 14, 1945, 19.

103. Bay, *Traveling Black*, 249.

104. Tushnet, *Making Civil Rights Law*, 73–74; *Morgan*, 328 U.S. 373.

105. "Woman Is Denied Damages in Suit," *Richmond News Leader*, June 12, 1946, 3.

106. "Segregation Act May Face New U.S. Test," *Richmond News Leader*, October 8, 1946, 3.

107. Milewski, *Litigating Across the Color Line*, 178–80.

Epilogue

1. For a discussion of Black women in cities in the second Great Migration, see Levenstein, *Movement Without Marches*; R. Williams, *Politics of Public Housing*; Countryman, *Up South*; Sugrue, *Sweet Land of Liberty*; Moten, *Continually Working*; Ervin, *Gateway to Equality*; Purnell et al., *Strange Careers*; Biondi, *To Stand and Fight*; Howard, *Midwest Unrest*.

2. See, for example, Biondi, *To Stand and Fight*, 22; Countryman, *Up South*, 30.

3. R. Williams, *Politics of Public Housing*; Levenstein, *Movement Without Marches*.

4. Richard Gergel, *Unexampled Courage*.

5. See, for example, Eva Robin, New York City, to Department of Justice, Washington, DC, July 10, 1946, box 219, folder 2, NAACP-LC; "Nation Aroused Over Blinding of Negro Vet," *Chicago Defender*, July 27, 1946, 1; "31,000 at Woodard Rally, Mayor Attacks Brutality," undated and unknown clipping, box 219, folder 1, NAACP-LC.

6. "Attorneys Hail Morgan Decision," *Baltimore Afro-American*, June 15, 1946, 11.

7. "Attorneys Hail Morgan Decision," 11.

8. "Greyhound Bus Company Stops Interstate Jim Crow," *Baltimore Afro-American*, June 15, 1946, 11; "Interstate Bus Officials Abolish Jim Crow Signs," *Baltimore Afro-American*, June 15, 1946, 11; "Bus Companies Obey Law Against Jim Crow Travel," *Plaindealer*, June 21, 1946, 1.

9. "Court Jim Crow Decision Defied," *Baltimore Afro-American*, July 6, 1946, 17; "White Supremacy Reigns on Bus Despite New Law," *Baltimore Afro-American*, July 6, 1947, 17; "Benefits of Morgan Case Not Enjoyed by Public," *Baltimore Afro-American*, July 6, 1946, 17.

10. Arsenault, *Freedom Riders*, 20–21.

11. Arsenault, *Freedom Riders*, 15–55.

12. Catsam, *Freedom's Main Line*, 13–21.

13. The women who disagreed that members of the Ride of Reconciliation should be limited to men included seasoned NAACP organizer Ella Baker; Washington, DC, activist Natalie Moorman; and Pauli Murray, a lawyer who had been arrested for bus segregation in 1940. See Bollard, *Protesting with Rosa Parks*, 270–71.

14. Catsam, *Freedom's Main Line*, 13.

15. Bollard, *Protesting with Rosa Parks*, 288–90.

16. "Negro Bus Company Still Rolls in Baton Rouge," *Northwest Enterprise*, August 11, 1948, 3.

17. Fairclough, *Race and Democracy*, 158.

18. Frystak, *Our Minds on Freedom*, 62–69.

19. McGuire, *At the Dark End of the Street*, 82–83.

20. Rosa Parks, quoted in Theoharis, *Rebellious Life of Mrs. Rosa Parks*, 51.

21. For a discussion of Parks before the boycott, see McGuire, *At the Dark End of the Street*; Theoharis, *Rebellious Life of Mrs. Rosa Parks*.

22. Robinson, *Montgomery Bus Boycott*; McGuire, *At the Dark End of the Street*; Theoharis, *Rebellious Life of Mrs. Rosa Parks*.

23. McGuire, *At the Dark End of the Street*, 85–134; for the Mother Pollard quote, see p. 116.

24. McGuire, *At the Dark End of the Street*, 132–34; Theoharis, *Rebellious Life of Mrs. Rosa Parks*, 108–10.

25. For the McNeil family, see *Seventeenth Census of the United States*, 1950, Summit County, Ohio, sheet 71.

26. Arsenault, *Freedom Riders*, 112.

27. "President Clinton Awards the Presidential Citizens Medals," January 8, 2001, https://clintonwhitehouse5.archives.gov/WH/new/html/Mon_Jan_8_141714_2001.html.

28. American Negro Nurses, Tuskegee, to Attorney General Francis J. Biddle, Washington, DC, September 18, 1942, in Department of Justice Class 144, RG 60, stack 20, row 17, compartment 48, shelf 3, box 2, National Archives II, College Park, MD.

Bibliography

Manuscript Collections

Amherst, MA
University of Massachusetts, Amherst
University Archives
W. E. B. DuBois Papers
Baton Rouge, LA
Parish Clerk of Court
Appellate Brief and Trial Transcript, Grant v. Baton Rouge Bus Co., 15 So.2d 123 (1943)
Appellate Brief and Trial Transcript, Hughes v. Baton Rouge Electric Co., 188 So. 473 (1939)
Appellate Brief and Trial Transcript, Valdry v. Baton Rouge Bus Co., 5 So.2d 173 (1941)
Birmingham, AL
Alabama State Archives
Cooper Green Papers
Chicago, IL
Chicago History Museum
Abakanowicz Research Center
Greyhound Bus Company Papers
Cleveland, OH
Western Reserve Historical Association
Greyhound Management Company Collection
Chester Gillespie Papers
Jane Hunter Papers
College Park, MD
National Archives II
Department of Justice Papers, Record Group 60
Records of Headquarters Army Service Forces, Record Group 160
Columbia, SC
South Carolina Supreme Court Library
Appellate brief and trial transcript, *Eaddy v. Greensboro-Fayetteville Bus Lines*
Detroit, MI
Walter P. Reuther Library
Department of Street Railways Papers

Jackson, MS
Mississippi Archives
State Supreme Court Appellate Briefs and Trial Transcripts
Mississippi Power & Light Co. v. Garner, 179 Miss. 588 (1937)
Morrow, GA
Georgia Archives
Supreme Court, Clerk of Court Criminal Appeal Case Files, 1917–1946
Davis v. State, 202 Ga. 13 (1947)
Kansas City, MO
National Archives at Kansas City
Records of the United States District Court, Eastern District of Missouri-St. Louis, Record Group 21
Lexington, KY
Louie B. Nunn Center for Oral History
Blacks in Lexington Oral History Project
Raleigh, NC
Supreme Court of North Carolina Law Library
State Supreme Court Appellate Briefs and Trial Transcripts
State v. Harris, 213 N.C. 758 (1938)
Richmond, VA
Library of Virginia
Virginia Transit Company Papers
Supreme Court of Virginia Law Library
State Supreme Court Appellate Briefs and Trial Transcripts
Davis v. Commonwealth, 182 Va. 760 (1944)
Lewis v. Commonwealth, 184 Va. 69 (1945)
Morgan v. Commonwealth, 184 Va. 24 (1945)
New v. Atlantic Greyhound Corp. 186 Va. 726 (1947)
Randolph v. A. B. & W. Transit Co., 183 Va. 420 (1945)
Washington, DC
Library of Congress
Manuscript Division
National Association for the Advancement of Colored People Papers
Moorland Spingarn Research Center, Howard University
Manuscript Division
Mabel Keaton Staupers Papers

Organs & Periodicals

Aframerican Woman's Journal
Atlantic
Bags and Baggage
Bus Transportation
Crisis
Decatur
Greyhound Traveler
Harper's Magazine
Highway Traveler
Highway Log
Journal of Negro Education
New Republic
Opportunity
Transit Journal

Black Newspapers

Alabama Daily World
Atlanta Daily World
Baltimore Afro-American
Birmingham Daily World
Carolina Times
Chicago Defender
Cleveland Call and Post
Cleveland Gazette
Detroit Tribune
Kansas American
New Journal and Guide
New York Amsterdam News
Philadelphia Tribune
Pittsburgh Courier

White Newspapers

Abilene Reporter News
Alexandria Daily Town Talk
Commercial Appeal
Crowly-Post Signal
Daily Clarion-Ledger
Daily News
Daily Press
Detroit Evening Times
Detroit Free Press
Durham Herald-Sun
Gazette & Daily
Hartford Courant
Jackson Sun
Knoxville News Sentinel
Lansing State Journal
Ledger-Star
Los Angeles Times
Macon Evening News
Meridien Record
Montgomery Advertiser
Monroe News Star
Nashville Tennessean
News and Observer
Plaindealer
Richmond News Leader
Richmond Palladium
Richmond Times Dispatch
Richmond Times Leader
Roanoke Times
Selma Times Journal
St. Joseph News Press
St. Louis Globe Democrat
St. Louis Star & Times
Washington Post
Weekly Review

Published Primary Sources

The Busman's Operating and Maintenance Guide Book. McGraw-Hill, 1945.
Green, Victor Hugo, ed. *The Negro Motorist Green Book.* Victor H. Green, 1939.
Murray, Pauli. *Song in a Weary Throat: An American Pilgrimage.* Harper and Row, 1987.
Selling the Bus Passenger. Greyhound Management, 1934.

Court Cases

Alabama Power Co. v. Adams, 31 Ala. App. 438 (1944)
Browder v. Gayle, 142 F. Supp. 707 (M.D. Ala. 1956)
Brumfield v. Consolidated Coach Corporation, 240 Ky. 1 (1931)
Buckley v. Green Bus Lines, 254 A.D. 702 (1938)

Davis v. Commonwealth, 182 Va. 760 (1944)
Davis v. State, 202 Ga. 13 (1947)
Dixie Gas & Fuel Co. v. Jacobs, 47 S.W.2d 457 (1932)
Dunn Bus Service v. Wise, 140 Fla. 341 (1939)
Eaddy v. Greensboro-Fayetteville Bus Lines, 191 S.C. 538 (1939)
Fry v. Dixie Motor Coach Corp., 142 Tex. 589 (1944)
Grant v. Baton Rouge Bus Co., 15 So.2d 123 (1943)
Higgins v. Southern Kansas Stage Lines Co., 141 Kan. 641 (1935)
Hughes v. Baton Rouge Electric Co., 188 So. 473 (1939)
Interurban Transp. Co. v. Reeves, 194 Ark. 321 (1937)
Johnson v. City of Monroe, 164 So. 456 (1935)
Jones v. Youngstown Municipal Ry. Co., 1937 WL 2366 (1937)
Kinchlow v. Peoples Rapid Transit Co., 66 App. D.C. 382 (1936)
Lewis v. Commonwealth, 184 Va. 69 (1945)
McFarland v. City of Monroe, 11 So.2d 19 (1942)
Mississippi Power & Light Co. v. Garner, 179 Miss. 588 (1937)
Missouri Pacific Transp. Co. v. Porter, 199 Ark. 225 (1939)
Morgan v. Commonwealth, 184 Va. 24 (1945)
Morgan v. Virginia, 328 U.S. 373 (1946)
Morris v. Public Service Co-ordinated Transport, 120 N.J.L. 261 (1938)
New v. Atlantic Greyhound Corp., 186 Va. 726 (1947)
Owens v. Monzingo, 191 So. 581 (1939)
Panhandle Stages v. Aston, 171 S.W.2d 911 (1943)
Patillo v. State, 120 Tex.Crim. 568 (1932)
Randolph v. A. B. & W. Transit Co., 183 Va. 420 (1945)
Shankle v. Tri-State Transit Co. of Louisiana, 8 So.2d 714 (1942)
State v. Harris, 213 N.C. 758 (1938)
Tri-State Transit Co. v. Martin, 181 Miss. 388 (1938)
Valdry v. Baton Rouge Bus Co., 5 So.2d 173 (1941)
Waters v. Brooklyn Bus Corp., 258 A.D. 755 (1939)

Government Documents

Negro Women War Workers, Bulletin No. 205, Women's Bureau, United States Department of Labor. Government Printing Office, 1945.
Tenth Census of the United States
Eleventh Census of the United States
Twelfth Census of the United States
Thirteenth Census of the United States
Fourteenth Census of the United States
Fifteenth Census of the United States
Sixteenth Census of the United States
Seventeenth Census of the United States

Secondary Sources

Alexander, Shawn Leigh. *An Army of Lions: The Civil Rights Struggle Before the NAACP.* University of Pennsylvania Press, 2012.

Amalgamated Transit Union Staff. "From Rags to Riches." In *A History of the Amalgamated Transit Union.* Amalgamated Transit Union, 1992.

Anderson, Karen Tucker. "Last Hired, First Fired: Black Women Workers During World War II." *Journal of American History* 69, no. 1 (1982): 82–97.

Arnesen, Eric. *Brotherhoods of Color: Black Railroad Workers and the Struggle for Equality.* Harvard University Press, 2001.

———. "Reconsidering the Long Civil Rights Movement." *Historically Speaking* 10, no. 2 (2009): 31–34.

Arsenault, Raymond. *Freedom Riders: 1961 and the Struggle for Racial Justice.* Oxford University Press, 2011.

Ayers, Edward L. *The Promise of the New South: Life After Reconstruction.* Oxford University Press, 1992.

Baldwin, Davarian. *Chicago's New Negroes: Modernity, the Great Migration, and Black Urban Life.* University of North Carolina Press, 2007.

Balto, Simon. *Occupied Territory: Policing Black Chicago from Red Summer to Black Power.* University of North Carolina Press, 2019.

Barkley Brown, Elsa. "'What Has Happened Here': The Politics of Difference in Women's History and Feminist Politics." *Feminist Studies* 18, no. 2 (Summer 1992): 295–312.

Barnes, Catherine A. *Journey from Jim Crow: The Desegregation of Southern Transit.* Columbia University Press, 1983.

Bates, Beth Tompkins. *The Making of Black Detroit in the Age of Henry Ford.* University of North Carolina Press, 2012.

———. *Pullman Porters and the Rise of Black Protest Politics in Black America, 1925–1945.* University of North Carolina Press, 2001.

Bavery, Ashley Johnson. *Bootlegged Aliens: Immigration Politics on America's Northern Border.* University of Pennsylvania Press, 2020.

Bay, Mia. *Traveling Black: A Story of Race and Resistance.* Harvard University Press, 2021.

Benson, Susan Porter. *Counter Cultures: Saleswomen, Mangers, and Customers in American Department Stores, 1890–1940.* University of Illinois Press, 1986.

Berrey, Stephen A. *The Jim Crow Routine: Everyday Performances of Race, Civil Rights, and Segregation in Mississippi.* University of North Carolina Press, 2015.

Biondi, Martha. *To Stand and Fight: The Struggle for Civil Rights in Postwar New York City.* Harvard University Press, 2003.

Boehm, Lisa Krissoff. *Making a Way Out of No Way: African American Women and the Second Great Migration.* University of Mississippi Press, 2010.

Bollard, John K. *Protesting with Rosa Parks: From Stagecoaches to Driving While Black.* University of Georgia Press, 2025.

Bolton, Charles C. *Home Front Battles: World War II Mobilization and Race in the Deep South.* Oxford University Press, 2025.

Bolzenius, Sandra M. *Glory in Their Spirit: How Four Black Women Took on the Army in World War II*. University of Illinois Press, 2018.

Boris, Eileen. "'You Wouldn't Want One of 'Em Dancing with Your Wives,' Racialized Bodies on the Job in World War II." *American Quarterly* 50, no. 1 (1998): 77–108.

Boyle, Kevin. *Arc of Justice: A Saga of Race, Civil Rights, and Murder in the Jazz Age*. Henry Holt, 2004.

Brimmer, Brandi Clay. *Claiming Union Widowhood: Race, Respectability, and Poverty in the Post-Emancipation South*. Duke University Press, 2020.

Buckner, Jocelyn. "The Angel and the Imp: The Duncan Sisters' Performances of Race and Gender." *Popular Entertainment Studies* 2, no. 2 (2011).

Burnham, Margaret. *By Hands Now Known: Jim Crow's Legal Executioners*. W. W. Norton, 2022.

Camp, Stephanie M. H. *Closer to Freedom: Enslaved Women and Everyday Resistance in the Plantation South*. University of North Carolina Press, 2004.

Canaday, Margo. *The Straight State: Sexuality and Citizenship in Twentieth-Century America*. Princeton University Press, 2009.

Capó, Julio. *Welcome to Fairyland: Queer Miami before 1940*. University of North Carolina Press, 2017.

Carter, Dan T. *Scottsboro: A Tragedy of the American South*. Louisiana State University Press, 2007.

Catsam, Derek Charles. *Freedom's Main Line: The Journey of Reconciliation and the Freedom Rides*. University Press of Kentucky, 2009.

Chateauvert, Melinda. *Marching Together: Women of the Brotherhood of Sleeping Car Porters*. University of Illinois Press, 1998.

Chatelain, Marcia. *Franchise: The Golden Arches in Black America*. Liveright, 2020.

———. *South Side Girls: Growing Up in the Great Migration*. Duke University Press, 2015.

Cortner, Richard C. *A "Scottsboro" Case in Mississippi: The Supreme Court and Brown v. Mississippi*. University of Mississippi Press, 1986.

Countryman, Matthew J. *Up South: Civil Rights and Black Power in Philadelphia*. University of Pennsylvania Press, 2006.

Cronenberg, Allen. *Forth to the Mighty Conflict: Alabama and World War II*. University of Alabama Press, 1995.

Dailey, Jane. "The Sexual Politics of Race in World War II America." In *Fog of War: The Second World War and the Civil Rights Movement*, edited by Kevin M. Kruse and Stephen Tuck. Oxford University Press, 2012.

Dailey, Jane, Glenda Elizabeth Gilmore, and Bryant Simon, eds. *Jumpin' Jim Crow: Southern Politics from Civil War to Civil Rights*. Princeton University Press, 2000.

Daniels, David J. *Rights, Liberties, and Ideals: The Contributions of Milton R. Konvitz*. Fred B. Rothman, 1983.

Delmont, Matthew. *Half American: The Epic Story of African Americans Fighting in World War II*. Random House, 2022.

Deutsch, Tracey. *Building a Housewife's Paradise: Gender, Politics, and American Grocery Stores in the Twentieth Century*. University of North Carolina Press, 2010.

Devlin, Rachel. *A Girl Stands at the Door: The Generation of Young Women Who Desegregated America's Schools*. Basic Books, 2018.
Downs, Jim. *Sick from Freedom: African American Illness and Suffering During the Civil War and Reconstruction*. Oxford University Press, 2015.
D'Weston, Haywood. *Let Us Make Men: The Twentieth-Century Black Press and a Manly Vision for Racial Advancement*. University of North Carolina Press, 2018.
Eatmon, Myisha Shauntez. "Public Wrongs, Private Rights: African Americans, Private Law, and White Violence During Jim Crow." PhD diss., Northwestern University, 2020.
——. "Wielding an Unlikely Weapon: Black Americans, White Violence, and Damage Suits During the Early Days of Jim Crow." *Journal of American History* 111, no. 2 (2024): 267–68.
Enstad, Nan. *Cigarettes Inc.: An Intimate History of Corporate Imperialism*. University of Chicago Press, 2018.
Ervin, Keona K. *Gateway to Equality: Black Women and the Struggle for Economic Justice in St. Louis*. University Press of Kentucky, 2017.
Fairclough, Adam. *Race and Democracy: The Civil Rights Struggle in Louisiana, 1915–1972*. University of Georgia Press, 1999.
Farmer, Ashley D. "In Search of the Black Women's History Archive." *Modern American History* 1 (2018): 289–93.
Felkor-Kantor, Max. *Policing Los Angeles: Race, Resistance, and the Rise of the LAPD*. University of North Carolina Press, 2018.
Fergusson, Erna. *Dancing Gods: Indian Ceremonials of New Mexico and Arizona*. University of New Mexico Press, 1931.
——. *New Mexico: A Pageant of Three Peoples*. Knopf Press, 1951.
Finkleman, Paul. "The Promise of Equality and the Limits of Law." In *The History of Michigan*. Ohio University Press, 2007.
Fischer, Anne Gray. *The Streets Belong to Us: Sex, Race, and Police Power from Segregation to Gentrification*. University of North Carolina Press, 2022.
Freedman, Estelle. "The New Woman: Changing Views of Women in the 1920s." *Journal of American History* 61, no. 2 (1974): 372–93.
——. *Redefining Rape: Sexual Violence in the Era of Suffrage and Segregation*. Harvard University Press, 2015.
Frystak, Shannon. *Our Minds on Freedom: Women and the Struggle for Black Equality in Louisiana, 1924–1967*. Louisiana State University Press, 2009.
Fuentes, Marissa. *Dispossessed Lives: Enslaved Women, Violence, and the Archive*. University of Pennsylvania Press, 2016.
Gabrick, Robert. *Go the Greyhound Way: The Romance of the Road*. Enthusiast Books, 2009.
Gallagher, Julie. *Black Women and Politics in New York City*. University of Illinois Press, 2012.
Gergel, Richard. *Unexampled Courage: The Blinding of Sgt. Isaac Woodard and the Awakening of President Harry S. Truman and Judge J. Waties Waring*. Macmillan, 2019.

Gilmore, Glenda Elizabeth. *Defying Dixie: The Radical Roots of Civil Rights, 1919–1950*. W. W. Norton, 2008.

——. *Gender and Jim Crow: Women and the Politics of White Supremacy*. University of North Carolina Press, 1996.

Glymph, Thavolia. "Paper Tracings in the Spectacularly Boisterous Archive of Slavery." *American Historical Review* 130, no. 1 (2025): 1–18.

Goings, Kenneth W. *Mammy and Uncle Mose: Black Collectibles and American Stereotyping*. Indiana University Press, 1991.

Goluboff, Risa L. *The Lost Promise of Civil Rights*. Harvard University Press, 2007.

Gordon, Linda. *The Second Coming of the KKK: The Ku Klux Klan of the 1920s and the American Political Tradition*. Liveright, 2017.

Green, Laurie B. "'Where Would the Negro Women Apply for Work?': Gender, Race, and Labor in Wartime Memphis." *Labor: Studies in Working-Class History of the Americas* 3, no. 3 (2006): 95–117.

Greene, Julie. *Box 25: Archival Secrets, Caribbean Workers, and the Panama Canal*. University of North Carolina Press, 2025.

Greer, Brenna Winn. *Represented: The Black Imagemakers who Reimagined African American Citizenship*. University of Pennsylvania Press, 2019.

Gregory, James N. *The Southern Diaspora: How the Great Migrations of Black and White Southerners Transformed America*. University of North Carolina Press, 2005.

Gross, Kali N. *Colored Amazons: Crime, Violence, and Black Women in the City of Brotherly Love, 1880–1910*. Duke University Press, 2006.

Grossman, James. *Land of Hope: Chicago, Black Southerners, and the Great Migration*. University of Chicago Press, 1989.

Guariglia, Matthew. *Police and the Empire City: Race and the Origins of Modern Policing in New York*. Duke University Press, 2023.

Guglielmo, Thomas A. *Divisions: A New History of Racism and Resistance in America's World War II Military*. Oxford University Press, 2021.

Hale, Grace Elizabeth. *Making Whiteness: The Culture of Segregation in the South, 1870–1940*. Random House, 1998.

Haley, Sarah. *No Mercy Here: Gender, Punishment, and the Making of Jim Crow Modernity*. University of North Carolina Press, 2015.

Hall, Jaqueline D. "The Long Civil Rights Movement and the Political Uses of the Past." *Journal of American History* 91, no. 4 (2005): 1233–66.

Harris, LaShawn D. *Sex Workers, Psychics, and Numbers Runners: Black Women in New York City's Underground Economy*. University of Illinois Press, 2016.

——. *Tell Her Story: Eleanor Bumpers and the Police Killing that Galvanized New York City*. Beacon Press, 2025.

Hernández, Kelly Lytle. *Migra! A History of the U.S. Border Patrol*. University of California Press, 2010.

Hicks, Cheryl D. *Talk with You Like a Woman: African American Women, Justice, and Reform in New York, 1890–1935*. University of North Carolina Press, 2010.

Hill, Daniel Delis. *Advertising to the American Woman, 1900–1999*. Ohio State University Press, 2002.

Hine, Darlene Clark. "Black Migration to the Urban Midwest: The Gender Dimension, 1915–1945." In *The Great Migration in Historical Perspective: New Dimensions of Race, Class, and Gender*, edited by Joe William Trotter, Jr. Indiana University Press, 1991.

———. *Black Women in White: Racial Conflict and Cooperation in the Nursing Profession, 1890–1950*. Indiana University Press, 1989.

———. "Rape and the Inner Lives of Black Women in the Middle West." *Signs* 14, no. 4 (1989): 912–20.

Hirsch, Arnold. *Making the Second Ghetto: Race and Housing in Chicago, 1940–1960*. University of Chicago Press, 1983.

Hixson, Kenneth R. *Pick of the Litter: Greyhound's Once Finest Bus Line*. Henry Clay Press, 2001.

Hobbs, Allyson. *A Chosen Exile: A History of Racial Passing in American Life*. Harvard University Press, 2014.

Hollars, B. J. *The Road South: The Personal Stories of the Freedom Riders*. University of Alabama Press, 2018.

Honey, Maureen, ed. *Bitter Fruit: African American Women in World War II*. University of Missouri, 1999.

Howard, Ashley. *Midwest Unrest: 1960s Urban Rebellions and the Black Freedom Movement*. University of North Carolina Press, 2025.

Hunter, Tera W. *Bound in Wedlock: Slave and Free Black Marriage in the Nineteenth Century*. Harvard University Press, 2019.

———. *To 'Joy My Freedom: Southern Black Women's Lives and Labors After the Civil War*. Harvard University Press, 1996.

Hurt, Douglas R. *The Great Plains During World War II*. University of Nebraska Press, 2008.

Ingram, Tammy. *Dixie Highway: Road Building and the Making of the Modern South, 1900–1930*. University of North Carolina Press, 2014.

Jackson, Carlton. *Hounds of the Road: History of the Greyhound Bus Company*. Bowling Green Press, 1984.

Jackson, Jerma. *Singing In My Soul: Black Gospel Music in a Secular Age*. University of North Carolina Press, 2004.

Johnson, Franklin. *The Development of State Legislation Concerning the Free Negro*. Columbia University Press, 1919.

Johnson, Walter. *River of Dark Dreams: Slavery and Empire in the Cotton Kingdom*. Harvard University Press, 2013.

Jones, Jennifer Dominique. *Ambivalent Affinities: A Political History of Blackness and Homosexuality After World War II*. University of North Carolina Press, 2023.

Kelley, Blaire L. M. *Right to Ride: Streetcar Boycotts and African American Citizenship in the Era of Plessy v. Ferguson*. University of North Carolina Press, 2010.

Kelley, Robin D. G. "Congested Terrain: Resistance on Public Transportation." In *Race Rebels: Culture, Politics, and the Black Working Class*. Free Press, 1994.

———. *Race Rebels: Culture, Politics, and the Black Working Class*. Free Press, 1994.

Kimble, Lionel, Jr. "I Too, Serve America: African American Women War Workers in Chicago, 1940–1945." *Journal of the Illinois State Historical Society* 93, no. 4 (2000): 414–35.

King, Shannon. *Whose Harlem Is This, Anyway? Community Politics and Grassroots Activism During the New Negro Era*. New York University Press, 2015.

Klanderud, Jessica D. *Struggle for the Street: Social Networks and the Struggle for Civil Rights in Pittsburgh*. University of North Carolina Press, 2023.

Korstad, Robert Rogers. *Civil Rights Unionism: Tobacco Workers and the Struggle for Democracy in the Mid-Twentieth-Century South*. University of North Carolina Press, 2003.

Kruse, Kevin M., and Stephen Tuck, eds. *Fog of War: The Second World War and the Civil Rights Movement*. Oxford University Press, 2012.

Kuper, Hilda. *Sobhuza II, Ngwenyama and King of Swaziland: The Story of an Hereditary Ruler and His Country*. Duckworth, 1978.

LeFlouria, Talitha. *Chained in Silence: Black Women and Convict Labor in the New South*. University of North Carolina Press, 2015.

Lemke-Santangelo, Gretchen. *Abiding Courage: African American Migrant Women and the East Bay Community*. University of North Carolina Press, 1996.

Levenstein, Lisa. *A Movement Without Marches: African American Women and the Politics of Poverty in Postwar Philadelphia*. University of North Carolina Press, 2009.

Lewis, Earl. *In Their Own Interests: Race, Class, and Power in Twentieth Century Norfolk*. University of California Press, 1992.

Long, Gretchen. *Doctoring Freedom: The Politics of African American Medical Care in Slavery and Emancipation*. University of North Carolina Press, 2016.

Mack, Kenneth W. "Law, Society, Identity, and the Making of the Jim Crow South: Travel and Segregation on the Tennessee Railroads, 1875–1905." *Law and Social Inquiry* 24, no. 2 (1999): 377–410.

———. *Representing the Race: The Making of the Civil Rights Lawyer*. Harvard University Press, 2014.

Marchand, Roland. *Advertising the American Dream: Making Way for Modernity, 1920–1940*. University of California Press, 1985.

Masur, Kate. *An Example for All the Land: Emancipation and the Struggle over Equality in Washington, D.C.* University of North Carolina Press, 2010.

———. "Patronage and Protest in Kate Brown's Washington." *Journal of American History* 99, no. 4 (2013): 1047–71.

———. *Until Justice Be Done: America's First Civil Rights Movement from the Revolution to Reconstruction*. W. W. Norton, 2021.

Materson, Lisa G. *For the Freedom of Her Race: Black Women and Electoral Politics in Illinois, 1877–1932*. University of North Carolina Press, 2009.

McEyla, Micki. *Clinging to Mammy: The Faithful Slave in Twentieth Century America*. Harvard University Press, 2007.

McGirr, Lisa. *The War on Alcohol: Prohibition and the Rise of the American State.* W. W. Norton, 2015.

McGuire, Danielle. *At the Dark End of the Street: Black Women, Rape, and Resistance from the Montgomery Bus Boycott to the Rise of Black Power.* Vintage, 2010.

McMillen, Neil R., ed. *Remaking Dixie: The Impact of World War II on the American South.* University Press of Mississippi, 1997.

Merrill, Dennis. *Negotiating Paradise: U.S. Tourism and Empire in Twentieth-Century Latin America.* University of North Carolina Press, 2009.

Meyerowitz, Joanne. "Beyond the Feminine Mystique: A Reassessment of Postwar Mass Culture, 1946–1958." *Journal of American History* 79, no. 4 (1993): 1455–82.

Michaeli, Ethan. *The Defender: How the Legendary Black Newspaper Changed America from the Age of the Pullman Porters to the Age of Obama.* Houghton Mifflin Harcourt, 2016.

Milewski, Melissa. *Litigating Across the Color Line: Civil Cases Between Black and White Southerners from the End of Slavery to Civil Rights.* Oxford University Press, 2018.

Milov, Sarah. *The Cigarette: A Political History.* Harvard University Press, 2019.

Mora, Anthony P. *Border Dilemmas: Racial and National Uncertainties in New Mexico, 1848–1912.* Duke University Press, 2010.

Moreton, Bethany. *To Serve God and Wal-Mart: The Making of Christian Free Enterprise.* Harvard University Press, 2009.

Morgan, Jennifer. *Laboring Women: Gender and Reproduction in the Making of New World Slavery.* University of Pennsylvania Press, 2004.

Moten, Crystal. *Continually Working: Black Women, Community Intellectualism, and Economic Justice in Postwar Milwaukee.* Vanderbilt University Press, 2023.

Murphy, Mary-Elizabeth B. "Empathetic Citizenship: Jewish Immigrants and the Struggle for Black Civil Rights in the Midwest." *Michigan Jewish History* 62, no. 5782 (2022): 8–23.

——. *Jim Crow Capital: Women and Black Freedom Struggles in Washington, D.C., 1920–1945.* University of North Carolina Press, 2018.

Murray, Pauli, ed. *States' Laws on Race and Color.* University of Georgia Press, 1997.

Nelson, Bruce. "Organized Labor and the Struggle for Black Equality in Memphis During World War II." *Journal of American History* 80, no. 3 (1993).

Ortiz, Paul. *Emancipation Betrayed: The Hidden History of Black Organizing and White Violence in Florida from the Reconstruction to the Bloody Election of 1920.* University of California Press, 2005.

Ortlepp, Anke. *Jim Crow Terminals: The Desegregation of American Airports.* University of Georgia Press, 2017.

Owns, Dierdre Cooper. *Medical Bondage: Race, Gender, and the Origins of American Gynecology.* University of Georgia Press, 2015.

Parascandola, John. "'Quarantining Women': Venereal Disease Rapid Treatment Centers in World War II America." *Bulletin of the History of Medicine* 83, no. 3 (2009): 431–59.

Parker, Traci. *Department Stores and the Black Freedom Movement: Workers, Consumers, and the Struggle for Civil Rights from the 1930s to the 1980s.* University of North Carolina Press, 2019.
Penningroth, Dylan C. "African American Divorce in Virginia and Washington, D.C., 1865–1930." *Journal of Family History* 33, no. 1 (2008).
——. *Before the Movement: The Hidden History of Black Civil Rights.* Liveright, 2023.
Phillips, Kimberley L. *AlabamaNorth: African-American Migrants, Community, and Working-Class Activism in Cleveland, 1915–45.* University of Illinois Press, 1999.
——. *War! What Is It Good For? Black Freedom Struggles and the U.S. Military from World War II to Iraq.* University of North Carolina Press, 2012.
Pryor, Elizabeth Stordeur. *Colored Travelers: Mobility and the Fight for Citizenship Before the Civil War.* University of North Carolina Press, 2016.
Purkiss, Ava. *Fit Citizens: A History of Black Women's Exercise from Post-Reconstruction to Postwar America.* University of North Carolina Press, 2023.
Purnell, Brian, Jeanne Theoharis, and Komozi Woodard, eds. *The Strange Careers of the Jim Crow North: Segregation and Struggle Outside of the South.* New York University Press, 2019.
Rabinovitch-Fox, Einav. "Baby, You Can Drive My Car: Advertising Women's Freedom in 1920s-America." *American Journalism* 33, no. 4 (2016): 372–400.
Randolph, Justin. *Mississippi Law: Policing and Reform in America's Jim Crow Countryside.* University of North Carolina Press, 2025.
Ransby, Barbara. *Ella Baker and the Black Freedom Movement: A Radical Democratic Vision.* University of North Carolina Press, 2004.
Reagon, Bernice Johnson. "African Diaspora Women: The Making of Cultural Workers." In *Women in Africa and the African Diaspora,* edited by Rosalyn Terborg-Penn, Sharon Harley, and Andrea Benton Rushing. Howard University Press, 1987.
Richter, Amy G. *Home on the Rails: Women, the Railroad, and the Rise of Public Domesticity.* University of North Carolina Press, 2005.
Robinson, Joanne Gibson. *The Montgomery Bus Boycott and the Women Who Started It: A Memoir of Joanne Gibson Robinson.* University of Tennessee Press, 1987.
Sanders, Crystal. *A Forgotten Migration: Black Southerners, Segregation Scholarships, and the Debt Owed to Public HBCUs.* University of North Carolina Press, 2024.
Schlanger, Margo. "Injured Women Before Common Law Courts, 1860–1930." *Harvard Women's Law Journal* 21 (1998): 79–140.
Schmidt, Christopher W. "Legal History and the Problem of the Long Civil Rights Movement." *Law and Social Inquiry* 41 (2016): 1081–103.
Schrader, Stuart. *Badges Without Borders: How Global Counterinsurgency Transformed American Policing.* University of California Press, 2019.
Schweninger, Loren. *Appealing for Liberty: Freedom Suits in the South.* Oxford University Press, 2017.

Sernet, Milton. *Bound for the Promised Land: African American Religion and the Great Migration.* Duke University Press, 1997.

Shockley, Megan Taylor. *"We Too, Are Americans": African American Women in Detroit and Richmond, 1940–1954.* University of Illinois Press, 2004.

Simmons, LaKisha. *Crescent City Girls: The Lives of Young Black Women in Segregated New Orleans.* University of North Carolina Press, 2015.

Sims-Wood, Janet. "'We Served America, Too!': Personal Recollections of African American Women in the Women's Army Corps During World War II." PhD diss., Union Institute, 1994.

Skwiot, Christine. *The Purposes of Paradise: U.S. Tourism and Empire in Cuba and Hawaii.* University of Pennsylvania Press, 2011.

Smith, J. Clay, Jr. *Emancipation: The Making of the Black Lawyer, 1844–1944.* University of Pennsylvania Press, 1993.

Smith, J. Douglas. *Managing White Supremacy: Race, Politics, and Citizenship in Jim Crow Virginia.* University of North Carolina Press, 2002.

Snorton, C. Riley. *Black on Both Sides: A Racial History of Trans Identity.* University of Minnesota Press, 2017.

Sorin, Gretchen. *Driving While Black: African American Travel and the Road to Civil Rights.* Liverlight, 2020.

Sosna, Morton. Introduction to *Remaking Dixie: The Impact of World War II on the American South.* Edited by Neil R. McMillen. University Press of Mississippi, 1997.

Stewart, Jaqueline Najuma. *Migrating to the Movies: Cinema and Black Urban Modernity.* University of California Press, 2005.

Sugrue, Thomas J. *Sweet Land of Liberty: The Forgotten Struggle for Civil Rights in the North.* Random House, 2008.

Sullivan, Patricia. *Lift Every Voice: The NAACP and the Making of the Civil Rights Movement.* New Press, 2009.

Sumler-Edmond, Janice. "The Quest for Justice: African American Women Litigants, 1867–1890." In *African American Women and the Vote, 1867–1890.* University of Massachusetts Press, 1997.

Taylor, Clarence. *Fight the Power: African Americans and the Long History of Police Brutality in New York City.* New York University Press, 2019.

Tetrault, Lisa. *Myth of Seneca Falls: Memory and the Women's Suffrage Movement, 1848–1898.* University of North Carolina Press, 2014.

Thaggert, Miriam. *Riding Jane Crow: African American Women on the American Railroad.* University of Illinois Press, 2022.

Theoharis, Jeanne. *The Rebellious Life of Mrs. Rosa Parks.* Random House, 2013.

Thornton, J. Mills, III. *Dividing Lines: Municipal Politics and the Struggle for Civil Rights in Montgomery, Birmingham, and Selma.* University of Alabama Press, 2002.

———. "Segregation and the City: White Supremacy in Alabama in the Mid-Twentieth Century South." In *Fog of War: The Second World War and the Civil Rights Movement,* edited by Kevin Kruse and Stephen Tuck. Oxford University Press, 2012.

Threat, Charissa J. *Nursing Civil Rights: Gender and Race in the Army Nurse Corps.* University of Illinois Press, 2015.

Tushnet, Mark. *Making Civil Rights Law: Thurgood Marshall and the Supreme Court, 1936–1961.* Oxford University Press, 1994.

Trotter, Joe William, Jr., ed. *The Great Migration in Historical Perspective: New Dimensions of Race, Class, and Gender.* Indiana University Press, 1991.

Turk, Katherine. "'A Fair Chance to Do My Part of Work': Black Women, War Work, and Rights Claims at the Kingsbury Ordinance Plant." *Indiana Magazine of History* 108, no. 3 (2012): 209–44.

Turner, Walter R. "Coming Home: The North Carolina Bus Companies That Became Part of Trailways and Greyhound." *North Carolina Historical Review* 90, no. 4 (2013): 255–84.

Walker, Susannah. *Style and Status: Selling Beauty to African American Women.* University of Kentucky Press, 2007.

Walsh, Margaret. *Making Connections: The Long Distance Bus Industry in the U.S.A.* Routledge, 2000.

Welch, Kimberly. *Black Litigants in the Antebellum American South.* University of North Carolina Press, 2018.

Welke, Barbara Young. *Recasting American Liberty: Gender, Race, Law, and the Railroad Revolution, 1865–1920.* Cambridge University Press, 2001.

Wilkerson, Isabelle. *Warmth of Other Suns: The Epic Story of America's Great Migration.* Vintage, 2011.

Williams, Kidada E. *They Left Great Marks on Me: African American Testimonies of Racial Violence from Emancipation to World War I.* New York University Press, 2012.

Williams, Rhonda Y. *The Politics of Public Housing: Black Women's Struggles against Urban Inequality.* Oxford University Press, 2004.

Williams-Forson, Psyche. *Building Houses out of Chicken Legs: Black Women, Food, and Power.* University of North Carolina Press, 2006.

Wolcott, Victoria. *Race, Riots, and Rollercoasters: The Struggle over Segregated Recreation in America.* University of Pennsylvania Press, 2014.

———. *Remaking Respectability: African American Women in Interwar Detroit.* University of North Carolina Press, 2004.

Woodward, C. Vann. *The Strange Career of Jim Crow.* Oxford University Press, 1966.

Woolner, Cookie. *The Famous Lady Lovers: Black Women and Queer Desire Before Stonewall.* University of North Carolina Press, 2023.

Yellin, Emily. *Our Mother's War: American Women at Home and at the Front During World War II.* Free Press, 2004.

Yellin, Eric. *Racism in the Nation's Service: Government Workers and the Color Line in Woodrow Wilson's America.* University of North Carolina Press, 2013.

Index

www.ingramcontent.com/pod-product-compliance
Lightning Source LLC
LaVergne TN
LVHW091025261026
850861LV00050B/149
* 9 7 8 1 4 6 9 6 9 8 3 1 1 *